# IT'S A GREAT DAY IN THE KINGDOM!

## RICHARD A. MORLEDGE

RAM PRESS
P.O. Box 155
Bakerstown, Pennsylvania
15007

# GREETING THE DAWN

*Let us greet the dawn with song! (Psalm 57:8, TLB).*

What a beautiful way to wake up to a great day in the Kingdom! Just sing a song with every new dawn. "This is the day which the Lord has made; let us rejoice and be glad in it" (Psalm 118:24). Sounds thrilling, but it is not easy. Most of us wake up with a moan or a groan, a sigh or a cry, or just a great big yawn, forgetting each dawn is a new beginning and God may have something exciting in store for us that very day.

"In the beginning God created the heavens and the earth" (Genesis 1:1). God is in all beginnings, and all great things begin with a seed of an idea planted by God in someone's mind. God bombards us daily with ideas that will bring great results if we have the courage to follow them, but He has trouble getting through to us when we wake up whimpering, whining, and wailing. If we greet each dawn with song, our hearts are receptive to Him and He is able to use us to bring forth marvelous new things for His Kingdom here on earth.

Greeting the dawn with song is an attitude we can choose to have. It does not mean every day of our lives will be carefree and fun. Far from it. For all of us, there are days that are dark. There are times that are tough. There are decisions to be made and we do not see how we can make them. We wonder if God is with us and if Christianity truly works. Even in the worst moments, though, we can choose to believe that God, who created the heavens, the earth, and each one of us, is working for good in our lives. No matter how dreary the day, how weary the body, how teary the eyes, and how leery you are of the future, merely believe you are loved and cherished by God, now and always. That is how to greet the dawn with song.

"Make a joyful noise to the Lord, all the lands! Serve the Lord with gladness! Come into his presence with singing!" (Psalm 100:1-2). Sing a song of joy and gladness in the dawns of tomorrow and you will find that your God-given ideas for glorifying the name of Jesus Christ soon turn into miracles.

*Read: Genesis 1:1-5; I Chronicles 16:23-34; Psalm 30:1-5*

# HOW TO ENJOY NOW

*The steadfast love of the Lord never ceases, his mercies never come to an end; they are new every morning (Lamentations 3:22-23).*

Yesterday is gone forever. Tomorrow may never come. Today is the only day of which we can be certain, and of that, now, this minute, is the only one of which we can be assured. We are created to enjoy now, but now is often hard to celebrate and enjoy. We miss now by dwelling on yesterday and anticipating tomorrow, rarely stopping to savor precious moments as they happen. Yet no special gift or education is needed to enjoy now. We simply must make the decision to develop a habit of enjoying now and support that habit with daily practice. Habits come from the mind. We have the power to form any habit we want and stop any habit we do not want. Just as we can choose to practice daily Bible reading, pray, attend worship regularly, and give generously, we can choose to enjoy each and every minute of our lives.

Do not let yesterday's mistakes or tomorrow's problems keep you from enjoying the now. Develop a security system to screen out negative, destructive thoughts. Certain ideas should be locked outside your mind: "it's impossible," "I'm too old," "I'm too sick," "I'm no good." Banish defeatist attitudes! If somebody, intentionally or unintentionally, tries to chain you to the past or limit your future, remember that although you cannot control what people say and do, you can control how their words and actions affect you. Learn to live by the calendar, not by the clock, and focus on the large picture, the big dimension. Keep your priorities straight and do not waste time in frustration over petty trifles. Jesus said, "Do not be anxious about tomorrow" (Matthew 6:34). Worry can keep you from achieving your potential, so make it a habit to trust in the steadfast love and mercy of the Lord, whatever happens.

Time is precious; don't waste it. Life is brief; don't miss it. Live every second in the now and enjoy the countless blessings God has given you. Make up your mind that right now is the greatest moment of your life, and thank God for it.

*Read: Matthew 6:25-34; Psalm 31:14-15; Ephesians 5:15-17*

3

# LOVEGROWERS

*Let love be genuine (Romans 12:9).*

Love: all of us talk about it, hope for it, and need it. We want to be loved, try to be loving, and know we are commanded to love, but not everybody realizes that love, like faith, hope, wisdom, and other spiritual qualities, needs to be nurtured and cultivated in order to grow. We frequently neglect two vital lovegrowers: appreciation and gratitude.

Love cannot grow unless **appreciation** shows. When Jesus ate with Simon the Pharisee and a prostitute, He could easily see who truly loved Him: the sinful woman, who let her hair down, kissed His feet, and shed her tears. Showing appreciation means personal sacrifice. In human relationships, we know if someone professes to love us but never shows appreciation, their love is a lie. It is the same with God; if we ignore Him, we reveal we do not sincerely love Him. When we are eager to attend worship and share all we have for His sake, we show genuine appreciation for His many kindnesses.

Love cannot grow unless **gratitude** shows. Usually we feel most grateful when we make some goof or commit a sin, yet are forgiven and loved in spite of everything. I do not know when I was ever more grateful than when I dented the front fender of my dad's Roadmaster Buick and he did not get angry. Jesus told the parable of the two debtors to teach us that "he who is forgiven little, loves little" (Luke 7:47). It is good to give thanks to God, and it is good to give thanks also to godly people who offer us forgiveness and another chance.

Appreciation and gratitude should be daily habits, but we habitually forget them. Rarely do we tell people we are appreciative of all they do and grateful for their lives. Worse yet, we forget to offer appreciation and gratitude to our Creator. If you are miserable today, perhaps you are failing to use the two lovegrowers God provides to nurture and cultivate loving relationships. Love can grow in your life if you make the decision to show heartfelt appreciation and gratitude, starting now. When you do, you will be a lovegrower yourself.

*Read: Luke 7:36-50; Romans 13:8-10; Psalm 92:1*

## POWER YOU POSSESS

*To all who received him, who believed in his name, he gave power to become children of God (John 1:12).*

You are a powerful person. God has given you power to live triumphantly, to move mountains instead of tripping over anthills, and to transform the world instead of conforming to it. Think about the tremendous God-given power you possess.

You have power to **change** for the better. The good news of the Bible is that you do not have to remain as you are. If you feel discouraged, fearful, angry, or confused, you have power to find dynamic new life in Christ. God Himself will help you become more like Jesus, our model for holiness, goodness, righteousness, and perfection. "We all ... are being changed into his likeness from one degree of glory to another; for this comes from the Lord who is the Spirit" (II Corinthians 3:18). You can change for the better today, if you want to.

You have power to **choose** for the right. Since the beginning of history, God has given people power to choose the course of their destiny. "I have set before you life and death, blessing and curse; therefore choose life" (Deuteronomy 30:19). No living being has more power to choose than you. Though you cannot control events, you can control your response to them. Conditions color life, but you choose the color! You can choose to rise above mistakes and hurts, love the unlovable, forgive the unforgivable, and open your heart to the transforming love of Christ. Today, choose right. Choose life. Choose blessing. Choose Jesus! You have that power.

You have power to **challenge** yourself and others. "Be strong, and of good courage. Fear not; be not dismayed" (I Chronicles 22:13). Be bold in your faith! Challenge yourself and others to change for the better and choose for the right.

Today, use the power you possess. God grieves when Christians fail to show evidence of His strength. Concentrate on your power, not your problems. The world needs to see the children of God courageously challenging themselves and others to change for the better and choose for the right.

*Read: Ephesians 4:25-32; Psalm 28:8-9; Ephesians 3:20-21*

# THE ONLY FAILURE

*By the encouragement of the scriptures we might have hope (Romans 15:4).*

Why is it that we enjoy seeing other people fail? When a prominent individual fails, in the political arena, in athletics, in business, or in personal morality, we gloat, snicker, make and repeat jokes, and zero in at close range to watch every moment of agony and pain. Yet we have quite a different standard when it comes to our own mistakes and misjudgments. When we goof, we want to be left alone; we claim our right to privacy; we do not want anyone to know anything about our foolish blunder; we try to cover up our feelings of shame and disgrace. A sense of failure can cause such intolerable humiliation, hurt, and embarrassment that we wonder if life is worth living or even if we can go on another day.

It is a shame we are so ashamed of failure. It is a shame failure makes us want to give up on ourselves. God never gives up on us, no matter what we do, no matter how horrible we are. No one knew this better than Peter, who passionately declared that although other disciples might betray Jesus, he never, ever would. Just hours later, a teenage girl pointed her cute finger at that rugged fisherman, Rocky, and he crumbled in the sight of his beloved Master. But Peter's life did not end there. Sometime after His resurrection on Easter morning, Jesus met Peter and convinced him not to quit, not to give up on himself, but to go on. Peter got the message. He was transformed from a dejected, hopeless failure into a dynamic, hope-filled leader in the early Christian Church.

If you feel like a failure today, hear the encouragement of Scripture. Jesus is telling you, "I forgive you. I have not given up on you, so do not give up on yourself." No matter what you have done, you can rise above failure and go on to do great things for the Kingdom of God. As you start again, try to be a little more encouraging to other people who are suffering with a sense of failure. Do not gloat and snicker. Give them the same hope God through Jesus Christ speaks to you. God gives up on no one. The only failure is in giving up on ourselves.

*Read: Luke 22:54-62; Luke 24:34; I Thessalonians 5:9-11*

6

# HOW DO YOU OPERATE?

*"If you would believe you would see the glory of God" (John 11:40).*

We operate within three realms. **Knowledge**: information, facts, certainties. We know things because we can see, touch, or prove them. **Feelings**: emotions, affections, sentiments. We respond to circumstances by feeling good or bad, healthy or sick, optimistic or pessimistic. **Belief**: faith, confidence, and trust in something for which there is no demonstrable proof. Though we cannot explain or understand, we can believe.

Our knowledge, feelings, and beliefs all are important, but if we operate primarily in the areas of knowledge or feelings, we will get into trouble. It is imprudent to depend solely on knowledge because there is so much we do not know; God alone knows all things. Feelings can change dramatically in five minutes, with our emotions spiking from the heights to the depths like a roller coaster; only God is unchanging. The wisest, steadiest way to operate is to walk by faith, basing our lives not on what we know or feel, but on what we believe.

What should we believe? Look to Scripture. The Bible tells us God created the world and each one of us. He loves us more than we love ourselves. Jesus Christ redeemed the world through His life, death, and resurrection. He is alive and will live forever. His Holy Spirit is active in the world today, though we cannot see Him or understand everything He does. He who created the world has not given up on the world or on any of us, whatever we have done. When we believe in Him, we have forgiveness of sin, new life on earth, and eternal life in Heaven. We see the glory of God when we believe.

We can never live triumphantly by floundering around in the realms of our imperfect knowledge and unstable feelings. Victory comes through belief! "Whatever is born of God overcomes the world; this is the victory that overcomes the world, our faith. Who is it that overcomes the world but he who believes that Jesus is the Son of God?" (I John 5:4-5).

How do you operate? If you want your operation to be successful, base your life on belief in Jesus and His Word.

*Read: I John 3:19-20; Malachi 3:6; John 5:24*

# HOW GOD GETS THINGS DONE

*"What is impossible with men is possible with God" (Luke 18:27).*

Whenever God wants to do something wonderful and special here on earth, He can create something new, perform a miracle, or do what He usually does: work through people.

When God works through people, He does not tell us His whole plan from the start. He knows we could not comprehend it. We could not take it. We would try to find a different way to do it. Worse yet, we would appoint a committee to study the options! No, God gives us just a little bit of information at a time and when we are faithful, He leads us further.

God may be trying to get something done through you today. Have you had any ideas lately? That is where it always begins. God constantly bombards us with ideas and puts corresponding ideas in the minds of other people. He allows time for the ideas to germinate, then brings people together in holy hook-ups so His plan can be accomplished.

God sends ideas at all hours, but one of His favorite times is during the middle of the night. If you get an idea then and you think it is a little crazy, do not automatically assume you have a case of indigestion! Think about it. Look around and see if somebody else has a complementary idea. Your idea may seem impossible, but do not let that stop you! Remember, by faith, all things are possible. Jesus said, "If you have faith as a grain of mustard seed, you will say to this mountain, 'Move from here to there,' and it will move; and nothing will be impossible to you" (Matthew 17:20-21). Your seemingly impossible idea may be part of God's plan to reach people with His gracious love. Ask God for help in pursuing your idea unashamedly, imaginatively, enthusiastically, and creatively.

God is not finished with the world yet. There are many things He is waiting to reveal to us. His plans will be carried out by people who have the courage to believe in ideas, no matter how ridiculous and incredible they first appear. What is impossible with us is possible with God, so have faith and allow God to get great things done through you today.

*Read: Luke 18:18-27; Matthew 17:14-21; Mark 11:1-10*

# TRUST

*Trust in him at all times (Psalm 62:8).*

It is beautiful to see what God can do when people trust in Him.

Jesus Christ was born in Bethlehem of Judea because a young peasant girl and a simple carpenter trusted God with their lives. Mary and Joseph were real people, and we should not forget that. We idealize the Christmas story so much through greeting cards and nativity scenes that we lose sight of the true humanity of Jesus's earthly parents.

Mary and Joseph were confused and frightened by all that happened. When the angel Gabriel came to Mary and said, "Hail, O favored one, the Lord is with you!" (Luke 1:28), Mary was "greatly troubled at the saying" (v. 29). Joseph also had an unsettling visit from a heavenly messenger; "an angel of the Lord appeared to him in a dream, saying, 'Joseph, son of David, do not fear to take Mary your wife'" (Matthew 1:20). Those experiences were stressful for Mary and Joseph, as they would be for any of us today. I would not be surprised if the two of them exchanged a few unpleasant words on the eighty-mile trip from Nazareth to Bethlehem. There was Mary, eight months and three-and-a-half weeks pregnant, riding bareback on a donkey without shock absorbers. "Joseph, slow down. Joseph, when is the next rest stop? Joseph, I don't feel well." Imagine her anxiety when labor began and there was no room at the inn!

How did they get through it? Trust.

"Let it be to me according to your word" (Luke 1:37).

I think those are the nine most beautiful words in all of the Gospels. If you want to know the secret of trusting God no matter what happens, there it is. "Let it be." Whatever it is, let it be. You may not like it. You may not agree with it. You may be confused and frightened because of it. Nevertheless, just let it be according to God's Word. Let it be the way He wants it to be and believe He is working for good in the situation. Trust in Him at all times in spite of your confusion and fear and see what beautiful things He will do in your life.

*Read: Luke 1:26-38; Matthew 1:18-25; Isaiah 26:4*

# THINKING ABOUT YOUR THINKING

*"What do you think?" (Matthew 18:12).*

Whoever dreamed up the quaint saying, "A penny for your thoughts," had no appreciation of the value of our thoughts.

The Bible says, "For as he thinketh in his heart, so is he" (Proverbs 23:7, KJV). It is our thoughts that essentially make us who we are. And so today, I am asking you to think about your thinking. What are you thinking about right now? What books are you reading these days? What ideas and challenges are confronting your mind? Are you thinking about things that are good, or all the bad news in the world? Do you think about harsh words people have said to you, or the many undeserved kindnesses you have received? Are you thinking negatively or positively? Do you dwell so much on mistakes you have made that you cannot think beyond to forgiveness and new life? Are you thinking about how you can help another person, or how you can hurt somebody who has hurt you? Do you think appreciatively about your blessings, or gripe incessantly about your problems? Are you thinking about how much you can get, or how much you can give? Are you thinking critically about people, judging them by their worst hour instead of their best? Just what are you doing with the mind God has given you? Jesus asked His first disciples, "What do you think?" How would you answer that question from Jesus Christ?

Your thought processes are under your control, no one else's. You can think good thoughts. You can think evil thoughts. Some people seem to think no thoughts! It is up to you. With His help, your mind can be captivated by God's love, power, and glory and you can enjoy a fascinating pilgrimage in spiritual insight. First, though, you must think about your thinking to be sure you are thinking right!

Paul advises, "Whatever is true, whatever is honorable, whatever is just, whatever is pure, whatever is lovely, whatever is gracious, if there is any excellence, if there is anything worthy of praise, think about these things" (Philippians 4:8).

I would not give up thoughts like those for a million dollars, let alone a penny. Would you?

*Read: Proverbs 1:1-7; I Corinthians 14:20; Psalm 104:33-34*

# THE ONLY ANSWER TO ABUSE

*"You meant evil against me; but God meant it for good"*
*(Genesis 50:20).*

The history of Joseph has just about everything: heartbreak and hope, deceit and death, love and lust, jealousy and mystery. We tend to remember Joseph for his greatness, but he was a man with many woes, many misfortunes. Joe's woes easily could have destroyed him. He was abused cruelly by family and friends: his brothers conspired to kill him, then sold him as a slave; the wife of Potiphar falsely accused him and had him imprisoned; the butler forgot to tell Pharaoh about him for two years. Yet Joseph, like Jesus, forgave those who perpetrated sins against him, believing God was with him and though others may have meant it for evil, God meant it for good.

If you have been abused, you, too, can believe God is working for good, no matter how devastating the effects of abuse have been to your emotional, physical, and spiritual well-being. The only answer to abuse is forgiveness. You can talk about abuse, go to support groups for abuse, and read books on abuse, but none of that will make the hurt go away. Only when you forgive your abuser can you begin to work through the hurt, pain, and anger. If you harbor bitterness toward someone, you hurt only yourself; you allow that person to control you by keeping you imprisoned in hatred and vengeance. When you forgive your abuser, you are free! You are free from negative, degrading emotions and memories. You are free to use your talents and gifts for your fulfillment and God's glory. You are free to discover the great destiny God has planned for you.

You may think it is impossible to forgive the person who hurt you so deeply, but the Bible tells us there is absolutely no one you cannot forgive through the power of God's Holy Spirit. In addition, you have the ability to believe that although others may have meant evil against you, God meant it for good. If you have suffered abuse, remember the history of Joseph, who overcame abuse, lived triumphantly, and grew strong in faith because he knew the only answer to abuse is forgiveness.

*Read: Genesis 50:15-21; Romans 8:28; Matthew 18:21-22*

13

## PERPLEXITY

*We are afflicted in every way, but not crushed; perplexed, but not driven to despair; persecuted, but not forsaken; struck down, but not destroyed (II Corinthians 4:8-9).*

Can a Christian live with perplexity? Many people say, "No, a Christian should never be perplexed. A Christian should be certain of everything, no doubts, no questions, no perplexity, period!" Just the opposite is true. Perplexity can be a sign of God's presence. Jesus said God's Holy Spirit lives and dwells in us. Think about it: the eternal, all-knowing, all-powerful Lord lives and dwells in our finite, ignorant, weak human bodies. "All who keep his commandments abide in him, and he in them. And by this we know that he abides in us, by the Spirit which he has given us" (I John 3:24). What a profound mystery! How can we help but be perplexed?

Perplexity means confusion, bewilderment, puzzlement. The Latin derivation suggests being entangled, twisted, intertwined. We know perplexity when we are not completely sure about our standing with God; when we want people to think we are saints but inside know we are unclean sinners; when we are filled with joy and sadness at the same time; when we hurt and do not know why; when things happen that we dislike; when we have some doubts and wonder, "Is it really true? Is Jesus the Son of God? Did He rise from the grave?"

Perplexity need never drive us to despair, for perplexity is part of faith. In faith, we believe what we cannot fully understand or explain. "The secret things belong to the Lord our God" (Deuteronomy 29:29). Do not worry if you experience perplexity. Maybe you should be concerned if you do not! If you think you know all things, well, congratulations, you do not need the Lord because you are a god in your own mind. But those of us who know we need His help have the assurance that God understands our perplexity. It is part of our humanity, and God never wants us to deny our humanity.

Can a Christian live with perplexity? Truly, we cannot live without it.

*Read: Romans 11:33-36; Acts 2:1-12; I Corinthians 2:6-16*

14

# RESTORING RELATIONSHIPS

*Let all that you do be done in love (I Corinthians 16:14).*

Broken relationships happen among Christians. It is unfortunate and regrettable, but true. In fact, if we are trying to do great things for God's Kingdom and His Church, we will have strained relationships occasionally with people who claim to be just as devoted to Christ as we are. When heartbreaking divisions with family and friends occur, try the **A A A A Program** for rebuilding and restoring those separations.

**A -- ATTITUDE.** That is where it all begins. You will not be reunited unless you have the positive attitude that your relationship, though damaged and scarred, can be helped, healed, and made stronger than before. Once you believe nothing can separate your love, you are on the way to healing.

**A -- ACTION.** You can think about the damage done to you, talk about your hurt feelings, and pray about forgiveness, but reconciliation will not occur without action. Stubbornness and pride are barriers to reconciliation. Make the first move or you will shortchange and impoverish the rest of your life.

**A -- APPEAL.** Appeal to the only power that works: the power of love. Do not make anyone grovel or plead for mercy. Be generous, be kind, and especially, be loving. You can do it, for the love of God's Holy Spirit lives and dwells in you.

**A -- ACCEPTANCE.** You went through a distressing battle, but now you are together again. Accept your brother or sister in Christ in a new, healthy relationship. Though you probably will never forget the painful ordeal, forgive! Bridge over the hurt and begin anew. As a Christian, your love is greater than your memory; your heart is bigger than your mind.

Do not grieve God by fighting with another Christian, whatever the reason. Jesus prayed for believers to be united, to be one, as He and the Father are one. Work today to restore the broken relationships in your life, for you cannot truly love God if you are separated in any way from another one of His children. Let love overcome all things in the name of Him who tells us we can do all things through Jesus Christ our Lord.

*Read: Philemon 4-14; I John 2:9-11; John 17:9-11*

15

## VOICES IN THE WILDERNESS

*"Behold, I send my messenger before thy face, who shall prepare thy way; the voice of one crying in the wilderness: Prepare the way of the Lord, make his paths straight --" John the baptizer appeared in the wilderness, preaching a baptism of repentance for the forgiveness of sins (Mark 1:2-4).*

John the Baptizer. He is the dean of preachers and an inspiration for all people trying to be disciples of Jesus Christ. An estimated 300,000 people were converted under his ministry, and he delivered his dynamic, life-changing message without auditoriums, advertising, and public address systems!

John was a preacher who identified with suffering people. When he was called by God to proclaim a message, he did not go downtown to the prestigious pulpits of worship. He did not stand on the street corners of Jerusalem. He did not even go to the university. He went to the wilderness. John knew how to preach to people who were having a difficult time. "Repent! Change your ways! Behold the Lamb of God, Jesus Christ, who takes away the sin of the world!" John told people to straighten out their lives and he pointed them not to himself, but to Christ. So much of John's effectiveness resulted from his understanding of wilderness experiences. Only people who have spent time in the wilderness themselves can identify with the pain, hopelessness, and loneliness of intense suffering.

If you have been in some wilderness and God has led you through it, do not forget about the experience or keep it to yourself. Use it! Share it! Turn it into a blessing. There are people near you who are hurting. They need help from someone who understands. You may be the one person who can help them straighten out their lives, the one person who can point them to Jesus. Listen for those voices in the wilderness! You know what they sound like because you have cried out yourself. When you hear them, go to those people as fast as you can with the hope, love, and peace of Jesus Christ. That is why God led you out, so you could go back in and help other people to find the way, the truth, and the life in Jesus Christ.

*Read: Mark 1:1-8; John 1:19-23; John 14:6*

# AN ALARMING DEVICE

*By rejecting conscience, certain persons have made shipwreck of their faith (I Timothy 1:19).*

Each one of us has a conscience. I am not quite sure where the conscience is located (maybe next to the spleen, below the gallbladder, in the pituitary gland?), but God created the conscience and He placed it within us. We human beings add guilt to the conscience through sin. Even a little bit of guilt makes us disheartened and restless. We cry ourselves to sleep night after night. We scratch our heads and wonder how we could have been so foolish and unthinking. We have a hard time looking squarely in the eyes of someone we respect. Many of us are like Adam and Eve, the first two people to experience a guilty conscience. They tried to run away and hide from the Lord, then blamed one another and even God for their disobedience. It was a guilty conscience that drove Adam and Eve into the sewing industry with those fig leaves!

The conscience is disturbing, but Scripture tells us God creates all things good and works for good in all things, and that includes the conscience. God uses the conscience to sound an alarm for us when we are not doing what we are supposed to be doing, when we are in danger of turning our backs on the Lord, when we are drifting from our faith. The Bible warns, "Take care, brethren, lest there be in any of you an evil, unbelieving heart, leading you to fall away from the living God" (Hebrews 3:12). A guilty conscience is a signal to change, get back on the right track, and be renewed into Christ-like living through God's forgiveness and grace. Sometimes a guilty conscience is the greatest teacher we have, for it forces us to admit our need for the Savior. The conscience, blessed by God's Spirit, fed by His Holy Word, sustained by preaching of biblical truth, can revive our commitment to Jesus Christ.

If an alarm rings in your conscience today, do not shut it off. Wake up! Correct what needs to be corrected without delay. Be grateful for the alarm God uses to restore you to righteousness. Your faith would be shipwrecked without it.

*Read: I Timothy 1:12-20; Genesis 3:1-13; I John 3:19-24*

19

# MEANNESS

*A man who is kind benefits himself, but a cruel man hurts himself (Proverbs 11:17).*

We are cruel to one another with the things we say and do. The irony is, we do not mean to be cruel; we are cruel because we are mean. All of us have a mean streak. We temporarily relish the seconds of sadistic satisfaction we feel when we spitefully get even with our adversaries. We "aim bitter words like arrows" (Psalm 64:3) at people who irritate or offend us. Later, we are sorry, but it is too late. The mean words have been spoken, the damage done. Usually then we realize our cruelty has hurt not only someone else, but ourselves. We pierce our own hearts with the sharp arrows we shoot at others.

Meanness brings disunity and disharmony. That is why God created forgiveness. He knows we can be mean and He does not want us to suffer interminably in anger and anguish. He offers forgiveness so we can rise above mean situations and move on in a positive, harmonious way. Forgiveness occurs when one person honestly says, "I'm sorry," and another says from the heart, "I forgive you." It is a two-way street, difficult for both individuals. Some people think we have to "forgive and forget." True forgiveness is not forgetting. If we can forget an offense, it probably did not even matter to us. God does not require us to forget meanness, cruelty, and indignities done against us, but He commands us to forgive. Forget about forgetting the ugliness; we cannot do it. But with God's help, we can forgive even the most heinous mistreatment.

Thank God He has given us a way to overcome meanness. I just wish we did not need it! Paul wrote, "Make love your aim" (I Corinthians 14:1). Love, not bitter words! If only we consistently aimed to follow the command to love God, others, and ourselves, if only we aimed to treat one another with dignity, we would not have to forgive and be forgiven so often.

Try to get rid of all cruelty and pettiness in your words and your conduct today. Forgiveness can cure the effects of meanness, but isn't prevention better than a cure?

*Read: Romans 12:19; Matthew 6:7-15; Proverbs 17:9*

20

# GOD KNOWS

*"The Lord searches all hearts, and understands every plan and thought" (I Chronicles 28:9).*

It is pathetic, the way we pretend we have all the answers, everything is certain in our minds, and we never have doubts about faith. We go to church, smile, and nod as though we understand every intricacy of Christian theology. We dare not ask a single question for fear someone will think we are stupid or be shocked by our apparent disbelief. Even more pathetic, we seem to think if we keep silent and do not tell anyone about our private doubts, then God will not know either.

God knows. God knows everything in our minds and hearts. God knows of our occasional skepticism. God knows what we are wrestling with this very moment. Why should that frighten us? The Lord is loving, merciful, and kind. He will not throw us out of the Kingdom because we ask questions. We will not get on God's bad list when we say, "I doubt sometimes the resurrection of the body. I wonder if I truly will see my loved ones again on the other side. I question if love and forgiveness really work." God knows our doubts, and it is all right. What is not all right is to stay away from His Church, for it is only there that we can find help in dealing with doubts.

Bring your questions to church and have the courage to express them. You will be amazed. Some of those smiling, confident, secure-looking people you see all the time have doubts, too! Honest discussion is healthy. No one has all the answers, but we can help one another with many of the questions. In my seminary education, the professors who taught me the most were those who had the frankness to admit they did not know everything. Somehow, when we share our concerns, God helps us to deal with them, through His Word, preachers, and the insights and experiences of other believers.

Most of us would never dream of stating, "I am omniscient!" Yet when we deny our questions, we are, in a way, claiming to comprehend all things. God knows we have doubts, so let's be honest. He is waiting patiently to give us help with them, and God knows, we need it.

*Read: Psalm 139; I John 3:19-20; Psalm 94:8-11*

# DEACON PHIL

*An angel of the Lord said to Philip, "Rise and go toward the south to the road that goes down from Jerusalem to Gaza." This is a desert road. And he rose and went (Acts 8:26-27).*

Through His Holy Word, God allows us to learn from the giants who have gone before us. One of those great individuals was Philip, a deacon of the first church of Jerusalem. Deacon Phil's outstanding characteristic was obedience. He was obedient to "holy nudges," ideas and insights sent by God. He was obedient to inquiry and did not hesitate to ask questions. He was obedient to invitations, especially the invitation to talk about Jesus. His obedience was immediate and instantaneous, just the way God likes it. Deacon Phil's obedience to the Spirit of the Lord led to the conversion of an Ethiopian official and the spread of Christianity to a new part of the world.

Obedience is as important for us as it was for deacon Phil nearly 2,000 years ago. Without obedience, we will never learn God's plan for our lives. Understanding the providence of God comes not through knowledge or maturity, but through obedience. To know what God wants us to do tomorrow, we must obey what He wants us to do today. He will not give the complete blueprint or final picture at once. He presents His plan in installments and we are to obey one step at a time. It can be unsettling and spooky. We may feel a tremendous, inexplicable urge to do something creative that we have never attempted before. We may be nudged into a holy hook-up and find God links us with somebody who is obeying His will in a complementary area. To discover our personal destiny, we must follow Him wherever He leads. Paul writes, "If we live by the Spirit, let us also walk by the Spirit" (Galatians 5:25). Walking by the Spirit is mysterious, but the reward is great, for "he who does the will of God abides for ever" (I John 2:17).

It is beneficial to learn God's eternal truths through history, but we are not just to study history; we are to make history in our own era by allowing God to do His will through us. If you sense the leading of God's Holy Spirit today, rise and go!

*Read: Acts 8:26-40; Isaiah 48:17-18; Psalm 143:10*

## KINDERGARTEN FAITH

*Therefore let us leave the elementary doctrine of Christ and go on to maturity (Hebrews 6:1).*

We all start out somewhere in our walk of faith with Jesus Christ, but where we start out is never where God wants us to end up. The Christian pilgrimage is a continual process of growth, of maturing, of increasing depth and understanding. Yet some people who enroll in the kindergarten of faith never progress to first grade. They catch a little glimpse of Jesus Christ and suddenly think they have all the answers in God's complex, beautiful, baffling world. Frequently they get hung up on love. Love, love, love! They talk so much about the love of God that they forget to show the love of God. They become religious bores, and there are few things worse.

Jesus said His Holy Spirit would come to lead us into all the truth. Lead! There are many things God has yet to reveal to us, and the only way we can be led into spiritual truth is by being open to new ideas and insights. Christians continuously must be refining and reforming that which they already believe. We need firm convictions and strong faith, of course, but when we are not willing to expose our convictions and faith to the light of fresh revelation, we live in fear, too timid to grow and learn. We cower nervously in our familiar kindergarten classroom, afraid of moving on to first grade.

Very few of us would want to repeat kindergarten twelve times until we reach the age of eighteen. That would be tedious. We would not be able to do much good for ourselves or for the world if that were the limit of our education. It is the same in the Christian life. "Brethren, do not be children in your thinking; ... in thinking be mature" (I Corinthians 14:20). We are to advance and progress, always seeking new challenges and opportunities. If we do not, we will bore ourselves and everyone else. We cannot turn people on for Jesus if we turn them off in our homes, businesses, and churches. Let us try today to graduate to a higher grade of faith and accept the exciting possibilities of each new level. Growing in Christ is a thrilling education that lasts a lifetime.

*Read: Hebrews 5:7-6:3; I Peter 2:2-3; Psalm 71:17-19*

23

# MADE TO MAKE A DIFFERENCE

*For who sees anything different in you? (I Corinthians 4:7).*

Right this second, each of us is making a difference in God's world. The important question is, what kind of a difference? Are we helping or hurting? Are we being positive or negative? Are we bringing healing or destruction, joy or misery? We cannot live without making some daily difference, any more than we can live without breathing. Of course, God wants it to be a positive difference. That is why He created us. We are not here only to take up space. We have been made, remade, redeemed, and blessed by God's Holy Spirit to make a difference for good -- today! Paul called himself "an apostle, set apart for the gospel of God" (Romans 1:1). We, too, are to be set apart, different, so the world will see Jesus Christ in us.

In the greatest sermon ever preached, Jesus called His disciples salt and light. Consider the make-up of these eternal symbols. If we examine salt under a microscope, we find it is not one mass, but individual little grains; no two look alike or have the same dimensions. Light is made up of rays of different colors, all working together to give a spectrum, the rainbow. Jesus is saying that nobody is too small and nobody is too ordinary to make a positive difference in the world. He needs all of us. Everyone is important. He gave us our individual gifts so we could uniquely serve Him. God loves all colors, sizes, shapes, and ages. Everybody! Each of us is equipped to do great things for His Kingdom on earth.

I wonder if anybody sees anything different in people who claim to be Christians these days. If only Christians stayed in character as followers of Jesus Christ twenty-four hours a day, every day of the year! So often we forget that by the way we speak and the things we do, we influence other people for good or for evil. Let us rededicate ourselves to knowing Christ better, trusting Him completely, spending time daily in His Word, and allowing His Holy Spirit to transform us. The more Jesus Christ makes a difference in our own lives, the greater difference we will be able to make in His wonderful world.

*Read: Matthew 5:13-20; Mark 9:50; Ephesians 5:8-9*

24

# JONAH, THE RELUCTANT PREACHER

*"For as Jonah was three days and three nights in the belly of the whale, so will the Son of man be three days and three nights in the heart of the earth" (Matthew 12:40).*

The Book of Jonah is a whale of a tale, but sometimes we get so caught up in details of the fish that we miss the meat of the message. Jesus spoke of Jonah as a real person, and I think all of us can learn from this reluctant Old Testament preacher.

**We cannot hide from God.** It is possible to run away from God, but impossible to outrun God. Jonah did not fool God by boarding the ship to Tarshish. God was right there. In trying to escape his calling, Jonah brought trouble on himself and others. Those poor sailors were thrown into a huge storm. Though they fought valiantly to save him, they probably were burdened with guilt when they had to throw Jonah into the sea.

**God gives second chances.** If we ask for forgiveness, God will give us another chance. Jonah was saved when he called for help. "The waters closed in over me, the deep was round about me; weeds were wrapped about my head at the roots of the mountains. I went down to the land whose bars closed upon me for ever; yet thou didst bring up my life from the Pit" (Jonah 2:5-6). What an extraordinary rescue! We should never think we are beyond hope of a new start with God's help.

**We may be unhappy with God's will.** Jonah preached an eight word sermon: "Yet forty days, and Nineveh shall be overthrown!" (3:4). His sermon was successful. The entire town of 120,000 people repented. Yet Jonah was not gratified or glad. He was angry! Many of us pray for God's will, expecting to be thrilled about it. Where do we get that idea? God's will is likely to make us unhappy. To obey God's will, we need to sacrifice our own, and that is never easy to do.

There is a little bit of Jonah in all of us. Like him, we often discover reluctantly that we can never get away from God, no matter how long and hard we run to escape the calling and responsibility He places upon us. Today, try to overcome any reluctance to do God's will, whether you like it or not.

*Read: The Book of Jonah*

# TALKING TO THE TEMPTER

*"It is written" (Luke 4:4).*

Are you ever tempted? If you answer No to that question, you must think you are holier than Jesus Christ Himself. Either that or you are denying your humanity, a very foolish thing to do. Temptation is a universal experience. All people are affected by temptation throughout their lifetimes. Jesus was tempted. Jesus was full of the Holy Spirit, and anyone who is full of the Holy Spirit will know moments of desire and temptation. Being tempted is no sin; sin comes in yielding to temptation. There is no temptation we will ever face that Jesus did not confront, but Jesus, "one who has been tempted as we are, yet without sin" (Hebrews 4:15), never yielded. By His example and with His help, we need not yield either.

How can we avoid walking into temptation? By talking to the tempter! The tempter, the power of evil, goes by many names: serpent, devil, Satan, sin, selfishness. There is an evil spirit in the world that Christians must confront. Jesus never ran from the tempter. He talked to the tempter, using the only language the tempter fears: the Word of God. "It is written," said Jesus. Quoting from Deuteronomy, He used the power of Scripture to defeat the power of evil, and the devil "departed from him until an opportune time" (Luke 4:13). The tempter always returns, so we must watch out for the next attack.

We have the same weapon against temptation Jesus Christ used: the Word of God. But the Word of God can only help us with our struggles if we know it. Get into the Scriptures and see what is written. It is written for you! Memorize as many Bible passages as you can. Otherwise, you will not have much to say to the tempter, who may be sneaking up on you this very moment. Your life can turn into a disaster overnight if you do not know how to talk to the tempter. All the help you need is probably sitting on your bookshelf: your Bible. Pick it up and study it. Learn it. Think about it. Trust it. Believe it!

Be prepared today to talk to the tempter, for the tempter might be preparing today to talk to you.

*Read: Luke 4:1-13; Deuteronomy 8:8, 6:13, 6:16; Hebrews 2:17-18*

# WHEN THERE IS SICKNESS IN YOUR HOME

*Now Simon's mother-in-law lay sick with a fever, and immediately they told him of her. And he came and took her by the hand and lifted her up, and the fever left her; and she served them (Mark 1:30-31).*

Simon Peter probably threw his wife into a panic when he brought Jesus and some disciples home after a synagogue service one day. He did not give his wife time for the frantic, elaborate ritual I call "P.H.F.P.V.": Preparing House For Preacher's Visit. People rearrange the house with hurricane speed when they know the preacher is stopping by, leaving it barely recognizable to its regular occupants. Still, Peter did the right thing. His mother-in-law was ill and Jesus healed her. Because Peter invited Jesus in, she was made completely well.

If there is sickness in your home or confusion in your life, it may be you have never taken the time to invite Jesus Christ in. Maybe you think you do not know Him well enough. Maybe you think your problems are not big enough. No one or no thing is too little for Jesus! Invite Him in and ask Him to take over. Like Peter, do not tell Him how to heal. Just be patient and trust Him, even if it looks as though more disaster and disease are coming. He will heal in His own time and way.

When healing comes, turn thanksgiving into thanks-living. Notice, Peter's mother-in-law immediately arose from her sickbed and began to serve people, and Jesus let her. He did not urge her to lie down and take it easy because she had been ailing with that fever. By serving, she expressed gratitude for what Jesus had done for her. When you are healed from some disease or problem, thank Jesus for the miracle by serving other people. Share the good news of your recovery with your neighbors so they can learn how to find healing for sicknesses in their homes. Whether the healing is small or great, talk about it! Remember, Jesus came to help other people, too. He came to offer salvation to all the world.

Invite Jesus Christ into your life today. You do not have to prepare your house for the Preacher's visit. Just prepare your heart for His mercy, love, and healing.

*Read: Mark 1:29-39; Colossians 2:6-7; Psalm 138*

# FORGIVE YOURSELF

*"Every one who believes in him receives forgiveness of sins through his name" (Acts 10:43).*

Probably the hardest person you ever will have to forgive is yourself. The Bible tells us, "If we confess our sins, he is faithful and just, and will forgive our sins and cleanse us from all unrighteousness" (I John 1:9). We are forgiven by the risen Lord, but sometimes we have trouble forgiving ourselves for the silly, stubborn, sinful things we have done. We allow past mistakes to hound us and hinder us from moving forward.

Jeremiah wrote, "Every man is stupid" (10:14). We tend to forget that even great leaders of the Lord in biblical times made stupid, senseless mistakes, just as we do today. Consider Peter, who boldly proclaimed to his beloved Master, "If I must die with you, I will not deny you" (Mark 14:31), but quickly made a fool of himself by denying Jesus three times. Because Peter "broke down and wept" (v. 72) over his sin, he was forgiven and he went on to be a powerful preacher in the early Church. Consider also King David, who was tormented with remorse after committing adultery and murder. When he admitted his transgressions and confessed with "a broken and contrite heart" (Psalm 51:17), he, too, received the release of forgiveness.

Some people fear their sin is too horrible, too base, to be forgiven, but there is no sin too great for God's mercy if we humbly pray, "I confess my iniquity, I am sorry for my sin" (Psalm 38:18), and mean it. The Lord promises His people, "Though your sins are like scarlet, they shall be as white as snow; though they are red like crimson, they shall become like wool" (Isaiah 1:18). Forgive yourself, whatever you have done. If you do not, you are still in your sin and that means Jesus Christ was crucified in vain for you. Do not be a prisoner of the past. You cannot change what happened, but you can make the decision today that your past will not ruin your future or prevent you from growing as a disciple of Christ.

God has forgiven you; that is why Jesus Christ died on the Cross. Other people have forgiven you; that is why they love you. Do not be the lone holdout.

*Read: Psalm 69:5; Mark 14:26-31, 66-72; Psalm 51*

# PAGEANT PORTRAYALS

*He did as the angel of the Lord commanded (Matthew 1:24).*

If you were involved in Sunday School Christmas pageants as a child, I imagine you remember them vividly. Back home, they were staged by the junior high department. One teenager read the Christmas story and the rest of us portrayed the characters. It was an honor to be a shepherd, and fun, too; they used a mop pole or piece of cardboard tubing as a staff and when the teacher was not looking, they dueled and poked each other. (I never got to be a shepherd.) The bigger boys were the wise men; they would dress up in bathrobes, carry cigar boxes covered with tin foil, and march magnificently down the aisle. (I never got to be a wise man.) The choir members represented the heavenly angels; they wore cut-out pillowcases, sat in the balcony, and sang pretty hymns. (I never got to be an angel.) Mary was always a beautiful young girl, one the teacher especially liked. She would smile and beam at the shepherds who adored, the wise people who worshipped, and the angels who sang. Me? I was the preacher's kid. That means I got the part of Joseph. Poor Joe. He just stood there. Didn't speak, didn't sing, didn't smile. Most embarrassing of all, he stood beside a girl. For a junior high guy, there is nothing worse.

I always have felt great sympathy for Joseph. There are no Christmas carols written about Joseph. He is not featured by himself on holiday greeting cards. We just do not hear too much about him. That is ironic, because without Joseph, the birth of Jesus would not have taken place as history records it. Joseph was a good, righteous, loving man. In a difficult, bewildering situation, he had the courage to follow his dreams, rise above his fears, and forget his pride. To Joseph, obedience to the Lord was more important than any other consideration. No wonder he was chosen to be Jesus's earthly father!

Looking back, I am very glad I had the opportunity to portray Joseph in so many Christmas pageants, because I learned a valuable lesson: we do not have to be the star of the show to play an important role in God's plan.

*Read: Matthew 1:18-25; Luke 2:1-7; Matthew 2:13-23*

## YOUR DESTINY DEPENDS UPON YOU

*"For I have no pleasure in the death of any one, says the Lord God; so turn, and live" (Ezekiel 18:32).*

Long before you were born, God planned your unique gifts, abilities, and personality. He sent you to earth for a reason and it is His will that you grow daily toward your destiny. Yet God can only bring your destiny to completion with your help, response, and participation. Your destiny depends not only upon God, who created it, but upon you, to fulfill it.

It is up to you to study and know the Word of God, believe in God's love, accept Jesus Christ as Lord and Savior, and follow with courage the leading of His Holy Spirit.

It is up to you to take personal responsibility for your life. Stop blaming parents, employers, or mates for your mistakes. Grow up and do something constructive about your problems instead of just moaning about them. Everyone is responsible for his own actions in God's sight. "The soul that sins shall die. The son shall not suffer for the iniquity of the father, nor the father suffer for the iniquity of the son; the righteousness of the righteous shall be upon himself, and the wickedness of the wicked shall be upon himself" (Ezekiel 18:20).

It is up to you to respond thoughtfully to whatever comes your way. Do not focus on your immediate desires. Filter experiences through your mind to see the long range view.

It is up to you to determine how you change and grow. You are changing daily, either growing closer to your destiny or farther away. If you like to be dejected and miserable, go ahead, but if you want to find the joy, peace, power, and happiness God intends you to have, make up your mind to do it, with the help of the Word of God, the forgiveness of Christ, and the power of His Spirit. Turn to the Lord God and live!

"God our Savior ... desires all men to be saved and to come to the knowledge of the truth" (I Timothy 2:3-4). God wants you to be saved, but He did not make you a puppet. You are free to choose your course. God equips you with the tools you need to bring you to your destiny, but you have to use them.

*Read: Ezekiel 18; Isaiah 65:11-12; I Thessalonians 5:9-10*

# THORNS

*A thorn was given me in the flesh (II Corinthians 12:7).*

Doesn't it seem as if nothing on earth could be more useless than a thorn? Nobody collects or exhibits thorns. They are hideous, like toothaches. They do not kill us; they just pierce and puncture and perturb us. No wonder Paul referred to a problem in his life as "a thorn in the flesh." We do not know what Paul's thorn was, but we know he prayed often to the Lord to take his thorn away. Each time the answer was No.

Most of us have thorny, bothersome problems. We think we would be so much better without them. Oh, we could be such tremendous witnesses for Jesus if we did not have those thorns! We blame them for our failures, and usually either hide them in shame or bellyache so much that we repel people.

If only we followed the apostle Paul's example. Through prayer, Paul came to see his thorn in the flesh as something meant by God for good, a friend instead of a foe. Prayer is the means by which we can differentiate between those things God is using in our lives for good, and those things God wants out of our lives because they are not good for us. Like Paul, we are to go to the Lord and ask Him to remove the thorn, believing God will hear and answer our prayer. The thorn will either go away or it will remain. If it remains, we can be sure God means it for good. In fact, the Lord can know that the worst thing in the world for us would be to take that thorn away, for it is through our thorns that we come to know and experience the sufficient grace and matchless love of God.

Paul said, "For the sake of Christ, then, I am content with weaknesses, insults, hardships, persecutions, and calamities, for when I am weak, then I am strong" (II Corinthians 12:10). When we are weak, the power of the Lord within us is greatest, for our thorns force us to rely on His strength, not our own.

Jesus Christ, hanging on the Cross, wore a crown of thorns, and through His death brought salvation to all who believe.

Thorns are not so useless after all.

*Read: II Corinthians 12:1-10; John 19:1-2; I Corinthians 1:26-31*

# THE ODDEST REBUKE

*A rebuke goes deeper into a man of understanding than a hundred blows into a fool (Proverbs 17:10).*

We all need to be rebuked from time to time, but most of us do not like that experience. Even when the rebuke is made in love and we know we deserve it, even when the rebuke straightens us out and we are grateful afterward, we tend to be a little embarrassed and resentful at the moment of reprimand.

Surely the oddest rebuke in history came to Balaam, a Mesopotamian prophet who made the fatal error of trying to please both God and man. Asked by King Balak to pronounce a curse upon the Israelites, Balaam prayed a prayer he never should have prayed. Because of his willful disobedience, he was unable to see the Lord's messenger, an angel with a large drawn sword, standing directly in front of him until he was rebuked by his donkey. Peter recalled Balaam, "who loved the wages of wickedness. But he was rebuked for his wrongdoing by a donkey -- a beast without speech -- who spoke with a man's voice and restrained the prophet's madness" (II Peter 2:15-16, NIV). The dumb donkey spoke! Balaam and his donkey had a conversation, and only then were Balaam's eyes opened to recognize his sin. Unfortunately, the rebuke failed to turn Balaam back to God and he died a horrible death.

No matter how far you wander from God, you probably never will hear a rebuke as odd as Balaam's. If one day some loving, caring person comes to you with words of warning that you are trying to please man and not God, that you are going in the wrong direction and your willful disobedience might destroy you, do not be embarrassed. Be happy! "Happy is the man whom God reproves; therefore despise not the chastening of the Almighty" (Job 5:17). Do not be resentful. Be wise! "Reprove a wise man, and he will love you. Give instruction to a wise man, and he will be still wiser" (Proverbs 9:8-9). Heed the warning before it is too late, and thank God for sending you His special messenger to turn you around. The one who rebukes you just might be the best friend you ever have.

*Read: Numbers 22:21-35; Jude 8-13; Revelation 2:14*

# TURNING TENSIONS INTO TREASURES

*"Son, why have you treated us so?  Behold, your father and I have been looking for you anxiously" (Luke 2:48).*

One would think if ever there was a harmonious, ideal family in our world, it had to be the earthly family of Jesus Christ: Joseph, the strong, honest carpenter; beautiful, obedient Mary; Jesus, the Son of God born in a manger.  What joy and laughter and closeness they must have shared day by day!

Well, the only biblical passage that speaks of Jesus's childhood tells a different story.  Returning to Nazareth after the Passover feast, Mary and Joseph assumed twelve-year old Jesus was in the company of friends and relatives.  When they could not locate Him, they frantically rushed back to Jerusalem, where, after three days, they found Him among the teachers in the temple.  That stressful situation shows there was tension in the household of Christ, just as there is in Christian homes today.  Within the best of families, people get lost.

Do not apologize for family discord.   Occasional disagreements are quite natural.  It is difficult for children to find their destiny, and difficult for parents to help.  Growth comes not in trying to avoid tension, but in being willing to change, to adapt.  Sometimes old customs must be broken and we feel sad, but if we believe God is working for good, we soon find we are blessed with better customs, deeper communication, and new levels of love in our relationships.

Parents, if you cannot understand your child's behavior, ponder it in your heart and be patient.  God has an agenda for each child.  Your plan is not as important as God's plan.  Give your child steady encouragement to discover God's will.

Children, if you dislike your parents' demands and rules, obey them anyway.  Jesus Christ knew more at twelve than His parents ever would, but He obeyed them, and He increased in wisdom and stature and in favor with God and man.

Always be loving, always be kind, but be realistic as well.  If Jesus's family knew tension, so will yours.  Do not deny it or ignore it.  Learn from it.  Tension brings change and growth.  With the power of Christ, tensions can be treasures in disguise.

*Read:  Luke 2:41-52;  Exodus 20:12;  Ephesians 6:1-4*

# SAINT MAKING

*Let thy saints shout for joy (Psalm 132:9).*

Many of us feel uncomfortable when, as Christians, we are called saints. That is because we know we do not always think, look, act, or talk like saints. Redeemed sinners, yes, but saints? The apostle Paul teaches that everyone who believes in Jesus Christ as Lord and Savior is a saint. We are saints not because of what we do or what we are doing, but because of what God has done and is doing to us. A saint is an ordinary person through whom God does extraordinary things. What things?

**Forgiveness of sins.** The message of our faith is that Jesus Christ came to earth and died so we could be forgiven of our sins. We cannot forgive others or know forgiveness of sin ourselves through our own efforts. God gives us ordinary people the extraordinary power to forgive and to be forgiven.

**The spirit of wisdom and revelation.** Jesus knew the mind of God and was wise in all ways. He promised, "When the Spirit of truth comes, he will guide you into all the truth" (John 16:13). Extraordinary wisdom and revelation come to us ordinary people from on high through God's Holy Spirit.

**A heart of hope.** All of us face problems, decisions, and grief, yet God places in our hearts something only He can give: hope. In the midst of trouble, we ordinary people have extraordinary hope to believe things are going to work out the way God wants them to and He is always working for good.

**Availability of power.** God gives His saints extraordinary power. We have resurrection power: power to die to self and be born again into new life. We have ascension power: power to rise above any situation, any conditions. We have dominion power: power to defeat temptation, hate, and sin, and be ruled instead by love and self-control. Saints are powerful!

Shout for joy that God has given you sainthood! Today, thank God in prayer for all the ordinary people you have known who were and are examples of His extraordinary love, and ask Him to make you a bigger, better, brighter, more extraordinary saint than you have ever been before.

*Read: Ephesians 1:11-23; Romans 8:27; Psalm 97:10*

# BRANCH MANAGERS

*"Abide in me, and I in you. As the branch cannot bear fruit by itself, unless it abides in the vine, neither can you, unless you abide in me. I am the vine, you are the branches. He who abides in me, and I in him, he it is that bears much fruit, for apart from me you can do nothing" (John 15:4-5).*

A truth taught throughout the Bible is that although no two of us are alike and no two of us have the same combination of gifts, there is one thing required of us all: whatever work we do, whatever abilities we possess, whatever days we are given to live, we are expected by God to produce. We are put on this earth to enjoy life and to serve the Lord by producing good, lasting fruit for the Kingdom. Nobody can be productive without Jesus's help. He is the Vine and we are the branches. Jesus is Headquarters and we are His branch managers.

Being a productive branch manager is the key to joy. "These things I have spoke to you, that my joy may be in you, and that your joy may be full" (v. 11). Joy is found as a result of doing something worthwhile. It is not a root, but a fruit! It takes discipline, obedience, and sacrifice, but the happiest people in the world are those who creatively produce good for themselves, their family, nation, and church. Burnout and depression come when people feel useless and wasted.

Branch managers not only find joy, but also receive the highest honor that can be given: friendship with Jesus Christ. Some people think God is against them, but Jesus says, "You are my friends if you do what I command you" (v. 14). We cannot earn Jesus's friendship. He gives it to us when we obey Him and produce good fruit to glorify His name.

We are important to Jesus and He still has work for us to accomplish. Do not tell Him how to run the branch. Just strive hard to please your Master. "Be steadfast, immovable, always abounding in the work of the Lord, knowing that in the Lord your labor is not in vain" (I Corinthians 15:58). Live as an effective, efficient, productive branch manager and know the inexpressible joy of being a friend of the Lord Jesus Christ.

*Read: John 15:1-18; Matthew 7:16-17; Proverbs 6:6-11*

# SILENT LIGHT

*"Blessed are the poor in spirit, for theirs is the kingdom of heaven. Blessed are those who mourn, for they shall be comforted. Blessed are the meek, for they shall inherit the earth. Blessed are those who hunger and thirst for righteousness, for they shall be satisfied. Blessed are the merciful, for they shall obtain mercy. Blessed are the pure in heart, for they shall see God. Blessed are the peacemakers, for they shall be called the sons of God. Blessed are those who are persecuted for righteousness' sake, for theirs is the kingdom of heaven" (Matthew 5:3-10).*

How beautifully the Beatitudes in Jesus's Sermon on the Mount describe what Christians are meant to be! Just four verses later, Jesus calls disciples "the light of the world." A marvelous attribute of light is that it is silent. Light makes no noise, yet always has a great impact. In times of darkness, Jesus expects His followers to be silent lights whose luminous radiance guides people toward God's everlasting light.

Silent lights are people of integrity who daily try to do what is right. When they have the power to hurt, they choose instead to help. Silent lights are people who never grumble about what they do not have, but are grateful for what they have and eager to share it. Silent lights are people we can count on. No matter how dark it is, we know they will be there with warmth and love. With their sense of humor and quiet confidence, they brighten any dull day. Silent lights are people who do their jobs without demanding recognition and gratitude. They give of themselves modestly so God gets the honor and glory.

Most of us think we need to yell and scream and shout to be noticed, but the best way to be noticed is to be a sincere, committed, consistent Christian, a silent light for Jesus Christ. Meditate today on the profound beauty of the Beatitudes. Allow them to challenge and enrich your faith. Accept your responsibility to reflect Jesus Christ in all you do, and before you fall asleep during your next silent night, pray, "Father, help me to be a shining, sparkling, silent light for you."

*Read: Matthew 5:1-16; John 9:5; Proverbs 13:9*

# DEMANDING DISCIPLINES OF DISCIPLESHIP

*"Enter by the narrow gate; for the gate is wide and the way is easy, that leads to destruction, and those who enter by it are many. For the gate is narrow and the way is hard, that leads to life, and those who find it are few" (Matthew 7:13-14).*

Jesus warns us that the gate to His way of living is narrow and the way is hard. Feeding our appetites, acting as our own god, following our personal wishes -- that is much easier, but it is the sure road to destruction. To dedicate our lives to Jesus Christ, we must practice some demanding disciplines.

**Discernment**. We have to discern the difference between authentic and evil teachers, truth and falsehood. "Beware of false prophets, who come to you in sheep's clothing, but inwardly are ravenous wolves" (Matthew 7:15). We should not be fooled by how people sound or look, but judge their teachings by their adherence to the Bible. To apply discernment, we must develop an understanding of Scripture.

**Deeds**. Jesus gets upset with people who sing hymns and recite creeds but have no expression in their confession, people who try to worship without the work of mission that goes along with it. "Not every one who says to me, 'Lord, Lord,' shall enter the kingdom of heaven, but he who does the will of my Father who is in heaven" (v. 21). It is not lip service Jesus wants, no matter how beautiful it sounds. It is life service!

**Decision-making.** Whether we realize it or not, we make decisions every day that shape our destiny. We are either building our lives upon the rock of Jesus Christ or upon shifting sand. Let us be wise, not foolish, for Jesus tells us someday, somewhere, the rains are going to pour, the floods are going to rise, the winds are going to howl. We are going to be hit with turbulence that will shake our foundations. If we build upon rock, we will stand. If we build upon sand, we will fall. The outcome depends upon the decisions we make today.

The disciplines of discipleship are demanding, but exercising them daily will bring joy and meaning to life here on earth and keep us safe on the narrow road to Heaven.

*Read: Matthew 7:13-29; II Corinthians 5:15; Proverbs 12:1*

# THE MELODY OF THE HEART

*Be filled with the Spirit, addressing one another in psalms and hymns and spiritual songs, singing and making melody to the Lord with all your heart (Ephesians 5:18-19).*

We human beings are unique among God's creatures in our ability to express deep, heartfelt emotions in song. The Psalms are songs, and throughout the Bible we are told to make a joyful noise, sing to the Lord, and praise God with gladness and thanksgiving. Singing is good for the soul. We sing when our hearts are full, not when we are depressed and angry. We would never dream of stopping to call a time-out in the middle of an argument to suggest, "Hey, let's sing a chorus!" We probably would be better off if we did, but we would have to duck for cover if we made a suggestion like that. Singing does not go with negativity and hostility. Singing goes with joy.

It is interesting to watch people during worship services. Many sing hymns with gusto and fervor. Others stubbornly keep their mouths shut. Some will not sing because they know they do not have a good voice. That never stops me! Singing expresses our attitude toward God. It is not the accuracy of the notes He cares about. It is the melody of the heart.

Music is a great inspiration to me. I am sure my love of music is a legacy from my mother, a professor of music. She had a beautiful voice. For the last six years of her life, from the effects of a stroke, she could speak only one word, my sister's name. Yet though she could not talk, she still could sing. How grateful I was to be able to sing great choruses and anthems of the church with her! The melody in her heart lasted to the end.

"O sing to the Lord a new song; sing to the Lord, all the earth! Sing to the Lord, bless his name; tell of his salvation from day to day. Declare his glory among the nations, his marvelous works among all the people! For great is the Lord, and greatly to be praised" (Psalm 96:1-4). Sing unto the Lord today. It is a tremendous way to praise God and you do not need a great voice to do it. Just keep the melody of love in your heart and your song will be beautiful to the Lord.

*Read: Exodus 15:2; Psalm 98; I Corinthians 14:5*

# LEARNING, YEARNING, AND EARNING

*"Turn to me and be saved, all the ends of the earth! For I am God, and there is no other" (Isaiah 45:22).*

We all have the same problem. Some people just do not recognize it or know what to do about it. This problem comes to every man, woman, and child: sin. We call it original sin for it is original within each person. Sin makes us do and say things we know we should not, and keeps us from doing and saying things we know we should. Paul lamented, "I know that nothing good dwells within me, that is, in my flesh. I can will what is right, but I cannot do it. For I do not do the good I want, but the evil I do not want is what I do" (Romans 7:18-19). Sometimes sin appears tantalizing and provocative, but it always leaves us wretched, depressed, and full of regrets.

People try to be saved from sin in different ways.

**Learning.** "I'll read books, take classes, study hard, and soon I'll be strong, confident, and capable of resisting sin."

**Yearning.** "I'll just yearn and search for a way to defeat the power of sin, and I'll keep looking till I find it."

**Earning.** "I'll go to church, give money, lead a good life, and earn credit in God's bank. He'll have to save me!"

Knowledge is a great achievement; searching for answers is commendable; works are important; but learning, yearning, and earning do not bring victory over sin. There is only one way.

**Turning.** Turn to God and accept the gift of salvation He offers through the life, death, and resurrection of Christ! "The saying is sure and worthy of full acceptance, that Christ Jesus came into the world to save sinners" (I Timothy 1:15). Salvation is the work of the Savior. It is on no merit of our own, not our learning, yearning, or earning. Jesus Christ, who never committed a sin, became sin for us. He took the penalty for sin upon Himself and paid the ransom. When we turn to Him and believe He died for us, we have forgiveness.

"Whoever calls on the name of the Lord shall be saved" (Acts 2:21). There is no other name by which a person can be saved except the name of Jesus Christ, so turn to Him today.

*Read: Romans 7:15-25; Acts 4:12; Galatians 1:3-5*

# WHAT DID YOU MISS TODAY?

*A man's mind plans his way, but the Lord directs his steps (Proverbs 16:9).*

Most of us feel irked and irritated when our plans do not work out the way we want. If we miss something we think we deserve or need, we become downright indignant. Did you miss anything today? Maybe you had to work late and you missed dinner. Maybe you missed a chance to go somewhere new or meet somebody interesting. Maybe you missed a concert or a television program you were eager to see. In our fast-paced, hurry-up society, some people act as though their day is ruined if they miss one section of a revolving door!

Those disappointments are frustrating, but did you ever stop to think about things that might have missed you today? There could have been a close call you did not even notice. You might have been near injury or death in an automobile accident. Perhaps a nasty germ was flying around and you could have caught it, but you did not. We denounce God when we think things go wrong, but forget to glorify Him for the countless times He protects us with His goodness and grace. We neglect to look for His presence in all circumstances, those we welcome as well as those we wish we could change.

Of course, we might not understand exactly how God is leading and directing our lives, but Scripture declares, "I know the plans I have for you, says the Lord, plans for welfare and not for evil, to give you a future and a hope. Then you will call upon me and come and pray to me, and I will hear you. You will seek me and find me; when you seek me with all your heart, I will be found by you" (Jeremiah 29:11-13). Our irksome, irritating disappointments are sometimes just the jolt we need to turn our earnest attention to the Lord.

God works for good in everything with those who love Him and who are called by Him. Nothing can separate us from His love. Surely, then, our little frustrations should never cause us to doubt His care. Do not be sad about what you missed today. Be glad about what missed you, and thank God for everything.

*Read: Romans 8:28-39; James 4:13-5:11; Psalm 36:5-9*

# ENJOYING THE MYSTERY

*For the kingdom of God is not food and drink but righteousness and peace and joy in the Holy Spirit (Romans 14:17).*

Have you ever thanked God for mystery? Though most of us realize we must live with mystery, we do not always enjoy it. That is too bad, because it is the mystery of the spiritual world that makes life so awesome, surprising, and exciting.

Nicodemus was a man who had no mystery, no wonder, no sense of the miraculous. He concentrated on facts and figures, dates and data, explanations and equations. He would fit into many churches today! He was outgoing, outspoken, but a little left out; intelligent, inquisitive, but insecure and inconsistent. Knowing something was wrong, he went to question Jesus and was stunned to learn that he needed to be reborn. "How can a man be born when he is old? Can he enter a second time into his mother's womb and be born?" (John 3:4). To explain spiritual rebirth, Jesus used the word "pneuma," meaning both wind (or breath) and Spirit. Nicodemus saw that he did not know where wind came from or where it went. He could not describe what it looked like, if it was big or little, male or female, or how it worked. He simply believed wind existed because he saw its effects. So it is with Holy Spirit. The Spirit evades description and definition. He is ceaseless and sovereign in His freedom. The Spirit does not ask our approval or operate by consensus. We do not know where He comes from, and only Heaven knows where He is going, but thank God for Holy Spirit! We are born anew by the Spirit, and in Him we find the righteousness, peace, and joy of the Kingdom.

Those who are born again do not have answers to all the questions and do not understand all things. They are excited and happy to live in a transcendent experience that is beyond human comprehension, accepting God's miracles and believing that, no matter what, He is in control. God is good. He gives us more than our physical world. He gives us a spiritual Kingdom! He allows us to be part of a mystery we are not required to explain, but only asked to believe in and enjoy.

*Read: John 3:1-15; Matthew 13:10-17; I Corinthians 2:1-13*

41

# A SAD END

*Jesus looking upon him loved him, and said to him, "You lack one thing; go, sell what you have, and give to the poor, and you will have treasure in heaven; and come, follow me." At that saying his countenance fell, and he went away sorrowful; for he had great possessions (Mark 10:21-22).*

I wonder what happened to the rich young ruler who approached Jesus but went away sorrowful when he was told to give up his riches. He seems to have been a fine man. He was educated, he obeyed the law, he was eager to ask Jesus how to inherit eternal life, and Jesus loved him. But when Jesus said, "Go, sell what you have, and give to the poor," his face fell and he turned away. Most people Jesus encountered during His earthly ministry found healing and new life. This man, sadly, was different. Why? Jesus's command to go, sell, and give was too great a sacrifice. He could not part with his wealth and possessions, even to obtain treasure in Heaven. Unless he had a change of heart later on, his life came to a sad end.

Many people today are sorrowful, for they have not found the purpose, peace, and power God promises through Christ. Even some who march under the Christian banner have yet to find the meaning of life. They are hesitant to go, sell, and give, but that is what it takes to inherit eternal life! Go: get involved, be active in the cause of Christ. Sell: take material blessings and turn them into spiritual blessings, exchange your riches for heavenly treasures. Give: take what you have and share it, give abundantly to the needy. Jesus warns of the dangers of wealth. The wrong attitude toward material possessions can keep us out of the Kingdom of Heaven. "The cares of the world and the delight in riches choke the word" (Matthew 13:22). When the Word is choked, we cannot grow as disciples of Jesus Christ.

Nobody plans to come to a sad end, but it can happen to any of us if we are afraid to go, sell, and give. Do not walk away sorrowful from the only One who can lead you to eternal life. When you offer all you have to Christ, you will not come to a sad end; rather, you will secure a glorious new beginning.

*Read: Mark 10:17-31; Proverbs 11:28; Matthew 6:21*

# METHODS OF FORGETFULNESS

*"O my God, I am ashamed and blush to lift my face to thee, my God, for our iniquities have risen higher than our heads, and our guilt has mounted up to the heavens" (Ezra 9:6).*

A guilty conscience is unpleasant and uncomfortable, and in our society nobody wants to be bothered. We do not like a sense of shame. Not many people blush anymore, even when they ought to! That is why most of us prefer to forget our guilt, push it aside and pretend it does not exist. We use plenty of ingenious methods to try to forget we have done something stupid, selfish, and senseless that breaks the laws of God.

**The Mathematical Method.** "Everybody's doing it. I'm no different than anybody else. People are sinners, that's all."

**The Comparative Method.** "I never killed anybody. I never robbed a bank. I'm not nearly as evil as some people."

**The Busy Method.** "I'm too busy to think about this right now. I will have to take care of my guilt another time."

**The Projected Method.** "I'm guilty, but it's not my fault. It's my tyrannical parents, my lousy environment. It's not me!"

These different methods of forgetfulness have one thing in common: they do not work. Even if we temporarily fool ourselves, we never fool God. "Can a man hide himself in secret places so that I cannot see him? says the Lord" (Jeremiah 23:24). Eventually, unconfessed guilt is bound to creep out somewhere, in some way, and when it does it can destroy us.

King David experienced both the anguish of guilt and the release of forgiveness. "When I declared not my sin, my body wasted away through my groaning all day long. For day and night thy hand was heavy upon me; my strength was dried up as by the heat of summer. I acknowledged my sin to thee, and I did not hide my iniquity; I said, 'I will confess my transgressions to the Lord'; then thou didst forgive the guilt of my sin" (Psalm 32:2-5). Guilt cannot be forgotten. Guilt must be faced and forgiven. However huge our guilt may be, we can be redeemed if we face it and ask God to forgive it. That is the Christian method of handling guilt, and never forget it.

*Read: Deuteronomy 8:11; Proverbs 28:13; Ephesians 1:7-8*

# BORN-AGAINERS

*From now on, therefore, we regard no one from a human point of view; even though we once regarded Christ from a human point of view, we regard him thus no longer. Therefore, if any one is in Christ, he is a new creation; the old has passed away, behold, the new has come. All this is from God, who through Christ reconciled us to himself (II Corinthians 5:16-18).*

Are you turned off by people who are turned on by Christianity? Some born-againers tend to be a bit over-zealous, intimidating, and misinformed. They come on too strong and make others feel inferior, like second-class citizens. Though nobody has ascended from Heaven to earth except Jesus, they give the impression they know everything there is to know about the Kingdom. Some seem to know more than Christ!

I understand people who get upset with religious fanatics, but please realize that each of us must be born again. It is not a suggestion, an alternative, or an option. It is the command of Jesus. "Unless one is born anew, he cannot see the kingdom of God" (John 3:3). That does not mean we have to stand in front of a crowd to give a lengthy, dramatic, spicy testimony with every intimate detail of our conversion experience (the exact date, place, hour, minute, and second we were reborn), or close our eyes, raise our hands, and sing boisterous hallelujahs day and night. Being born again has a much deeper meaning.

Spiritual rebirth is a beautiful process of growth into new life. Paul writes, "Put off your old nature which belongs to your former manner of life and is corrupt through deceitful lusts, and be renewed in the spirit of your minds, and put on the new nature, created after the likeness of God in true righteousness and holiness" (Ephesians 4:22-24). As we grow in likeness to God, we are not only born into eternity, but we live as we never lived before on earth. We learn as we never learned before. We love as we never loved before. The old passes away and new life comes. So if you hope to see the Kingdom of Heaven, make sure you never get so worked up over born-againers that you fail to be born again yourself.

*Read: John 6:63; I John 5:1-12; Revelation 21:5*

# HOPHNI AND PHINEHAS

*Fathers, do not provoke your children to anger, but bring them up in the discipline and instruction of the Lord (Ephesians 6:4).*

Hophni and Phinehas. There are two names we do not hear anymore! They were PKs: Preacher's Kids. Sons of Eli, chief judge and high priest of Israel, they grew up in a religious home and became priests themselves, but fell into evil and disrepute. "The sons of Eli were worthless men; they had no regard for the Lord" (I Samuel 2:12). They were infamous, uncontrollable, despicable, a disgrace to the clergy. They died violent deaths on the same day, and when Eli, ninety-eight years old, heard the news, he fell, broke his neck, and also died.

The names Hophni and Phinehas faded out of our language long ago, but their story prompts questions that still are asked today. What went wrong? How can bad children come from good parents? Why do children from pious homes become prodigals? Who fouls up? Various experts blame such factors as heredity, environment, school, and peer pressure, but God put the blame for Hophni and Phinehas on Eli. Eli did not know his children. About seventy years old when they were born, preoccupied with fulfilling his important responsibilities, he was simply too busy to take an active interest in them. He did not know what was happening in their lives. He was afraid to say No and unwilling to put boundaries on their behavior when they were young. By the time he tried to deal with them, it was too late. Once the boys set their selfish, destructive course, there was nothing Eli could do to turn them around.

Hophni and Phinehas. Those names seem weird to us, but it is a good idea to remember them if you are raising a family, or thinking about it. Children do not need moms and dads as pals. They need parents who are involved and loving enough to say No when they have to, despite protests and pestering. Bringing up children with godly discipline and instruction is tiring, frustrating, and unappreciated at the time, but if it ever starts to seem easier to stand back and let things slide, just recall Hophni and Phinehas and consider the consequences.

*Read: I Samuel 2:12-4:18; Proverbs 22:6; Proverbs 29:17*

# JEHOVAH - JIREH

*Abraham lifted up his eyes and looked, and behold, behind him was a ram, caught in a thicket by his horns; and Abraham went and took the ram, and offered it up as a burnt offering instead of his son. So Abraham called the name of that place The Lord will provide (Genesis 22:12-14).*

Jehovah-Jireh, "The Lord will provide." We quote that phrase to calm our nerves, answer our questions, and think about the future. It is a mistake, though, to interpret Jehovah-Jireh as meaning we can sit back and do nothing because God will take care of everything for us. Jehovah-Jireh means the Lord will provide and produce if we do our part and live by faith. Even God cannot provide if we do not provide Him the opportunity to lead with His providence. We do that by faith.

The substance of faith is obedience. When the Lord says to do something, we are to obey immediately, no matter how ridiculous, unwise, incredible, and unloving it seems, whether we like it or not. Surely Abraham did not like God's command. "Take your son, your only son Isaac, whom you love, and go to the land of Moriah, and offer him there as a burnt offering" (v. 2). Abraham loved Isaac deeply, and besides, how could God keep His promise to multiply his descendants as the stars of heaven and the sand on the seashore if his only son were to die? Yet Abraham obeyed, not understanding but believing God had the power to raise Isaac from the dead to fulfill His Word. Abraham proved his love for the Lord, and God provided a ram for the sacrifice. Abraham, known as the father of the faithful, had true understanding of Jehovah-Jireh.

Do not expect the Lord always to make sense to you. We have a limited scope of perception, and it is not for us to judge what God does. Our part is to be faithful, and we cannot be faithful unless we are obedient. Walk by faith and the Lord will provide, though you cannot know when or where or how.

Jehovah-Jireh: it is a great phrase. You probably could dazzle your friends by quoting it once in a while, but if you want it to have real meaning in your life, believe it!

*Read: Genesis 22:1-19; Hebrews 11:17-19; I Samuel 15:22*

# SEEKING THE SIMPLE

*Then children were brought to him that he might lay his hands on them and pray. The disciples rebuked the people; but Jesus said, "Let the children come to me, and do not hinder them; for to such belongs the kingdom of heaven" (Matthew 19:13-14).*

Wouldn't it be wonderful if life were simple? Then we could mean what we say and say what we mean. We could express emotions unashamedly. We could keep our promises and not make up complicated excuses for our behavior. We could quit pretending we understand everything. We could stop spending money we do not have to impress people we do not like. We could go to sleep without guilt or grief and get up the next day with enthusiasm, not dread. If only life were simple! Then the Kingdom of Heaven would be the Kingdom on earth. That is the way we are meant to live, and most of us know it. Our problem is how to do it, how to seek simplicity in everyday living. Some people try by retreating from life and shutting out the world; they flee the rat race to live in a lonely cabin. Others join study groups, boycotts, and organizations; their lives become more complicated than before!

Jesus says the way to seek simplicity is to turn to God with the mind of a child. "Unless you turn and become like children, you will never enter the kingdom of heaven. Whoever humbles himself like this child, he is the greatest in the kingdom of heaven" (Matthew 18:3-4). We are not to be childish, but child-like, showing openness, dependence, and trust. Children have no secrets or pretenses. They are not ashamed to take their parent's hand. They believe what they are told. Greatness in the Kingdom always has its roots in such child-like simplicity. "Let the greatest among you become as the youngest, and the leader as one who serves" (Luke 22:26). Today, be child-like. Open yourself up. Trust God's Holy Word. Depend upon Him. Be a seeker of simplicity, for then you will be meek, and it is the meek who inherit the earth.

If you want Heaven and earth, and there is nothing more, become as a little child and enter the Kingdom forever.

*Read: Matthew 18:1-6; Matthew 5:37; James 4:10*

47

# JAIL TIME

*Now the Lord is the Spirit, and where the Spirit of the Lord is, there is freedom (II Corinthians 3:17).*

Many Bible heroes suffered trials and hardships for God. Just read Hebrews 11 about Noah, Abraham, Moses, and more individuals who dared to live by faith. "Some were tortured, refusing to accept release, that they might rise again to a better life. Others suffered mocking and scourging, and even chains and imprisonment. They were stoned, they were sawn in two, they were killed with the sword" (v. 35-37). Joseph, John the Baptizer, Peter, John -- all spent time in prison. Paul referred to himself as "an ambassador in chains" (Ephesians 6:20).

Most of us have never visited a jail or penitentiary, let alone spent time there as a criminal. We take pride in obeying the laws of the land and keeping our record clean. Our good citizenship does not mean, though, we are not imprisoned. We do not have to be behind bars to be in jail. Some people live in a prison of despair or hopelessness. Others are held captive in a prison of fear, bitterness, or low self-esteem. Maybe it is the prison of an addiction or habit we cannot control. "Whatever overcomes a man, to that he is enslaved" (II Peter 2:19).

If you are trapped in some dark spiritual prison today, try to understand that very likely, you are your own jailer. Those words sound harsh, I know, but I offer them in love. The message of the Gospel is that you do not have to serve a life sentence in a dismal cell. You can unlock the prison door and live in the light if you are willing to ask Jesus to save you. Jesus is the truth, and the truth will set you free. "If the Son makes you free, you will be free indeed" (John 8:36). Your release into new, triumphant life in Christ begins the moment you invite Him into your heart and surrender to His control. The Spirit of the Lord will liberate you from the oppression of sin and deliver you to unfettered love, joy, peace, and power.

The length of time you spend in jail is up to you. If you are tired of the constraints of prison life, pray today, "Lord, make me a captive of yours, and then I shall be truly free."

*Read:  John 8:31-36; Isaiah 61:1; Galatians 5:1*

# GIVING GENUINE GIFTS

*Mary took a pound of costly ointment of pure nard and anointed the feet of Jesus and wiped his feet with her hair; and the house was filled with the fragrance of the ointment (John 12:3).*

The Bible says, "It is more blessed to give than to receive" (Acts 20:35), but that does not mean it is easy to give genuine gifts. Mary anointed the feet of Jesus Christ with a costly ointment less than one week before His crucifixion. Out of love, she gave Jesus a genuine, extravagant gift that was special, significant, and symbolic, and she gave it all. Yet her generous sacrifice created commotion and controversy among the disciples. Judas said, "Why was this ointment not sold for three hundred denarii and given to the poor?" (John 12:5). Three hundred denarii equaled about $60.00, a year's wages. To the disciples, the gift seemed unduly lavish and exorbitant. Jesus, though, saw the love in Mary's heart and commended her. Genuine, extravagant gifts are understood and appreciated only by those who speak the language of love.

The salvation of the world came through an extravagant gift. Nearly 2,000 years ago, God gave a genuine gift out of His love for all mankind. He gave His only begotten Son, Jesus Christ, to die upon the Cross. To some, the Cross is foolishness; to others, a stumbling block. Yet to those who believe, God's gift is the power of salvation. "Thanks be to God for his inexpressible gift!" (II Corinthians 9:15).

Giving genuine gifts is risky. Gifts can be rejected, misused, misunderstood, or criticized. Christians take the risk, realizing that selfless generosity is essential for a rewarding life. When we give freely to God and others, our hearts are enriched beyond measure. In addition, our gifts touch and transform people. The fragrance of Mary's ointment filled the house and touched everyone. Genuine gifts change attitudes, inspire people to be more godly, and help them to grow.

It is beautiful to give genuine gifts, and God allows us to feel great when we do. That is one of His beautiful gifts to us.

*Read: John 12:1-8; I Corinthians 1:18-25; Proverbs 11:24-25*

# USE IT OR LOSE IT

*The apostles said to the Lord, "Increase our faith!" (Luke 17:5).*

Like the apostles, many of us want to increase our faith. Some wonder where to get faith. Others pray for faith. I believe the teaching of Jesus is that we do not have to get faith or pray for faith, because we already have faith! God places faith within us, and all the faith we will ever need, we already have. As God grants us the capacity to love and the will to survive, He grants us the gift of faith. To increase in faith, ask God for courage to use the faith you have now. Using your faith is vital, because if you do not use it, you lose it. If faith is not growing, it is dying. How do you use your faith?

**Walk praising God.** "Praise the Lord, all nations! Extol him, all peoples! For great is his steadfast love toward us; and the faithfulness of the Lord endures for ever. Praise the Lord!" (Psalm 117). Praise God from whom all blessings come and do not blast people from whom all evils come. Praise God for what is right and do not dwell on what is wrong. Seek to please Jesus, who loves you, and not your enemies, who do not even like you. Just keep walking and praising the Lord.

**Talk positively.** Do not knock people down; build them up! "Encourage the fainthearted, help the weak, be patient with them all" (I Thessalonians 5:14). Be optimistic! Pessimism seems to rule our times. If we hear there is a 20% chance of rain, we forget there is an 80% chance of sunshine. God gave us a spectacular world. Let's inspire one another to enjoy it.

**Do not balk.** Refuse to give up. Never balk when things do not go your way. We see children cry, stomp their feet, take their marbles, and go home when they lose. That is no way for a Christian to respond to disappointments. "Blessed is the man who endures trial, for when he has stood the test he will receive the crown of life which God has promised to those who love him" (James 1:12). Keep going, no matter what happens.

God has placed faith within you. Use it or lose it! The choice is that simple. Choose to use your faith today.

*Read: Romans 1:16-17; Psalm 148; I Timothy 6:11-12*

## GETTING INTO THE WHEELBARROW

*Commit your way to the Lord; trust in him, and he will act (Psalm 37:5).*

A tightrope walker stretched his cable across Niagara Falls and said to a crowd of people, "Do you believe I can walk on that cable to the other side?" They didn't know. The man took his rod and, one foot in front of the other, made his way across, then turned around and came back. Everybody applauded! "Now do you believe I can do it?" "Yes! We believe!" Next he asked, "Do you believe I can balance a wheelbarrow across that tightrope?" They didn't know. He took the wheelbarrow and carefully, a bit shakily, went the whole way over, then came back -- in reverse! They clapped and cheered! "Do you believe now that I can balance the wheelbarrow on this tightrope?" "Yes! We believe!" "Do you trust that I can do it?" "What do you mean?" "Get into the wheelbarrow!"

I am very grateful for this much-used illustration, for it demonstrates clearly the difference between belief and trust. One can believe without trust. In belief, we have faith in ideas; in trust, we have a relationship with somebody. Belief is an action of the head; trust is an action of the heart. It is possible to believe Jesus is the Son of God, He was crucified, dead, and buried, He rose again, ascended into Heaven, and sits on the right hand of God; it is possible to believe all that and still not trust Him with our lives. Trusting Jesus with our lives is hazardous. We have to be willing to get into the wheelbarrow!

If Jesus wanted to push you in a wheelbarrow on a tightrope over Niagara Falls, would you go? Would you trust Him? How about if He wanted to guide you through this day, on the job, with your friends, in your home? What if He wanted you to follow some impossible idea? Would you trust Him then? I have news for you. Jesus does want to guide you through this day and He does want you to follow an impossible idea He might send you this very week. What will you do?

If you have the courage to commit your way to the Lord, get into the wheelbarrow! Trust in Him, and He will act.

*Read: Psalm 56:3-4; Jeremiah 17:5-8; Proverbs 22:17-19*

# THE MOST EXCITING PLACE IN TOWN

*"Zeal for thy house will consume me" (John 2:17).*

My great hero, teacher, and friend, the late Dr. John Mackay, past President of Princeton Theological Seminary, used to say, "Whenever you see a church building, do not automatically assume God is there. No, just because there is a building, that does not mean the Spirit is present. Wherever the Spirit is, that is where the Church of Jesus Christ is!" It is tragic, but some churches are merely monuments to the past. They are dead. The Holy Spirit is not at work there.

It takes the Holy Spirit to make churches exciting and alive and vital. There was no mistaking His presence on the first Pentecost! To tell if the Spirit is present in a church today, just look at the members for obvious signs of the Spirit.

**Enthusiasm.** The people at Pentecost were so enthusiastic that observers thought they were drunk! "Enthusiasm" comes from two Greek words: "en" meaning "in"; "Theos" meaning "God". People who have enthusiasm are in God and God is in them. They exude excitement and joy. Their hearts are filled with love. They are channels for God's special energy. There is a twinkle in the eye and a skip in the step, and only positive statements come out of the mouth. They are truly alive!

**Unity.** At Pentecost, many languages were spoken, yet everyone understood one another. The Holy Spirit brings warmth, love, and harmony out of diversity. All of us feel misunderstood from time to time. God's Holy Spirit enables us to understand and to be understood; that results in unity.

**Spontaneity.** After the mysterious rush of a mighty wind and the tongues of fire, people at Pentecost were not afraid to ask, "What does this mean?" (Acts 2:12). In a Spirit-filled church, people eagerly look for challenges and opportunities to help others, fill needs, and bring their neighbors to Jesus.

The Church ought to be the most exciting place in town, and members should be walking advertisements for the joy and power of the Spirit. Let's make sure our zeal for God's house is so consuming, so magnetic, and so unmistakable that everyone we meet will think, "The Church -- that's the place for me!"

*Read: John 2:13-22; Acts 2:1-13; Ephesians 2:19-22*

# A VANISHING VIRTUE

*Help, Lord; for there is no longer any that is godly; for the faithful have vanished from among the sons of men (Psalm 12:1).*

Faithfulness is a virtue vanishing from our midst. In our culture, faithfulness does not seem to count for much anymore. What is worse, we just shrug our shoulders and say, "What are you going to do? That's the way things are these days."

The ironic thing is we expect faithfulness from God and other people; we just think we are exempt from it ourselves. How demanding we are! "God, you better be faithful and make sure the sun rises tomorrow. Jesus, you better be there when I need you. Mom, you better be ready when I want my cereal in the morning and need a clean pair of socks. Dad, you better bring home a big paycheck. Teacher, you better teach me the truth. Employer, you better come through with everything in my contract. And preacher, don't you dare step out of line or I'll leave the church! But me? Well, it's OK for me to do what I want to do. My actions are my own business. It's my life!"

When we think like that, we need to get into the Bible and see what Jesus Christ says about faithfulness. Jesus demands faithfulness. "He who has my commandments and keeps them, he it is who loves me" (John 14:21). Faithfulness to His commands is proof of our love for Him. There are no exemptions. Each of us is accountable for everything we do, say, and think. It is our responsibility to be faithful to Jesus even if faithfulness is a vanishing virtue throughout society.

A great hymn starts, "O Jesus, I have promised to serve Thee to the end." That does not mean to the end of an hour-long worship service or to the end of the day. It means to the end of life! "Be faithful unto death, and I will give you the crown of life" (Revelation 2:10). Our God is faithful to us, and we are called to be His faithful servants now and always.

"Fear the Lord, and serve him in sincerity and in faithfulness" (Joshua 24:14). Faithfulness -- let us never allow that godly virtue to vanish in us.

*Read: I Corinthians 1:9; Luke 12:41-48; Proverbs 3:3-4*

# THE LAWS OF THE HARVEST

*He who sows sparingly will also reap sparingly, and he who sows bountifully will also reap bountifully (II Corinthians 9:6).*

Though Jesus was a carpenter and several of His disciples were fishermen, He often used agricultural language in His lessons. He told parables about sowers, vineyard laborers, mustard seeds, tares, and fig trees, among others. Jesus knew that people who live close to the soil appreciate the mystery of growth. The laws of the harvest are universal and timeless.

**The qualitative law:** whatever we sow, we reap. A good tree bears good fruit and a bad tree bears bad fruit.

**The quantitative law:** the reaping will be greater than the sowing in number. Seeds have power. The seeds we plant in word, thought, and deed will be multiplied many times.

**The consequential law:** after the sowing, the reaping is not far behind, and the harvest will be visible to everyone.

The laws of the harvest continue to teach us eternal truths. First, we are responsible for the harvest we produce. On the day of reaping, we will not be able to blame our harvest on anyone else. "Each man will have to bear his own load" (Galatians 6:5). We determine if our fruit decays or flourishes. Second, we should examine carefully every seed before we let it drop to the ground. The seeds we plant today bring about the reaping we have in the future. God will forgive us for sowing our wild oats, but the results of our sin and selfishness could be devastating to people for years to come. Unless we consider the consequences of our actions, we could reap evil instead of good. Third, we can make up our minds now to sow only good seeds. We cannot do it without God's help, but if we allow the mind of Christ to be in us, He will show us how to sow good seeds that benefit His Kingdom, other people, and ourselves.

"The fruit of the Spirit is love, joy, peace, patience, kindness, goodness, gentleness, faithfulness, self-control" (Galatians 5:22-23). If that is the fruit you hope to cultivate in your life, then do not waste this day. Sow bountifully, because what you sow right now, you will reap in eternity.

*Read: Galatians 6:1-10; Luke 6:43-45; Proverbs 22:8-9*

# DON'T BLAME GOD

*"Far be it from God that he should do wickedness, and from the Almighty that he should do wrong. For according to the work of a man he will requite him, and according to his ways he will make it befall him. Of a truth, God will not do wickedly, and the Almighty will not pervert justice" (Job 34:10-12).*

How morality has changed! When we do wrong today, we do not call it sin, and we regret it only if we get caught. People think, "As long as I'm not hurting anyone, what difference does it make?" Many voice the false theology that has been around since the beginning: they blame God for sins they commit. It started in the Garden when Adam blamed God for his disobedience. "The woman whom thou gavest to be with me, she gave me the fruit of the tree, and I ate" (Genesis 3:12). Adam was claiming, "It's your fault, God, for giving me Eve!" In Isaiah's day, people grumbled, "O Lord, why dost thou make us err from thy ways and harden our heart?" (Isaiah 63:17). In other words, "You made us sin, God. We can't help it!"

Let's get this straight. God created us as free people. He created us with the ability to sin, but that does not mean He causes us to sin. He created us with the ability to swallow, and that means we can swallow anything, including poison. But if you swallow poison, do not say God caused you to do it!

A lot of people push their humanity and say, "I'm just doing my thing." They excuse all responsibility and blame God for the sin that brings so much suffering and gloom. The message of Scripture is that each of us is responsible for our own words, decisions, and actions. Jesus said, "On the day of judgment men will render account for every careless word they utter" (Matthew 12:36). Paul wrote, "Each of us shall give account of himself to God" (Romans 14:12). Accept responsibility for your life. Denying sin has deadly consequences, for only when you face your sin and confess it can you be forgiven.

Whatever you do, don't blame God, for God does not do wickedness or wrong. Blaming God for your personal sin is spiritual poison, and I sure hope you will not swallow that.

*Read: Genesis 3:8-24; Isaiah 63:15-19; Romans 2:1-11*

# THE NEXT STEP

*Then Moses stretched out his hand over the sea; and the Lord drove the sea back by a strong east wind all night, and made the sea dry land, and the waters were divided. And the people of Israel went into the midst of the sea on dry ground, the waters being a wall to them on their right hand and on their left (Exodus 14:21-22).*

Responsible individuals who are trying to love God and follow Jesus Christ hope the next step they take, in word or in action, will be beneficial to themselves and other people. Regrettably, it does not always work out that way. Alcoholism, divorce, feuds -- no one plans for these crises to come. They all start with a misplaced step. Therefore, the importance of what we say and do right now cannot be over-stressed.

The Israelites did not know where to take their next step when they were pursued by Pharaoh to the edge of the Red Sea. Through Moses, God instructed them to proceed. Remember the Lord's advice before you take your next step today.

**Quit crying.** Do not bellow and bawl. It is useless, and the negative effects are contagious and demoralizing. The pitiable wailing of the Israelites did not divide the Red Sea and defeat Pharaoh. It just made people more intensely frightened.

**Stand firm.** Be still and trust God. No matter how dark and menacing the horizon appears, no matter how frightening the reports against victory sound, look for signs of the Almighty working to bring deliverance from danger.

**Go forward.** Do not waste time scampering backwards or sideways. God wants to create miracles through us, but He cannot do it until we are ready to move ahead. It was only when Moses and the people went forward that the Red Sea divided. Miracles are made by people in motion!

The next step you take today will help to determine whether your life will be fruitful or fruitless, whether you will be considered a beauty or a beast. It will have lasting effects on you and on people who love you. So be careful with your next step. The paths of tomorrow lead from the steps of today.

*Read: Exodus 14:10-31; Isaiah 51:10-11; Psalm 77:19-20*

# YOUR JOY LEVEL

*Let our people learn to apply themselves to good deeds, so as to help cases of urgent need, and not to be unfruitful (Titus 3:14).*

Think about your joy level today. On a scale of 1 to 10, exactly where are you? Are you a 10, or a 9, or an 8 . . . or a 1? Are you filled with joy or stressed out and shriveled up, sullen and mean, on the verge of warning everyone to get out of your way or else? What is your joy level at this precise moment?

Why, on this day, do you suppose your joy level is there?

I will tell you why. It is because of what you did yesterday! If you were productive, if you took the initiative to go out and do something for someone else, your joy level is probably pretty high right now. Maybe you were swinging a hammer or a paintbrush, cleaning up a neighbor's yard, visiting a patient in the hospital, driving an elderly person to an appointment. Maybe something was wrong and you took time to make it right. A lonely soul longed to talk and you listened. A grief-stricken friend needed a hug and you gave it. Someone was down and you said, "Hang in there. I care about you."

Jesus commands His disciples to bear fruit and do good. When we obey His command, we quickly discover the best way to ease our own pain is to forget ourselves and offer practical service to ease the pain of another. Helping, caring, loving, sharing -- that is what life is all about. We are saved by faith, but faith is evidenced by good works. Jesus "went about doing good" (Acts 10:38), and John writes, "He who does good is of God; he who does evil has not seen God" (III John 11).

If your joy level is a little low today, get busy and do something wonderful for somebody else. You will not have to look far to find people who are sick, tired, hurting, sad, discouraged, and lost. In the name of Jesus Christ, apply yourself to good deeds and help people with urgent needs, using all the love, strength, and enthusiasm you have. When you do, your joy level will soar and you will make tomorrow a joyous, unforgettable day for many people, including yourself.

*Read: John 15:1-8; James 2:14-26; Proverbs 12:20*

## HOW CHRIST FINDS THE LOST

*"For the Son of man came to seek and to save the lost" (Luke 19:10)*

Little Zacchaeus was lost. Zacchaeus was a chief tax collector in Jericho and nobody liked him. He was rich, but cheerless. A man with no spiritual dimension, he made his plans without thinking of God, and anybody who does that is lost. No one, though, is too lost to be found by Jesus. Jesus found Zacchaeus through four characteristics we all possess.

**Curiosity.** "He sought to see who Jesus was" (Luke 19:3). Zacchaeus wondered what people found so special about Jesus and earnestly followed his curiosity to find out for himself.

**Opportunity.** Zacchaeus was short, short in stature and also in popularity and respectability. The crowd pushed him away, but "he ran on ahead and climbed up into a sycamore tree to see him" (v. 4). He saw an opportunity and took it.

**Obedience.** When Jesus told Zacchaeus He must have lunch at his house, Zacchaeus obeyed immediately. "He made haste and came down, and received him joyfully" (v. 6).

**Repentance.** Zacchaeus became a new man. "Half of my goods I give to the poor; and if I have defrauded any one of anything, I restore it fourfold" (v. 8). His public proclamation went far beyond the requirement of the law. Jesus said, "Today salvation has come to this house" (v. 9). Zacchaeus was found!

Most of us feel a bit lost from time to time. If you are lost today, do not despair. You can be found if you look to God. "Seek the Lord your God, and you will find him, if you search after him with all your heart and with all your soul" (Deuteronomy 4:29). Be curious about Jesus and get to know Him. Use every opportunity to draw close to Him; you may be forced up a tree and out on a limb, but there you will see the world from the right perspective. Obey His commands; obedience brings peace. Show repentance in tangible ways.

Salvation can come to you, just as salvation came to little Zacchaeus. In the Kingdom of Heaven, it does not matter how tall or short you are, as long as you are big in faith.

*Read: Luke 19:1-10; Psalm 105:1-4; I John 4:14*

# AN IMPORTANT PERSON TO LOVE

*"Which commandment is the first of all?" Jesus answered, "The first is, 'Hear, O Israel: the Lord our God, the Lord is one; and you shall love the Lord your God with all your heart, and with all your soul, and with all your mind, and with all your strength.' The second is this, 'You shall love your neighbor as yourself.' There is no other commandment greater than these" (Mark 12:28-31).*

We are commanded to love. Jesus does not present love as an option or a suggestion. Love is a command! Christians talk a lot about love and accomplish much good in the name of Jesus's love, but it is surprising how many believe self-love is forbidden and sinful. They confuse self-love with self-will. Self-will is selfishness and self-centeredness; that is sin. Self-love is biblical. It is a psychological and biblical principle that if we do not love ourselves, it is impossible for us to love other people and God. We cannot give to others what we do not have ourselves. Love, like all spiritual qualities, is something we do not lose when we give it away. We gain when we give. Unless we love ourselves, we cannot love people healthily and happily. If we cannot love people, we cannot love God.

Christian self-love is not narcissism. It does not say, "I love myself because I have status and renown. I live in a fancy house. I run a huge business. I write several degrees after my name. I know influential people." Christian self-love says, "I love myself because God loves me." It comes not from what we have done, but from who we are: people created, forgiven, and valued by God so much that He entrusts us with His Holy Spirit. We cannot find self-love through the adulation of obsequious flatterers. We cannot build self-love on silly games and charades. It takes honesty: accepting ourselves not as we want the world to see us, but as we truly are; realizing we are not perfect, but we are made in the image of God.

As a Christian, your duty is to love God first, other people second, yourself third. Yet though you are third, you are still an important person to love, so love yourself as God loves you.

*Read: Deuteronomy 6:4-7; Philippians 1:9-11; I John 4:7-17*

# EASY WAYS TO RUIN YOUR LIFE

*I have chosen the way of faithfulness (Psalm 119:30).*

Many people are satisfied with their lives because no great catastrophes or tragedies have happened to them. As long as they get by from day to day without a crisis, they think they are doing fine. Unfortunately, trouble and trauma are not the only threats to spiritual well-being. There are many easy ways to ruin your life. You can ruin your life by choosing to love no one but yourself. You can ruin your life by choosing to hold grudges against those who have wronged you. You can ruin your life by choosing to discourage everybody around you with hurtful, mean words and glances. You can ruin your life by choosing to be a victim of past mistakes, letting them tear you apart with regret and remorse. You can ruin your life by choosing to be sick, snide, cynical, and bitter. You can ruin your life by choosing to neglect God's Holy Word; even if somebody drags you to church, you can choose not to listen!

Go ahead and ruin your life if you want to. No one will stop you. You can ignore God, be indifferent to His Word, and choose the way of faithlessness, but Paul warns, "By your hard and impenitent heart you are storing up wrath for yourself on the day of wrath when God's righteous judgment will be revealed" (Romans 2:5). Not only that. If you choose to go through life never knowing the love, forgiveness, joy, peace, and power that come from faith in Jesus, you will miss out on all that really matters here on earth. Whether you realize it or not, you will be throwing your life away. Tragically, it is very easy to do. More lives are ruined by wrong choices than by catastrophes and tragedies. Suffering works to strengthen people of faith, while selfish, worldly decisions made over time subtly destroy faithless people's lives, little by little, bit by bit.

There are many easy ways to ruin your life. There is one sure way not to: make the decision to give your life to Jesus Christ and allow Him to control your words, your actions, and your choices. Choose the way of faithfulness to Christ and your life will be marvelous, miraculous, and victorious!

*Read: Proverbs 10:8; Hebrews 4:5-7; Zephaniah 1:14-2:3*

## SHEEP VALLEY AND GOAT HILL

*"When the Son of man comes in his glory, and all the angels with him, then he will sit on his glorious throne. Before him will be gathered all the nations, and he will separate them one from another as a shepherd separates the sheep from the goats, and he will place the sheep at his right hand, but the goats at the left" (Matthew 25:31-33).*

Like it or not, there is going to be a Judgment. Jesus Christ, who was born in Bethlehem of Judea in the days of Herod, is going to come again and there will be no question in anybody's mind that He alone is King of kings and Lord of lords. Jesus will rule and every knee shall bow to the eternal, everlasting God. When He comes, Jesus will separate all of us into two groups. I call them Sheep Valley and Goat Hill. We will be with the sheep or the goats, the blessed or the cursed, on the right-hand side of God (the place of favor) or on the left-hand side of God (the place of torment and rejection).

Many people do not realize we have the responsibility and privilege of determining now how Jesus Christ will make His decision on the Day of Judgment. There are two criteria.

**Our beliefs.** "If you confess with your lips that Jesus is Lord and believe in your heart that God raised him from the dead, you will be saved. For man believes with his heart and so is justified, and he confesses with his lips and so is saved" (Romans 10:9-10). Belief in Jesus Christ is essential.

**Our actions.** "For we are his workmanship, created in Christ Jesus for good works, which God prepared beforehand, that we should walk in them" (Ephesians 2:10). We are commanded to work diligently for the Kingdom. Our actions reveal whether or not we are sincere and honest in our beliefs.

We do not like to think about Judgment, especially our own. If we could, most of us would arrange to be put on hold until we are ready to go, but we do not have that capability! Judgment is a reality. Sheep Valley or Goat Hill: those are the only destinations. There is no in-between. Where we spend eternity, whether we are going to be blessed or cursed, sheep or goats, depends upon what we decide to believe and do today.

*Read: Psalm 1:5-6; Ecclesiastes 12:13-14; Romans 14:10-12*

61

## HELPFUL PETER

*Peter answered him, "Lord, if it is you, bid me come to you on the water." He said, "Come." So Peter got out of the boat and walked on the water and came to Jesus; but when he saw the wind, he was afraid, and beginning to sink he cried out, "Lord, save me." Jesus immediately reached out his hand and caught him, saying to him, "O man of little faith, why did you doubt?" (Matthew 14:28-31).*

I like Peter. He was so much like many of us: impulsive, impetuous, spontaneous, always putting his foot in his mouth. He would have been an excellent pastor! He meant well, he loved so much, but at times, he was not too strong. Often he was chided by our Lord, but the great thing was, he never quit.

Jesus loved Peter and there was no question of Peter's love for Jesus. Yet when Peter could not accept Jesus's plan to go to Jerusalem to die, Jesus said, "Get behind me, Satan! You are a hindrance to me" (Matthew 16:23). How that must have stung. How humiliated Peter must have been in front of the other disciples. He must have wanted to get out of there. He didn't. In the Garden when Jesus was arrested, it was Peter who tried to defend Him with the sword, but Jesus said, "Put your sword back into its place; for all who take the sword will perish by the sword" (Matthew 26:52). Rebuked again. I think I'd have quit right there. He didn't. It was Peter who asserted he would never betray Christ. "Even if I must die with you, I will not deny you" (Matthew 26:35). Yet he soon denied his Lord three times, only to weep bitterly when he realized what he had done. How could he go on? I don't know, but he did, and he became an outstanding, faithful, courageous leader of the early Church.

Hallelujah for Peter of yesterday and for Peters of today, people who refuse to quit when the Lord corrects them. Our human tendency is to give up when we think we have failed. Resist that tendency! Jesus said, "He who endures to the end will be saved" (Mark 13:13). No matter how many mistakes you make, keep going. Forgive yourself as Jesus forgives you and move on. That is what it takes to be His disciple.

*Read: Matthew 26:30-75; Acts 4:8-22; Acts 11:1-18*

# TWO FATAL PHRASES

*"Talk no more so very proudly, let not arrogance come from your mouth; for the Lord is a God of knowledge, and by him actions are weighed" (I Samuel 2:3).*

Three little words form two little phrases that are deadly to spiritual health.

**"I am only..."** This phrase reveals a sense of inferiority. When God called Jeremiah, he responded, "Behold, I do not know how to speak, for I am only a youth" (Jeremiah 1:6). God gets upset with people who hesitate to follow His plan and offer excuses that they are "only" a boy, "only" a girl, "only" a senior citizen, or "only" anything else. That is saying No to God. Jeremiah's age was hardly any secret to the Lord. "Do not say, 'I am only a youth'; for to all to whom I send you you shall go, and whatever I command you you shall speak" (v. 7). God does not want excuses. He wants instant obedience.

**"I only am..."** This phrase shows an attitude of superiority. After defeating the 450 prophet of Baal, Elijah complained that he was the only one left doing God's will. "I have been very jealous for the Lord, the God of hosts; for the people of Israel have forsaken thy covenant, thrown down thy altars, and slain thy prophets with the sword; and I, even I only, am left; and they seek my life, to take it away" (I Kings 19:10). God had a little reminder for Elijah. "Yet I will leave seven thousand in Israel, all the knees that have not bowed to Baal" (v. 18). Elijah was not as lonely as he thought. Seven thousand other prophets also served the Lord! There is pride in thinking we alone are faithful, and God does not like that.

Disagreeing with God is arrogance. Evaluate honestly your willingness to serve Him in anything He calls you to do. We are in spiritual danger when we think we are too little to do a big job or too big to do a little job. Jesus said, "Why do you call me 'Lord, Lord,' and not do what I tell you?" (Luke 6:46). God knows the attitudes of our hearts and He weighs our actions. Banish the two fatal phrases from your thoughts and come alive with enthusiasm when God asks you to serve Him.

*Read: Jeremiah 1:4-10; I Kings 19:9-18; Proverbs 8:13*

# WAITING YOUR TURN

*For now we see in a mirror dimly, but then face to face. Now I know in part; then I shall understand fully (I Corinthians 13:12).*

On the Day of Resurrection when we are transported to the other side to spend eternity with our Lord, you may discover you are standing in line like you do at the bank, just waiting and waiting and waiting to see Jesus Christ. If you do, you will know why: I am up front ahead of you, asking questions!

At last count, I had 483 questions to ask the good Lord.

There are many, many mysteries in life. As a pastor, I see one mystery almost every Sunday. Two people come to church. They are identified by the same last name. They live in the same house. They drive to church in the same car. They attend the same worship service. They sit in the same pew. They sing the same hymns. They hear the same preacher say the same words. One is lifted to the seventh heaven; the other cannot wait to escape. One soaks up every word; the other falls asleep. Why, Lord? What is the answer to number 279?

And Lord, why are all those calories packed into chocolate cake with seafoam icing and not in turnips or rutabagas or onions? What is the answer to number 74?

Do you have a list of questions to ask Jesus? I hope you do, because Jesus wants us to use our minds in following Him as well as our hearts and souls. True, we have to live in mystery. We have to walk by faith, not by sight. But that should not deter us from trying to learn all we can about the Lord, ourselves, and His creation through His Holy Word, prayer and meditation, other people, and our experiences. The Lord gave us our minds and He expects us to use them!

"Be still before the Lord, and wait patiently for him" (Psalm 37:7). If I am ahead of you in that line, do not panic or grow restless. The Bible tells us we shall dwell in the house of the Lord forever, so there will be plenty of time for all of us to get answers to every question on our lists. Just be patient and wait your turn, and if you are ahead of me, I will wait, too.

*Read: Matthew 22:37-40; Psalm 23:6; Psalm 38:15*

# THE PRAY-AS-YOU-GO PLAN

*He was praying in a certain place, and when he ceased, one of his disciples said to him, "Lord, teach us to pray" (Luke 11:1).*

It is interesting to note that the disciples never asked Jesus how to organize a church, how to heal, or how to preach, but they did ask Him how to pray. Watching Jesus pray, they realized much of His peace and power came from prayer and prayer gave Him motivation and strength to carry out His mission. Jesus gives us His prayer plan in the Sermon on the Mount. "Pray then like this..." (Matthew 6:9). Though we rarely attain complete effectiveness in prayer, we should work diligently on our prayer lives. There are no easy lessons. The only way to learn to pray is to pray as you go through life.

There are some requirements in the pray-as-you-go plan.

**Sincerity.** Prayer is not just closing the eyes, dropping the head, and folding the hands. It is coming into the presence of the Almighty, sincerely believing He is your Father in Heaven.

**Secrecy.** Get away from confusion so you can pray in privacy. Do not tell people about your prayer life. Rather, let them see revealed through you the answers to your prayers.

**Simplicity.** Do not bother trying to impress the Lord with your erudite theological understanding and vocabulary. Be simple and specific, saying exactly what you think and feel.

**Silence.** If you are so busy talking that you forget to listen, you cannot receive an answer. Be still and allow God to reveal His will through circumstances, His Word, and other people.

**Submission.** This is the most difficult part. We must truly believe God is the Potter and we are the clay. Do not try to force the hand of God to get what you want. He is in charge! Pray, "Not my will, but thine be done," and mean it.

When you follow the pray-as-you-plan, surprising changes begin to happen: your requests get fewer, your joys and thanksgivings increase, and you find richer peace and power in your everyday living and greater motivation and strength to carry out your unique mission in life. The pray-as-you-go plan worked for Jesus Christ and it will work for you. Pray today!

*Read: Matthew 6:5-15; Colossians 4:2; Jude 20-21*

# THE NUMBERS GAME

*Do not be conformed to this world (Romans 12:2).*

One person on God's side is a majority, even if countless multitudes oppose Him. Unfortunately, since the dawn of humanity, people have preferred to look at the numbers, go with the crowd, base decisions on popularity, polls, and public opinion rather than on God's will. A dilemma faced by the Israelites demonstrates the tragic results that develop when people insist on playing the numbers game. Moses sent twelve men to spy out the land of Canaan. Though all reported the land flowed with milk and honey and its fruit was plentiful, ten hesitated to cross into the Promised Land because huge giants lived there. Only Caleb and Joshua bravely urged, "Let us go up at once, and occupy it; for we are well able to overcome it" (Numbers 13:30). Ten to two. Those were the numbers. How did people respond? "Would that we had died in the land of Egypt! Or would that we had died in this wilderness!" (14:2). What moaning! They got their wish about dying in the wilderness. God was so angry, He had them wander around for another generation. Only Caleb, Joshua, and people age twenty or younger received the gifts of the Promised Land.

Sometimes we imagine we are safest when we say and do and think what everybody else says and does and thinks. That is not true. Playing the numbers game is dangerous. Consider how God regarded the Israelites who refused to obey Him. "How long will this people despise me?" (14:11). Despise the Lord? None of us wants to despise the Lord! Yet apparently when we ignore His plan and allow people to control us rather than His Holy Word, we demonstrate we despise God. Keep that in mind the next time you are tempted to conform to this world and do things you know to be biblically wrong.

It is tough to stand firm when everyone around you is on the other side, but do not let the numbers scare you. Remember, you are not standing alone. God is standing with you. One person on God's side is a majority, so take courage and never let giants keep you out of the Promised Land!

*Read: Numbers 13 & 14; Psalm 73:23-28*

# A GREAT SPIRIT

*"I do not account my life of any value nor as precious to myself, if only I may accomplish my course and the ministry which I received from the Lord Jesus, to testify to the gospel of the grace of God" (Acts 20:24).*

The apostle Paul was an impressive individual. Many people admire Paul for his physical strength. He describes his trials in II Corinthians 11, beginning, "Five time I have received at the hands of the Jews the forty lashes less one. Three times I have been beaten with rods; once I was stoned. Three times I have been shipwrecked; a night and a day I have been adrift at sea" (v. 24-25), and going on to describe other dangers and hardships. What a giant of a man; he must have taken his vitamins! Other people respect Paul for his mind. Paul wrote the classic for systematic theology, the book of Romans, and more than half the New Testament. We are still learning from this man of intellect and understanding.

Paul had great strength and a great mind, but his most outstanding attribute was his great spirit. Paul was consistent and stable. He never fell into negativism or complaints. On good days and not-so-good days, on mountaintops and in valleys, he could cope and persevere. The marvelous benefit for us is that Paul tells us how he kept his spirit strong: through his beliefs. His writings abound with expressions of belief in the love, peace, presence, power, and grace of Jesus. In Philippians 4 alone, Paul urges us to rejoice in the Lord, have no anxiety, pray with thanksgiving, know the peace of God which passes understanding, keep our hearts and minds in Christ, be content in all circumstances, and do all things through Christ who strengthens us. Paul's unshakable beliefs gave him the great spirit to accomplish his special ministry.

Not everybody has the great strength to endure physical peril or the great mind to write theology, but everyone can have a great spirit. We develop a great spirit through belief in Christ. Today, believe in the love, peace, presence, power, and grace of Jesus. Your spirit will be great, and so will your life.

*Read: II Corinthians 11:16-31; Philippians 4:4-13; II Corinthians 6:3-10*

# OUR GOOD SHEPHERD

*"I am the good shepherd" (John 10:14).*

"The Lord is my shepherd, I shall not want; he makes me lie down in green pastures. He leads me beside still waters; he restores my soul. He leads me in paths of righteousness for his name's sake" (Psalm 23:1-3). The twenty-third Psalm is perhaps the most powerful piece of literature in all history. The power is there because Jesus Christ, God's Son, came and confirmed everything in the Psalm and identified Himself as the Good Shepherd. Jesus Christ, our Good Shepherd, is the way, the truth, the life, and the light of the world for all time.

Sheep are like people: defenseless, vulnerable, easily preyed upon, and frequently confused! Shepherds in biblical times carried a three-foot rod to beat off predators from their flocks. They used an eight-foot staff with a hook to pull fallen sheep out of holes and ditches. With their rods and their staffs, they comforted their sheep. Jesus Christ took two pieces of wood to make a Cross. With those two pieces of wood, He defeated every enemy that ever has or ever will come, even the enemy called sin and the last enemy, death. The Cross of Jesus Christ reaches down and hooks all people who cry unto Him for help and saves them for eternity. "He himself bore our sins in his body on the tree, that we might die to sin and live to righteousness. By his wounds you have been healed. For you were straying like sheep, but have now returned to the Shepherd and Guardian of your souls" (I Peter 2:24-25).

If today you are walking through the valley of the shadow of death or some other dark valley, open your heart to Jesus Christ, "the great shepherd of the sheep" (Hebrews 13:20), who laid down His life for you. You are one of His precious sheep. He loves you. He knows you by name. He wants the best for you. No matter where you are, He will supply your needs, restore your soul, and lead you in paths of righteousness. His rod and His staff will comfort you, His Cross will redeem you, and you will dwell in the house of the Lord forever.

Our Good Shepherd cares about you.

*Read: Psalm 23; John 10:1-18; Isaiah 40:11*

# LITTLE STEPS TO DISCIPLESHIP

*I am sure that he who began a good work in you will bring it to completion at the day of Jesus Christ (Philippians 1:6).*

Making the decision to accept Jesus Christ as our personal Lord and Savior does not require us to achieve instantaneous perfection in Christian discipleship the moment we believe. Discipleship is a lifelong process with many steps of growth along the way. Some people are afraid to make a commitment because of the sacrifices it might demand down the road. They know the gate is narrow and the way is long, so they fall into spiritual paralysis and cannot take the vital first step.

Jesus promises to provide for our needs if we follow Him. "Do not be anxious about your life... Do not seek what you are to eat and what you are to drink, nor be of anxious mind. For all the nations of the world seek these things; and your Father knows that you need them. Instead, seek his kingdom, and these things shall be yours as well" (Luke 12:22,29-31). We should not worry about what God has in store, for He will take care of us wherever we are. Rather, today, this hour, this minute, we should think of little steps we can take to become more like Jesus Christ: being less derogatory and judgmental; showing more love and forgiveness; praising people when they do right instead of berating them for errors; setting an excellent example in word and deed; enjoying life fully. As we take little steps, one at a time, we find that discipleship, though never easy, is exciting and liberating. "If you continue in my word, you are truly my disciples, and you will know the truth, and the truth will make you free" (John 8:31-32).

When infants speak their first words, moms and dads do not reproach them for poor grammar. Parents wisely wait until children are older to correct them. So it is with God. God is pleased with all the little steps we take to follow Jesus. The important thing is to get started and keep going! With each step, we make His world a better place and bring honor to His name. Today, take little steps to discipleship and allow God to bring the good work He has begun in you to completion.

*Read: Luke 13:24; Philippians 3:12; Proverbs 4:10-19*

69

# BELIEVING IN DISBELIEF

*He who believes in the Son has eternal life (John 3:36).*

Sometimes it is hard to believe. There is so much, and it is so mysterious. How can we be expected to believe without seeing or knowing? The Bible instructs us to believe God created us, loves us, and will never leave us nor forsake us; Jesus is the Son of God and His life and His death on the Cross have forgiven us once and for all; Holy Spirit living and dwelling in us wants the best for us and has great things in store for us. It all seems too complex and awesome to grasp.

It is difficult to believe. It does take tremendous faith. But it also takes a lot of effort not to believe. Though it requires great faith to believe in God's love and in Jesus Christ, God's Son, it takes even more faith not to believe in God's love and in the life, death, and resurrection of Jesus Christ. To say God does not love us is to claim the Bible is a pack of lies and the Church has been living a mistake for nearly 2,000 years. Such negativity takes great belief, yet many people do believe that way. They believe down instead of up, bad instead of good. They believe God is trying to tease, torment, or terrify them and people do not care about their needs. They believe life is a dismal, futile ordeal and reality consists of nothing but bad breaks, wrong decisions, and unfulfilled dreams.

Believing in disbelief can sap all the energy, enthusiasm, and life out a person. Of course, we have the power to believe whatever we want to believe. If you want to disbelieve the message of the Bible and believe instead that human existence is wretched, go ahead. It will be hard, but you can do it. I do not know why you would want to, though, because there is an easier, better, happier way to go through life. Believe in God's love. Believe in Christ. Believe in Holy Spirit. Believe in life, not death; hope, not despair; power, not feebleness; wholeness, not confusion. Disbelief is truly the hardest belief to live by, for it violates God's loving design for us. Jesus said, "This is the work of God, that you believe in him whom he has sent" (John 6:29), so believe in the Son of God, Jesus Christ, today.

*Read: John 8:39-47; Mark 16:16; Hebrews 3:12-19*

# CHRISTIAN ASSUMPTIONS

*Surely his salvation is at hand for those who fear him, that glory may dwell in our land. Steadfast love and faithfulness will meet; righteousness and peace will kiss each other. Faithfulness will spring up from the ground, and righteousness will look down from the sky. Yea, the Lord will give what is good (Psalm 85:9-12).*

To assume means to act as though it were fact. As a Christian, you can act on certain fundamental biblical assumptions in your walk of faith today and every day.

**Assume God is working in your life right now.** God works in particular people for particular reasons. He is within you this very moment by the power of His Holy Spirit and He has a unique and wonderful plan for your life.

**Assume the Lord has great things in store for you.** Do not be impatient about what those great things are. We may not understand God's time, but He is never too early or too late.

**Assume people love you.** Expect the best from everybody. Be honest, forgiving, kind, and loving to one another and look upon people you meet as potential friends, not adversaries.

**Assume your ideas come from the indwelling Christ.** You cannot prove it, but you can believe it! Overcome the human inclination to procrastinate and move forward with your ideas. You will discover whole new areas of potential.

**Assume you can do anything through Christ.** Do not be afraid to go out on a limb. Take chances! You are more alive when you run risks for Jesus Christ than at any other time.

So many people act on negative assumptions, their minds filled with anger, hate, disappointment. It is sad and depressing for them and everyone else. The Bible proclaims a God of salvation, a God of steadfast love and faithfulness, of righteousness and peace, a God who will give what is good. Believe that message! Give God a chance, in your life and in your outlook on life. God loves you. Cherish His love in your heart. When you assume you are a special, beloved child of the King of kings and Lord of lords, you soon will come to assume you are a fortunate, truly blessed person in God's world.

*Read: Ephesians 1:3; Luke 6:20-23; Psalm 108:1-4*

# WHERE TO FIND PEACE

*God is not a God of confusion but of peace (I Corinthians 14:33).*

Many people stay away from the Church because they think all the Church wants is a piece of them -- a piece of their time, a piece of their talent, a piece of their pocketbooks. That is not why the Church exists! The Church is not after a piece of you. The Church is here to offer you the peace of Jesus Christ.

It is the Church alone that dispenses the peace that passes all understanding. We cannot find the peace of Jesus Christ by going to the library and reading. We cannot find the peace of Jesus Christ by going to taverns and parties. We cannot find the peace of Jesus Christ in solitude. We cannot even find the peace of Jesus Christ in our homes unless we bring it there from His Church. People are looking everywhere in the world for peace and the world sure needs peace, but we can only find true, lasting peace in the Body of Jesus Christ, the Church.

If you do not have peace or if peace seems to be moving away from your life, assemble with Christian believers. I know, it can be intimidating to face people. Maybe you feel nervous, a little unworthy or embarrassed. Perhaps you have mistreated other people or yourself in the past and doubt you can be forgiven. No matter how timid you are, do not let anything keep you from that fellowship! You will find that you can bring your troubles and fears to the Body of Christ and leave them there, then go out in peace and be a peacemaker yourself in our turbulent world. "The peace of God, which passes all understanding, will keep your hearts and your minds in Christ Jesus" (Philippians 4:7). His peace lasts eternally.

If you have found peace already, be aware that this week you will meet people who urgently need spiritual tranquillity. They could be in your home, office, neighborhood, anywhere. Show them where to find it. Through your example and your loving concern, point them to the Church so they, too, can banish inner strife and experience lasting peace.

Today, thank the God of peace for giving you power both to find peace and to make peace in this world of confusion.

*Read: Romans 8:6; II Corinthians 13:11-14; Psalm 85:8*

# CRAVING THE HOLY WORD

*So put away all malice and all guile and insincerity and envy and all slander. Like newborn babes, long for the pure spiritual milk, that by it you may grow up to salvation; for you have tasted the kindness of the Lord (I Peter 2:1-3).*

Do you crave the Word of God, long for closeness with your Creator, and sincerely want to grow in faith? The plain truth is, if we do not desire to grow spiritually, we will not grow. Spiritual growth is not magically bestowed upon us. We must want it, seek it, devote ourselves to it. Peter says we must desire to grow as a child grows, craving the spiritual Word of God as much as a baby craves physical milk. We know what happens when babies want milk. They cry, scream, and create a disturbance. They do not care where they are or who gets annoyed. We never have to read them a book or send them to school to teach them how to find milk. They know they need milk and they cause non-stop commotion until they get it!

We have been made to crave the pure spiritual milk of God that is in His Word. The Psalmist wrote, "As a hart longs for flowing streams, so longs my soul for thee, O God. My soul thirsts for God, for the living God. When shall I come and behold the face of God?" (Psalm 42:1-2). The way to develop your craving for God's Holy Word is simply by tasting it. Most likely you have a Bible. Do you ever read it? Are you intermingling with the life and teaching of Jesus Christ? You cannot follow Him and obey Him if you do not know what He says. Taste the Word! If you have never done it before, get into the Gospels daily for one month. Soon you will find that if you taste the Word of God, the craving will be there. The more you get into the Word, the more you will want of the Word.

Jesus said, "If any one thirst, let him come to me and drink. He who believes in me, as the scripture has said, 'Out of his heart shall flow rivers of living water'" (John 7:37-38). Come unto Jesus Christ and drink deeply of His Word. When you begin to crave His Holy Word as a baby craves milk, you will see your life grow bigger, better, and brighter every day.

*Read: Psalm 84:1-2; John 4:14; Revelation 21:6*

# PART OF THE PLAN

*Thou didst form my inward parts, thou didst knit me together in my mother's womb. I praise thee, for thou art fearful and wonderful. Wonderful are thy works! Thou knowest me right well; my frame was not hidden from thee, when I was being made in secret, intricately wrought in the depths of the earth. Thy eyes beheld my unformed substance; in thy book were written, every one of them, the days that were formed for me, when as yet there was none of them (Psalm 139:13-16).*

I am amused when I hear a nonplused husband and wife say, "This child wasn't planned!" I want to ask, "By whom?" "We weren't expecting this. We don't know what happened!" I can tell them what happened. God! God planned for that child, as He planned for you and for me. Long before we were ever thought of, long before our parents even met, God planned for our lives. He protected us for nine months, then produced us to the world. He has provided for our needs and led us to this moment in our history. He continues to work out His plan, even when we question Him and lose our way occasionally.

God told Jeremiah, "Before I formed you in the womb I knew you, and before you were born I consecrated you; I appointed you a prophet to the nations" (Jeremiah 1:5). I believe God has an appointed plan for us as well. He places people and events in our lives to bring us to spiritual fulfillment and completion. Sometimes we get hurt, but that is how we learn life's biggest lessons; our disappointments lead to greater appointments! We are not governed by coincidence or chance, for "in everything God works for good with those who love him, who are called according to his purpose" (Romans 8:28).

Never think your life is a mistake or an accident. If you are living in darkness and sorrow today, depressed, lonely, uncertain which way to turn, believe in spite of it all that God's Holy Spirit has great things in store for you. Though you see but dimly now, though you know only in part, someday you will understand fully that God has a beautiful plan for the salvation of the world and your life is part of the plan.

*Read: I Corinthians 13:12; Isaiah 14:27; Job 33:4*

# YOUR R.S.V.P.

*"The kingdom of heaven is at hand" (Matthew 4:17).*

You are invited to the Kingdom of Heaven! Through His messengers, pastors, evangelists, missionaries, and His Word, the King Himself, Jesus Christ, sends each of us a personal invitation to join Him for eternity. Not everybody, though, accepts His gracious invitation. "The kingdom of heaven may be compared to a king who gave a marriage feast for his son, and sent his servants to call those who were invited to the marriage feast; but they would not come" (Matthew 22:2-3).

How will you respond to His invitation? Will you ignore it? Many people do; they toss it aside like a piece of junk mail and never think of it again. Will you take it lightly? Some people would love to come, but they have something better to do; business or pleasure has higher priority, so they regretfully decline the offer. Will you be hostile to the invitation? Some people react with fury, petulance, even violence; they resent the intrusion into their lives and tear the invitation to shreds. Will you happily accept the invitation? I hope so. If you accept the loving invitation of Jesus Christ, the Son of God and Savior of sin, you enter the Kingdom of Heaven for eternity.

Through the parable of the marriage feast, we see the Kingdom as a place of laughter, joy, and happiness, but in the parable of the wedding garment, we learn there is a serious responsibility on us as well. "When the king came in to look at the guests, he saw there a man who had no wedding garment... Then the king said to the attendants, 'Bind him hand and foot, and cast him into the outer darkness'" (v. 11-13). When we accept the invitation, we agree to put on a new garment. The new garment symbolizes our willingness to change. We come as we are, but once there, we put on a new heart and a new mind so we become more and more like our host, the King.

The Kingdom of Heaven is at hand. The invitation has been sent. Have you returned your R.S.V.P.? It is rude to keep the host waiting, so do not delay! Accept His gracious invitation today and join the Kingdom of Heaven forever.

*Read: Matthew 22:1-14; Revelation 19:9; Psalm 145:10-13*

# FRIDAY'S FAILURES

*He said, "It is finished"; and he bowed his head and gave up his spirit (John 19:30).*

Good Friday -- what a dark day in the history of the world! Jesus Christ was crucified on Golgotha Hill. Everybody thought He had failed. His disciples, who had forsaken everything to follow Him for three years, felt cheated and depressed. But events did not end there. Friday's failure turned to glory on Easter morn. The Cross knew triumph from the empty tomb. What seemed a failure on Friday became on Sunday the greatest historical event the world has ever known. "The Lord has risen indeed" (Luke 24:34), bringing salvation to all who believe in Him. The resurrection proves there is no stone strong enough, no death deadly enough, no grave deep enough, to keep Jesus Christ and His believers entombed.

Most of us have experienced the devastation of a sense of failure. Sadly, many people never get over it. They dwell on problems instead of solutions, death instead of life, tragedy instead of triumph. They never experience the power of the resurrection or discover the destiny for which they were created. "Failure" is a terrible, debilitating word. If I were God, I would make some immediate innovations in our world: I would make church attendance and tithing mandatory, take the calories out of chocolate cake and put them into turnips, and erase the word "failure" from every language under the sun!

If today you are demoralized by your apparent failures, remember there is no such thing as failure in God's sight if you have done your best with what you have. If you did not try hard enough, that is laziness, but if you attempted something and did not succeed after giving it your best, you have not failed! God has another plan for you. It is not just a different plan; it is a better plan, though you cannot understand it now. Not only that, but He is on the way to fulfill His better plan.

Do not be crippled by Friday's failures. A seeming failure today may set you off in a thrilling fresh direction tomorrow. God has a greater plan for you than you can ever imagine.

*Read: John 19:17-30; I Corinthians 2:9; Psalm 73:26*

# TALENTS AND GIFTS

*Now there are varieties of gifts, but the same Spirit; and there are varieties of service, but the same Lord; and there are varieties of working, but it is the same God who inspires them all in every one. To each is given the manifestation of the Spirit for the common good (I Corinthians 12:4-7).*

There is confusion among some Christians about natural talents and spiritual gifts. Talents come from physical birth. Perhaps we have superior manual dexterity, a beautiful voice, a quick mind. Those are talents. Spiritual gifts are special attributes given by the Holy Spirit according to God's grace to equip people for ministry. God may take our physical talents, multiply them, and present them as gifts, but natural talents are not the same as spiritual gifts. We cannot receive spiritual gifts unless we are born again. Spiritual gifts come only to believers. Everybody who is a believer in Jesus Christ has a spiritual gift, and most people have a gift-mix of two or more.

It is God who decides what spiritual gifts we receive. "All these are inspired by one and the same Spirit, who apportions to each one individually as he wills" (I Corinthians 12:11). God chooses who will be the apostles, pastors, teachers, who will have the gift of healing, intercession, mercy, or serving. We do not select our own gift, nor can any well-meaning parent, pastor, or friend tell us what our gift should be.

All gifts are vitally important in the work of the Kingdom. Paul compares the Body of Christ to the human body. "Just as the body is one and has many members, and all the members of the body, though many, are one body, so it is with Christ" (v. 12). Fulfillment and joy come when we use our spiritual gifts selflessly for the benefit of God and other people. "As each has received a gift, employ it for one another, as good stewards of God's varied grace" (I Peter 4:10). When we discover and develop our special gifts and apply them to the tasks assigned to us by the Lord, the Church is built up, people are happy, and great things are done for His Kingdom on earth.

You are blessed with spiritual gifts. Allow your gifts to be a blessing to you and a blessing to the world.

*Read: I Corinthians 12; I Peter 4:7-11; John 3:6*

# DISCOVERING YOUR SPIRITUAL GIFTS

*His gifts were that some should be apostles, some prophets, some evangelists, some pastors and teachers, to equip the saints for the work of ministry, for building up the body of Christ, until we all attain to the unity of the faith and of the knowledge of the Son of God (Ephesians 4:11-13).*

Many Christians lead spiritually impoverished lives simply because they do not know their spiritual gifts. Paul, Peter, and James talk about spiritual gifts, but they never say, "This is the precise way to discern your gifts." The discovery is left to us, and it requires attention and work. Here are some guidelines.

**Explore the prospects.** There are over twenty spiritual gifts listed in four passages of Scripture: I Corinthians 12, Romans 12, Ephesians 4, and I Peter 4. Study the gifts and try to understand their distinctiveness and possibilities.

**Experience the opportunities.** When you are asked to do something (teach a class, be a leader, give generously), do not humbly say, "Oh, I can't do that." That is a sin against the Holy Spirit if God has given you that gift. Experiment! You may fail, but you will not know which gifts you do and do not have until you experience the opportunities that come your way.

**Examine your feelings.** It is lousy theology to teach that unless we are glum and gloomy, we cannot possibly be doing God's will. That is ridiculous and there is no truth to it! Contentment, satisfaction, and vitality grow as we use our gifts.

**Evaluate the results.** Some people sincerely want a certain gift, but they just do not have it. If you never see positive results from your earnest efforts, try something else.

**Expect confirmation.** If you have a spiritual gift, other people within the Body of Christ will recognize it. Their confirmation will strengthen your belief that you have the gift.

Discovering spiritual gifts takes dedication, but it is worth the effort. As you learn and apply the abilities God has placed within you, your self-esteem will soar and you will be excited about the future. Your greatest days are always ahead of you when you are helping to build the Kingdom of God.

*Read: Ephesians 4:1-16; Romans 12:1-8; Luke 9:62*

# CONTINUE THE CUSTOM

*I was glad when they said to me, "Let us go to the house of the Lord!" (Psalm 122:1).*

As a pastor, I study worship and often wonder about worship services in the Bible. Mary, Joseph, and baby Jesus went to a worship service forty days after Jesus was born for Mary's ceremonial purification. It was the custom of the law.

I wonder if Joseph was glad to go to temple that day. Maybe the Jerusalem Jets were playing the Bethlehem Bull-Dogs and he hated to miss the big game. Maybe he wanted to get back to his carpentry shop in Nazareth; he had overdue work to catch up on. I wonder if Mary was glad to go. Maybe she had a headache. Maybe she had diapers to wash. Maybe she wanted to write thank-you notes to the shepherds and magi.

Jesus did not have much choice about going. He was less than six weeks old! He was there because His parents followed the custom of the law. Apparently they continued the custom of regular worship. When Mary and Joseph lost Jesus for a while when he was twelve, "they found him in the temple, sitting among the teachers, listening to them and asking them questions" (Luke 2:46). Later we read that Jesus "went to the synagogue, as his custom was, on the sabbath day" (Luke 4:16). Imagine all the boring worship services Jesus Christ, the founder of the Church, must have sat through! He did it because it was the custom of the law. If Jesus valued and followed the custom of regular worship, we should as well.

I hope we are glad when someone says, "Let's go to church!" But consider church attendance on Christmas and Easter as compared with attendance on Sundays in January or August. What happens? Well, for some people, weekly worship is a cherished, indispensable custom; for others, if they do not feel like it or if they have something better to do, they just skip it. For some people, regular worship is a top priority; for others, it is simply another option in their busy schedules.

Are you glad to go to the house of the Lord? The Holy Spirit works mightily when people assemble together, so continue the custom of regular worship, just as Jesus did.

*Read: Luke 2:22-52; Psalm 27:4-6; Hebrews 10:19-25*

# MY DAD'S ADVICE

*Listen to advice and accept instruction, that you may gain wisdom for the future (Proverbs 19:20).*

As a child, I loved to play ball with my dad. He always gave me practical pointers on how to take a catch. "Keep your eyes open and your hands ready. Be eager and be positive. When you catch it, pass it on!"

That is not simply good advice and instruction on playing catch. It is a wise philosophy of life for every Christian.

We all catch things from one another. We affect and influence people by our attitudes, beliefs, and behavior. What do people catch from you? I hope they catch more than the flu! "We all, with unveiled face, beholding the glory of the Lord, are being changed into his likeness from one degree of glory to another; for this comes from the Lord who is the Spirit" (II Corinthians 3:18). Changing into Christ-likeness means we are to be accurate reflections of His glory. If you have caught the love of Jesus Christ in your life, people ought to be able to catch a little bit of Jesus Christ in you. Joy, hope, meekness, control, encouragement, strength, truth, self-esteem, creativity, perseverance, contentment, peace, generosity, humility, love, forgiveness -- these are qualities you should exemplify daily.

"Set the believers an example in speech and conduct, in love, in faith, in purity" (I Timothy 4:12). As a disciple, you have the responsibility and privilege of helping people catch new life in Jesus Christ. Don't drop the ball!

It does not take skill to play catch poorly. If you want to excel, you have to practice. It does not take skill to live feebly and miserably, either. To have a dynamic, powerful, joy-filled life in Christ, you have to concentrate and work at it. Keep your eyes open to see the beauty and majesty of God's Holy Word. Keep your hands ready to help build up His Kingdom on earth. Be eager to learn all you can about Jesus Christ. Be positive and encouraging to everyone around you. When you catch Christianity, pass it on! Pass the Good News of the Gospel on to someone today and every day in the future.

*Read: Deuteronomy 5:16; Matthew 10:24-25; Psalm 68:3-4*

# MARTHA'S DESCENDANTS

*He entered a village; and a woman named Martha received him into her house (Luke 10:38).*

We do not know if Martha was married or had children, but she does have descendants, people just like her in temperament, ability, and emotions. Marthas are capable, conscientious, concerned, and competent. They take charge and get jobs done right. We cannot get along without them! But it is not easy being a Martha. Marthas are unappreciated, taken for granted, and misunderstood. They frequently become unhappy and unpleasant from the pressure of their responsibilities. Though Martha was a wonderful woman, history records her unkindly; she is remembered as being rebuked by Jesus on His way to dying on the Cross. Marthas alienate themselves from loved ones and even from God, and Jesus tells us why. "Martha was distracted with much serving" (Luke 10:40). She tried too hard! She became so troubled and anxious about preparing the meal that she presumed to tell Jesus to make Mary help in the kitchen. Not ask, not suggest, but tell! Trying to tell the Lord what to do about somebody else's life is not right. God is the Creator; we are the creation. He tells; we are to listen.

Martha's descendants do tremendous good in the world, but unless they are careful, they will miss the most important part of life. If you realize you resemble Martha and you have been overdoing it, working too hard, causing rifts, and feeling unappreciated, there is just one thing to do: like Mary, come to the feet of Jesus and listen to His teaching. Be still and allow God to speak to you. Wait upon Him, claiming the promise that those who wait upon the Lord renew their strength.

The Lord is waiting for you to wait upon Him. Jesus invites you to come to His feet, but He will never force you to do so by hitting you over the head and dragging you there against your will. The only way to come is through personal choice. Choose today to come to the feet of Jesus Christ. You will find more blessings than you have ever known and be remembered kindly and lovingly by your descendants.

*Read: Luke 10:38-42; Isaiah 40:28-31; Luke 12:22-31*

## YOU AND YOUR BURDEN

*Blessed be the Lord, who daily bears us up (Psalm 68:19).*

Each of us has to carry a burden. Sometimes, though, we confuse burdens with other things.

A burden is not an anxiety. Anxiety is usually caused by something we can do nothing about, such as our height, our age, or the weather. Jesus tells us not to be anxious, but rather to trust in Him. Anxieties are to be forgotten.

A burden is not a complaint. Complaints are not all bad, for without constructive complaints, inequities and wrongs would not be corrected. Complaints are to be talked through with the right person, at the right time, in the right way.

A burden is not a problem. Though we resent problems, adversity can make us more creative and ingenious as we try to find answers to the dilemma. Problems are to be solved.

A burden is different. A burden cannot be forgotten, talked through, or solved. It simply must be carried, as a soldier carries his backpack, a student carries his books, and a mother carries her baby. A burden may be some past sin that, though forgiven by God, is not forgotten by people; a physical or mental limitation; a sickness or disease; a heavy heart caused by a prodigal in a far country; friction and personality clashes at work. The solution to a burden is in the hands of God.

If a burden is crushing you now, here is biblical help. First, celebrate your strength. You are stronger than you think, for Jesus Christ Himself lives in you. Believe, "I can do all things in him who strengthens me" (Philippians 4:13). Next, share your burden. "Bear one another's burdens, and so fulfill the law of Christ" (Galatians 6:2). Do not be possessive with your burden. Accept help offered in love. Finally, "Cast your burden on the Lord, and He will sustain you" (Psalm 55:22). Carry your burden to the Lord in prayer. Believe today God is with you and will daily bear you up. You can carry your burden, whatever it is, because the Lord is carrying you.

Burdens are cumbersome and difficult, but God will never give us more than we can endure. We can carry any burden because Jesus Christ carried the Cross for us.

*Read: Isaiah 46:3-4; Matthew 11:28-30; I John 5:3-5*

# CHRISTIAN SECURITY

*The eternal God is your dwelling place, and underneath are the everlasting arms (Deuteronomy 33:27).*

Most of us look for a sense of security during tough times. Usually we think we must hold onto somebody or something: a strong person, an attitude of hope, words of reassurance. The Bible teaches instead that true security comes in believing God is holding onto us, today, tomorrow, and always. We are His little lambs and He has us close to His breast. He is taking care of everything and working for our good. We can rely on Him.

That is hard to remember sometimes. When illness intrudes, when death devastates, when world events seem out of control and threatening, it is difficult to think we are in the loving arms of God. At times we find ourselves in deplorable circumstances and do not see how we will make it to the end. We grow bitter, confused. We have questions and we want to understand all the mysteries right away, but we cannot, and we must accept that. Nevertheless, there is security here and now for the Christian. The security comes not in holding on, but in knowing we are being held onto by the grace of God.

Jesus said, "My sheep hear my voice, and I know them, and they follow me; and I give them eternal life, and they shall never perish, and no one shall snatch them out of my hand. My Father, who has given them to me, is greater than all, and no one is able to snatch them out of the Father's hand" (John 10:27-29). Jesus is the Good Shepherd who laid down His life for His sheep. Absolutely nothing will be able to snatch us from the grasp of His hand. Nothing in life. Nothing in death. Nothing in the present, in the past, or in things to come will ever separate us from the love of God in Christ Jesus our Lord. We need not be afraid. We are safe. We are secure.

If today your life has been shattered by illness or death or fear for the future, if you are facing a difficult dilemma, if you are bitter and confused, put your trust in the promises of God and believe you are safe in His care. Thank Him for His love for you and dwell in the security of His everlasting arms.

*Read: John 10:7-30; Romans 8:38-39; Psalm 4:8*

# THE JONADABS IN YOUR LIFE

*"Speak the truth to one another" (Zechariah 8:16).*

The Bible explicitly commands us to forgive our enemies, but also implies, through a tragic incident in King David's family, that we should be careful with our friends. Friendship is a precious gift to be cherished, yet we must be prudent, for often friends, not foes, bring us misery and grief. Invariably, alcoholics and drug addicts say they were introduced to their destructive habits by friends, not strangers or enemies.

Amnon listened to the advice of his friend, Jonadab, with terrible results: an innocent girl, Tamar, was molested and lived as "a desolate woman" (II Samuel 13:20); Absalom had his half-brother killed because of that incestuous act, then fled the country and lived in exile; David saw his family torn apart. The Bible describes Jonadab as "crafty" (v. 4), but I wonder if Jonadab was as bad as we would like to think. Jonadab loved Amnon and wanted to help him. He did not present his plan to gain anything for himself. He gave bad advice, certainly, but let us be frank and realize that it is very easy for all of us to be crafty friends. Don't we sometimes tell our friends what they want to hear instead of what they need to hear? That is dishonest. Oh, it is all done out of love. We cannot bear to see them suffering, frustrated, tormented, depressed, so we say things to make them feel better, things that may not be true or right. In the name of friendship and love, we unwittingly mislead them, causing disaster and heartache for many people.

The only way to resist craftiness is to replace it with strong Christian values: honesty, conviction, and courage. Honesty is the basic requirement in true friendship. Convictions about ethics, sexuality, and morality must be rooted firmly in our minds. Courage gives us the ability to stand alone when we believe our convictions are right. Without honesty, conviction, and courage, friendship easily can lead to calamity.

Be very careful with your friendships. To ensure that you do not act as a Jonadab or allow a Jonadab to ruin you, cling faithfully to Jesus Christ, the best Friend anyone can have.

*Read: II Samuel 13:1-22; III John 4; Proverbs 12:22*

# REMEMBERING TO FORGET

*"God has made me forget all my hardship" (Genesis 41:51).*

God equipped each of us with a memory. The memory has two functions. One function is to recall. We rely on memory to gather knowledge, retain a sense of identity, recognize one another, find the route home from the office, and remind us to get to church on time on Sunday. The other function of memory is to forget! That's right. Though we often become upset when we forget things, God gets upset with us when we remember things He wants us to forget. What things?

**Forgiven sins.** When you confess your sins and ask for God's forgiveness, do not keep playing those sins over and over in your mind. Painful regrets will drag you down. Forget them. What God forgives, He forgets. You forget them, too.

**Stupidities.** Those little goofs and foolish things we all say and do -- forget them. If you do not, you will lose all self-confidence and view yourself as a bumbling idiot who cannot do anything right. That is no way for a Christian to live.

**Criticisms.** If you are doing anything worthwhile in this world, you will be attacked with ugly, mean, jealous remarks. They hurt, but forget them. Rehashing them constantly will prohibit you from developing Christ-like love and mercy.

**Successes.** This is hard. We all like trophies and recognition, but if we dwell on past achievements, we become big bores and the remainder of our lives cannot help but be a letdown. Forget your successes. God has new, exciting things planned for you right now. Concentrate on what lies ahead.

Remembering the things God wants you to forget will stunt your growth as a Christian. The Bible tells us how to use the memory. "Remember Jesus Christ, risen from the dead" (II Timothy 2:8). Keep your mind focused on Jesus Christ, His love, His death on the Cross, the power of His resurrection, and His eternal promises in Scripture. You have the potential to achieve a great destiny, so do not let past sins, stupidities, criticisms, or successes become spiritual blockades that keep you from its fulfillment. Remember to forget them today.

*Read: Isaiah 43:25; Philippians 3:12-16; Psalm 119:16*

# MIRROR RELIGION, WINDOW RELIGION

*Be doers of the word, and not hearers only, deceiving yourselves. For if any one is a hearer of the word and not a doer, he is like a man who observes his natural face in a mirror; for he observes himself and goes away and at once forgets what he was like (James 1:22-24).*

Jesus said, "You, therefore, must be perfect, as your heavenly Father is perfect" (Matthew 5:48), but it is not always easy to discern what is good and right, even within a church. In congregations, there are two kinds of people: people with mirror religion and people with window religion.

**Mirror religion.** People with mirror religion try to reflect off themselves and other people. They are stern, harsh, and judgmental. They think each sermon was meant for somebody else. They notice who is absent from church on Sunday and feel superior. They sing hymns loudly, but without emotion. They close their eyes during prayer, but do not listen. They wear religious jewelry, carry Bibles, and look pious, but after a worship service, quickly forget what they saw and heard.

**Window religion.** People with window religion allow the light to shine in so they can see with clear understanding and insight. They do not have critical eyes on others, but rather believe the Lord is speaking a personal message to them. They are willing to change their hardness of heart and make a greater commitment to Christ. They joyfully recognize Him as their hero, Master, and Lord. Window religion is true religion.

Jesus told the rich young ruler, "If you would be perfect, go, sell what you possess and give to the poor, and you will have treasure in heaven; and come, follow me" (Matthew 19:21). The man "went away sorrowful" (v. 22). That is mirror religion: no sacrifice, no sincerity, no devotion, no love. Mirror religion is a subtle danger. Let us not deceive ourselves. Are we doers of the Word, or hearers only? Are we walking in light or darkness, truth or falsehood? Our destiny depends upon our answers to those questions. Today, open the window of your soul to Jesus and be a doer of His Holy Word.

*Read: James 1:16-27; Isaiah 60:19-20; Micah 7:7-8*

# GETTING READY TO BE READY

*"Be ready and keep ready" (Ezekiel 38:7).*

Jesus is coming back. That fact is as sure as the sun rising tomorrow. More sure, for it is a promise of Scripture. We do not know when or where, but He is coming. If we are ready and waiting, it will be the most glorious day in our lives. If we are found wanting, it will be the worst; for eternity, we will live in separation from God and Christian loved ones. All of us today should be getting ready for that day. Jesus tells us how.

**Believe the preachers of God's Word.** There are many wrong reasons to go to church. The right reason is to believe! Preachers are not trying to fill seats and entertain crowds. They are trying to help people to believe and understand the Word of God and incorporate biblical truth into daily living. Noah was chosen by God to preach, but his neighbors were too busy to listen and so most of the world perished in the flood.

**Fear the Heavenly Judge.** God is not only a loving Father, but an eternal Judge. Everybody who has ever lived will be in His courtroom. "God will bring every deed into judgment, with every secret thing, whether good or evil" (Ecclesiastes 12:14). People who fear judgment will be ready.

**Think like the thief of the night.** A thief is despicable, but at least he thinks creatively, works out details, and has nerves of steel! To be ready, we are to be just as watchful and alert. "The day of the Lord will come like a thief in the night. When people say, 'There is peace and security,' then sudden destruction will come upon them" (I Thessalonians 5:2-3).

Where we spend eternity depends on our readiness for Jesus's return. He will receive unto Himself all who are ready. We need not be afraid if we are right with God. "Our commonwealth is in heaven, and from it we await a Savior, the Lord Jesus Christ, who will change our lowly body to be like his glorious body, by the power which enables him even to subject all things to himself" (Philippians 3:20-21). When He comes, if we are ready, it will be the most glorious day in our lives, but to be ready then, we must start getting ready today.

*Read: Matthew 24:32-44; Hebrews 10:26-30; Titus 2:11-14*

# THE TRIP OF A LIFETIME

*"Follow me" (Mark 10:21).*

If we insist on traveling first-class whenever we go on a trip, we will have trouble with the journey of faith Jesus Christ has planned for us. Christian disciples are not just along for the ride in this life, sitting back in comfort, relaxing, being waited on and pampered, enjoying the view. No, Christian disciples are called to push and pull, help, get dirty, and devote themselves untiringly to the welfare of fellow travelers. Jesus said, "He who does not take his cross and follow me is not worthy of me. He who finds his life will lose it, and he who loses his life for my sake will find it" (Matthew 10:38-39). Unless we are willing to travel as dedicated servants of Jesus Christ, we should not embark on the Christian journey.

We will have trouble, too, if we like to have every detail of our itinerary planned ahead and know exactly where we are going, what stops will be made, and for how long. Christian disciples are people who respond to two words of Jesus: "Follow me." Jesus does not announce in advance His specific plans for us, saying "Follow me to the other end of the country" or "Follow me to Africa." Just, "Follow me." That is the risk, for we never know where He will lead. Most of us wish Jesus would share His schedule with us so we could think it over. "Give me a few days, Jesus. I'll get back to you." Our attitude is, "Show me, Jesus, then I will go." Discipleship does not work that way. Jesus says, "You go, then I will show." It is scary, but that is how the spiritual journey always begins.

Christians are third-class travelers on this earth: God first, other people second, self third. Are you prepared to set out on a trip without knowing where you are going? If you are, you will have a marvelous, exciting journey, the trip of a lifetime. You will pass through some deep valleys, but also soar to lofty mountaintops you never knew existed and explore mystical places you could not have imagined. Best of all, once you decide to follow Jesus Christ wherever He leads, your final destination is assured. You are on your way to Heaven.

*Read: Mark 10:17-25; Luke 9:23-24; Hebrews 11:8-10*

# A PRICELESS COMMENDATION

*He was a good man, full of the Holy Spirit and of faith (Acts 11:24).*

What a commendation!   There is only one person in Scripture described this way: Barnabas, who serves as a model for goodness for us today.   Barnabas acknowledged God as the giver of everything and knew he possessed nothing; when he became a Christian, he sold his property and generously gave the money to the disciples.   Barnabas believed in the possibility of anything; he helped Saul overcome the disciples' skepticism and gain acceptance into the early Church after his dramatic conversion.   Barnabas admitted he did not know everything; he was humble enough to ask for help with his mission work and did not plunge into jealousy when Paul became more prominent.   In the presence of failure, Barnabas could find good; he remained loyal to Mark, who left the first mission trip, even though his loyalty led to a public rift with Paul.

The secret of Barnabas's goodness is easy to see.   He was "full of the Holy Spirit and of faith."   That is what it takes.   The name Barnabas means "Son of encouragement" (Acts 4:36), and his example encourages us as we try to be our best.   The same Spirit who filled Barnabas nearly 2,000 years ago lives in us and will be with us forever.   "The Lord is good" (Nahum 1:7), and our goodness depends upon how much we believe in God's Spirit within us.   The power of His Spirit operates according to our faith.   If we doubt His presence, our faith is weak and we cannot please God.   If we believe He is alive in us, we have the fruit of the Spirit, which includes goodness.

The Bible exhorts us to "do good to all" (Galatians 6:10).  We should not strive to be great in our own eyes and neglect to do what is good in the sight of God.   "It is not the man who commends himself that is accepted, but the man whom the Lord commends" (II Corinthians 10:18).   A priceless commendation awaits all those who are full of the Holy Spirit and of faith: the beautiful, welcoming words of Jesus Christ, "Well done, good and faithful servant" (Matthew 25:21).

*Read:  Acts 11:19-26;  Psalm 37:27-28;  II Timothy 1:13-14*

## LEADING PEOPLE TO JESUS

*Do the work of an evangelist, fulfil your ministry (II Timothy 4:5).*

If I were to suggest to you right now that you put this book down, go outside, stand on a street corner, and start talking to people about your faith, you probably would put this book down for a long, long time. Most people fear the ministry of evangelism. However, all faithful disciples of Jesus Christ have a responsibility to lead other people to Him.

Fortunately, that is not as difficult as it sounds. One way to lead people to Jesus is simply to invite them to church. Statistics show that 75% of the people who join organized churches today do so not because of the beauty of the building, the denomination, or the popularity and intelligence of the pastors, but because somebody invited them to come along to church one Sunday. Another way is to bring people into our homes. Through our attitude, conversation, and conduct, we allow them to see the love of Jesus Christ living and dwelling in us. They should sense something different, a peace and power they would like to have themselves. We do not need a big house or a big budget, just a big heart for Jesus and a big desire to let other people know what He has done in our lives.

Paul wrote, "I am not ashamed of the gospel" (Romans 1:16). Are we? If we are afraid to share the Good News of the Gospel, how can we claim to serve the Lord? Today, try to tell someone about your Savior. Just be sincere and natural, and never, ever be ashamed. You will be surprised at the number of people who truly want to learn more about Jesus Christ. Once you do the work of an evangelist, you soon find that leading people to Jesus is not a dreadful chore; it is a joy.

Someone led you to Jesus Christ. If possible, contact that person today. Pick up the phone or write a letter and say, "Thank you for making a difference in my life. Thank you for helping me find new life. Thank you for leading me to Jesus." If you live as a devoted disciple of Jesus Christ, you just might receive some calls and letters like that yourself someday.

*Read: II Timothy 4:1-5; Ephesians 4:1-16; Psalm 40:9-10*

## SMILES AND LAUGHTER

*"A glad heart makes a cheerful countenance, but by sorrow of heart the spirit is broken" (Proverbs 15:13).*

Of all God's creatures, we alone are capable of smiles and laughter. God uses our sense of humor to help us keep a proper perspective on our humanity. Most of us take ourselves far too seriously and we do not take God seriously enough. We tend to resent our human limitations and act as though we are infallible and incorruptible. The Bible warns that when we deny our humanity, we hurt ourselves and others. Our sense of humor gives us the opportunity to see ourselves as we truly are: people who occasionally stumble and goof, yet people created, valued, and loved by God, who never stumbles or goofs. When we learn to laugh at our ludicrous blunders and slips, we realize how much we need God's grace, just like everyone else.

Jesus was not only a healthy, humble, honest Person, but a humorous Person as well. He talked about swallowing camels and about wood logs in the eye. He told stories with surprise endings that confounded and amused listeners. The Gospel is Good News, and good news always brings forth smiles and laughter. The Good News is that Jesus is alive, and the power that empowered Jesus can empower us to live triumphantly today. Though we have tribulation, we can smile and laugh with good cheer and joy that no one can take away from us.

There is a thin line between laughter and tears, a glad heart and a sorrowful heart, a cheerful countenance and a broken spirit, but when we are in depression or grief, that thin line appears to be an endless chasm. If you are tearful, sorrowful, or broken, hold on to Jesus's promise to His disciples. "You will be sorrowful, but your sorrow will turn into joy" (John 16:20). In spite of everything, smile a little right now. Laugh at yourself a bit. Try to be hopeful about what God can do in your life and in our thrilling world. You might think you cannot smile or laugh today, but you can. You will be glad you did! Smiles and laughter bring health and healing. "A cheerful heart is a good medicine" (Proverbs 17:22). Try a dose today.

*Read: Matthew 23:23-24; Luke 6:39-42; Proverbs 15:15*

91

# RESTING IN HIS WORD

*Let the word of Christ dwell in you richly (Colossians 3:16).*

We all yearn for inner peace in times of dilemmas, disasters, and difficulties. Sometimes, though, we search for peace in places that can generate only more confusion.

**In words.** The reassuring words we hear and speak often have little practical influence. Words are losing their impact. In the past, our word was our bond; now we need a lawyer for everything! Many people did not even believe the words of Jesus while He lived on earth. "The Jews gathered round him and said to him, 'How long will you keep us in suspense? If you are the Christ, tell us plainly.' Jesus answered them, 'I told you, and you do not believe'" (John 10:24-25).

**In works.** Some people who cannot believe words can believe works they can see and experience. Yet works have limitations. Jesus's mighty miracles confirmed Him as the Messiah, but people kept wanting to see more. "The works that I do in my Father's name, they bear witness to me; but you do not believe" (v. 25-26). Today, His Holy Spirit is actively working in the world, but many people do not believe it.

**In workers.** Christian workers are strong and faithful. In the storms of life, they show stability and courage, knowing they are safe in the hands of God and will be all right no matter what happens. But any worker can stumble and fall.

Words do not mean much. Works might not be enough. Workers can fail. Where, then, do we look for inner peace?

**In God's Holy Word.** We find rest for our souls when we rest in His Word. Inner peace begins with the Word of God. "Receive with meekness the implanted word, which is able to save your souls" (James 1:21). In the Word are truth, light, and eternal life. The Bible is "living and active" (Hebrews 4:12), God's personal message to believers. Hear and believe His Word. Trust His Word. Love His Word. Read His Word and commit your life to the Word made flesh, Jesus Christ.

Let the Word of Christ dwell in you richly, for only by resting there will you find the inner peace for which you yearn.

*Read: John 10:22-30; Hebrews 4:12-13; Matthew 24:35*

# INSTRUCTIONS FOR THE JOURNEY

*He called to him his twelve disciples and gave them authority over unclean spirits, to cast them out, and to heal every disease and every infirmity... These twelve Jesus sent out (Matthew 10:1,5).*

It is exciting to anticipate a journey, but difficult to get ready for one. Usually we leave the packing until last, then, in a rush, bring the wrong clothes, and too much. A journey's preparations begin when we decide to take a trip, and our preparations are as important as the trip itself. Jesus knew this as He sent His disciples out to turn the world upside-down. Before commissioning them, He gave instructions, guidelines He wants each of us to follow in our journeys of life today.

**Wherever you go, preach!** "Preach as you go, saying, 'The kingdom of heaven is at hand'" (Matthew 10:7). Proclaim the Good News. Through your lips and your life, point people to Christ, who alone brings healing, cleansing, and rebirth.

**Give, and do not worry about the pay.** "Give without pay. Take no gold, nor silver" (v. 8-9). It is in giving our lives for the glory of the Lord that we find the true meaning of life. If we do the job God assigns to us, He will supply our needs.

**Extend the peace of God.** "As you enter the house, salute it. And if the house is worthy, let your peace come upon it" (v. 12-13). Be first to extend peace. Proceed with open arms, not clenched fists; listening ears, not critical eyes; love, not anger.

**Grasp the promises of God.** "He who endures to the end will be saved" (v. 22). Jesus never guarantees anyone an easy voyage. He sends His disciples out "as sheep in the midst of wolves" (v. 16), but promises if we persevere in following Him, we will triumph over all obstacles along the route.

You are an emissary of the Lord Himself, so rejoice as you travel the King's highway. Wherever He takes you, He will be with you all the way, all the time. If the trail gets bumpy and you lose direction, do not quit half-way or hunt for some other avenue to take. Just refer back to your instructions and keep going. The best part is always ahead, for if you follow Jesus Christ, your journey leads to the Kingdom of Heaven.

*Read: Matthew 10:1-23; Proverbs 10:17; Psalm 16:7-13*

## SPINNING

*The vessel he was making of clay was spoiled in the potter's hand, and he reworked it into another vessel, as it seemed good to the potter to do (Jeremiah 18:4).*

Do you ever feel as though your life is spinning out of control? Jeremiah talked about the spinning wheel at a potter's house; the wheel hummed, clay spattered. Spinning is a force God uses when He creates and recreates. When He created the universe, He made planets revolve around the sun; when He formed the earth, He made it turn on its axis. God creates power, stress, and pressure through spinning. We all spin in our daily activities, and sometimes we get tired of the tension. We want to shout, "Stop! Enough!" We yearn to escape the weight of responsibilities and demands, but we can no more do that than birds can fly without wings or fish can live outside water. We are made to live in pressure, under stress, spinning. We may not like it, but that is how God designed us.

People handle the spinning in their lives in different ways. Pitifully, many are anxious and nervous, angry and upset, tossed to and fro like pieces of paper swirling in an empty parking lot on a breezy day. The Bible says, "Anxiety in a man's heart weighs him down" (Proverbs 12:25). God does not want us weighed down by stress. The teaching of the Bible is to adapt, to adjust, to advance. Like the bird that puts its wings to the wind, like the sailor who hoists his sail in the midst of a storm, we are to use positively the pressures of the day. How? By believing God is sovereign, He is always at work trying to bless us with new opportunities, and He is using the spinning to remake us into viable vessels for His will. Notice, when the potter came upon a marred piece of clay, he did not throw it away; he reshaped it, remodeled it, recreated it. Through the spinning of the wheel, he took something useless and turned it into an object of value, beauty, and purpose.

God is the Potter. We are the clay. Adapt to the spinning. Be grateful for it. Through the spinning, God places within our meager earthen vessels the treasure of His glory and power.

*Read: Jeremiah 18:1-11; Genesis 1:14-19; II Corinthians 4:6-7*

# PARADING DOWN THE AVENUE

*"What is your decision?" (Mark 14:64).*

Many people dislike decisions. It is scary to realize the choices we make today have a huge impact on our tomorrows. Often, though, we forget that our decisions also affect other people's decisions. When Jesus Christ decided to proclaim Himself as Messiah and march down the main street of Jerusalem, He forced everyone else to decide if they were for Him or against Him, if they would crown Him or crucify Him.

I wonder what we would have decided that first Palm Sunday. We love to believe we'd have been waving palms, spreading garments, and shouting Hallelujah, but would we? Many of us are slow to change. We very well might have been watching from the corner with the scribes and Pharisees, wishing Jesus would fall. We might have been standing on the curb of indifference, wondering, but anxious for the parade to pass so we could return to our routine. When Jesus paraded down the avenue, what do you think you would have done?

Thank God we live on this side of Easter. We do not have to make the decisions those Palm Sunday people had to make. We have the advantage of the resurrection, Pentecost, and the Church in action for nearly 2,000 years. We know enough to be for Jesus! But today, in our nation, communities, businesses, and homes, we have issues and problems parading down the avenue in front of us all the time. Look around. Read the newspaper. Drug and alcohol abuse, racism, world peace, the environment, crime and violence, poverty and homelessness -- we as Christians cannot and should not seek to avoid these difficult challenges. Claiming Jesus Christ as Lord and Savior, we must make decisions today to try, in His name, to make this world a better place.

What is parading down the avenue before you today? You might wish you could have more time, more information, more expertise, and more advice before making your decision, but the moment to act is now. Do not watch from the corner. Get off the curb of indifference. For the sake of the Kingdom, make your decision and get involved.

*Read: Matthew 21:1-11; Mark 14:53-65; Matthew 5:20*

# SURPRISED BY LOVE

*"What no eye has seen, nor ear heard, nor the heart of man conceived, what God has prepared for those who love him," God has revealed to us through the Spirit... Now we have received not the spirit of the world, but the Spirit which is from God, that we might understand the gifts bestowed on us by God (I Corinthians 2:9-10,12).*

God has great, wonderful, amazing surprises in store for those who love Him, but He can surprise only people who expect to be surprised. We need to believe in order to receive! That means we must live in the spirit of surprise and do some surprising things to show all the world our love for God.

**Love the unlovable and the unlovely.** Jesus told us to love one another, with no conditions. We must love those who do not love back and even look for unlovely people to love. When we love people who are crass and ornery, we will be surprised at the miracles that happen in their lives and our own.

**Believe the unbelievable.** Salvation, faith, miracles: these and other biblical ideas are hard to believe, but we can believe even when we do not understand. Possibly the most difficult idea to believe is that human life can change. Believe it! God changes lives through Christ. It is surprising, but true.

**Accept the unacceptable.** It is hard to face facts. Children grow up and move away. We get older. Loved ones die. Only time and God's grace get us through the heartbreak, but no matter how difficult, we must accept reality and put our trust in God. When we do, surprises come.

**Attempt the impossible.** If we are not attempting bold, beautiful things for God, life is dull. God surprises us when we follow our impossible dreams to bring honor to His name.

On a human level, the people we love most are the ones we most enjoy surprising. God loves us and wants to surprise us in ways we cannot imagine. Though eye has not seen, ear has not heard, and heart has not conceived the gifts God is preparing to bestow on us, let us be open to His Spirit and live in the spirit of surprise, and we will be surprised by His love always.

*Read: I Corinthians 2:9-16; I John 4:21; Isaiah 64:4*

# WHEN YOU INVITE JESUS IN

*"I entered your house, you gave me no water for my feet, but she has wet my feet with her tears and wiped them with her hair. You gave me no kiss, but from the time I came in she has not ceased to kiss my feet. You did not anoint my head with oil, but she has anointed my feet with ointment. Therefore I tell you, her sins, which are many, are forgiven, for she loved much; but he who is forgiven little, loves little" (Luke 7:44-48).*

Some people invite Jesus Christ in when they are not ready for Him to be Lord and Master of their lives. In the passage contrasting a Pharisee and a prostitute, Jesus illustrates what it means to be ready, or not to be ready. It is typical of Jesus's teaching that the individual we would expect to be ready is not the one who is ready.

Simon invited Jesus in with his lips, then held Him back. He withheld the customary kiss, bowl of water, and ointment, symbolically revealing that he would give Jesus no love, no service, and no anointing. We cannot hold back when we invite Jesus in. That is asking Him to come into our lives on our terms, saying, "I want you when I want you, but the rest of the time, I am going to restrain my devotion, my adoration, my love, my service." If Jesus Christ is not first in our lives, He is nowhere in our lives. We are only ready to invite Him in when we willingly and freely offer Him everything we have.

The prostitute did not hold back. She washed Jesus's feet with her tears and unashamedly let her hair down in front of people who were sure to criticize her. She cried openly, revealing deep love for Jesus. The woman saw herself in the promises of God and looked ahead to what she could become, and Jesus said, "Your faith has saved you; go in peace" (Luke 7:50). Because she held nothing back, she found new life.

Two people invited Jesus into their lives. One wasted Jesus's time; one was saved. The difference? One held back; one did not. You can find new life in Christ, but do not play games. If you do not mean business with Jesus, do not invite Him to become Lord of your life. It will only foul you up.

*Read: Luke 7:36-50; James 2:5; Psalm 24:7-10*

97

## BEING RIPPED OFF

*Therefore be imitators of God, as beloved children. And walk in love, as Christ loved us and gave himself up for us, a fragrant offering and sacrifice to God (Ephesians 5:1-2).*

Have you ever felt ripped off when you did not get what you expected? It has happened to me at the department store. Someone will shove a sample of after shave lotion in my face and it smells great. I buy it, take it home, open it up, and discover it does not smell at all the way it did at the store. I think they put stronger scents in the sample bottles than in the real thing! That irritates me. I resent it. I feel cheated!

That is how some people react when they look at a person who professes to be a Christian but do not see Christ. If we are truly Christian, we should be recognized as authentic, fragrant samples of Jesus Christ, for God places His Holy Spirit within believers. Paul wrote, "Do you not know that you are God's temple and that God's Spirit dwells in you?... For God's temple is holy, and that temple you are" (I Corinthians 3:16-17).

Being the temple of God's Holy Spirit means when people see us, hear us, and watch us, they have a right to experience the presence of Jesus Christ. What do we tell the world if we are joyless, grim, self-centered, smug, and materialistic? Christians are to live for Christ! "For the love of Christ controls us, because we are convinced that one has died for all; therefore all have died. And he died for all, that those who live might live no longer for themselves but for him who for their sakes died and was raised" (II Corinthians 5:14-15). Are we controlled by the love of Jesus Christ in all we do?

Many people are being ripped off today. They expect to see Jesus, hear Jesus, learn what Jesus would do in different situations. They expect to see love, forgiveness, compassion. If they do not see these qualities in us, we cheat them. Let us not deprive anyone of the chance to meet Jesus. People want to see Christ and need to see Jesus Christ. People will not find fulfillment until they experience Christ personally in their lives. Do not be a rip-off! Be such an authentic, fragrant sample of Christ that people will hunger to know Christ Himself.

*Read: Titus 2:7-15; Philippians 2:1-11; II Corinthians 6:16*

# INGREDIENTS OF FAITH

*Then Jesus answered her, "O woman, great is your faith! Be it done for you as you desire." And her daughter was healed instantly (Matthew 15:28).*

A Canaanite woman once pleaded with Jesus to heal her daughter. Her story reveals some essential ingredients of faith.

**Have a quest.** To have faith, we must have a quest, an intense, driving passion to help somebody or do something. The quest for the Canaanite woman was her daughter's healing. "Have mercy on me, O Lord, Son of David; my daughter is severely possessed by a demon" (Matthew 15:22). She had probably consulted priests, physicians, and everyone else she could think of. She would not quit! Strong faith comes when we have a quest that eats us up, a quest that is heavy on our hearts, a quest we will never forsake. Jesus tells us to ask, to seek, to knock. That is the beginning of great faith.

**Be a pest with your quest.** When the woman begged for help, Jesus at first was silent. "He did not answer her a word" (v. 23). Sometimes we call on Jesus and He seems to do nothing. The silence of Jesus is painful. We think He does not hear or care. Keep petitioning and pleading! Jesus hears, understands, and knows everything. Even in His silence, He loves us. He will answer in His own way, and whatever answer comes, it will be the right solution at the right time.

**Do your best.** When Jesus did respond, He referred to the distraught mother as a dog. "It is not fair to take the children's bread and throw it to the dogs" (v. 26). I really do not know what to make of that, but I know how she took it: she took it for the best; she had a positive attitude; she smiled and used her sense of humor. "Yes, Lord, yet even the dogs eat the crumbs that fall from their masters' tables" (v. 27). She accepted what Jesus had to say.

The great faith of the Canaanite woman brought complete healing to her daughter miles away. Remember the essential ingredients of faith the next time you come to Jesus with a problem. Your great faith can bring help to you as well.

*Read: Matthew 15:21-28; Matthew 7:7-8; Hebrews 11:6*

# A LITTLE ANATOMY LESSON

*Be quick to hear, slow to speak, slow to anger, for the anger of man does not work the righteousness of God (James 1:19-20).*

When God created us, He equipped us with everything we would need to live as He intended. He must have known we would have trouble with our emotions, especially that explosive emotion, anger. Consider how He designed our faces: we each have two ears and only one mouth; we have no muscles to close our ears but we are equipped with muscles to close our mouths. This little anatomy lesson points to an obvious truth: when we are angry, God wants us to open the ears and shut the mouth, to be long on listening and short on talking.

Anger is a positive force when used judiciously to correct inequities, but anger characterized by vicious, venomous insults hurled at people we dislike inflicts severe wounds. James calls the tongue "a fire" (James 3:6) difficult to control; "every kind of beast and bird, of reptile and sea creature, can be tamed and has been tamed by humankind, but no human being can tame the tongue -- a restless evil, full of deadly poison" (v. 7-8). It is easy to shoot off the mouth without engaging the brain and blurt out sarcastic, savage remarks. Instead, we should follow the example of Paul and Jesus. Paul wrote, "Let no evil talk come out of your mouths, but only such as is good for edifying, as fits the occasion, that it may impart grace to those who hear" (Ephesians 4:29). Jesus got angry, but His anger never destroyed; it improved people and situations, because Jesus used His ears more than His mouth. He listened kindly to everyone, and even when people mistreated, rejected, and misunderstood Him, He spoke only words of love.

We would be wise to remember today's little anatomy lesson. "Do you see a man who is hasty in his words? There is more hope for a fool than for him" (Proverbs 29:20). Let us ask the Lord's help in being quick to hear, slow to speak, and slow to anger so we can live righteously, as God intends us to live.

*Read: James 3:4-10; Psalm 140:1-3; Proverbs 14:17*

# RAISING UP PARENTS

*"Let the children come to me, and do not hinder them; for to such belongs the kingdom of God. Truly, I say to you, whoever does not receive the kingdom of God like a child shall not enter it" (Luke 18:16-17).*

It seems the logical order for parents to raise up children, but often the reverse is true and children raise up parents to a spiritual level they would not otherwise attain.

Children raise up parents to realize faith formation is a family affair. Couples often become reactivated in churches only after children are born. They grow conscious of their obligation to provide religious guidance for their youngsters.

Children raise up parents to recognize the huge impact of words. Little children have big ears, and wise parents learn to be careful with their own speech. Careless words of vulgarity, bigotry, and negativity can cripple a child spiritually for life.

Children raise up parents to celebrate the uniqueness of personality. Parents soon see that each child is an individual. God does not own a copier machine. He makes all things new. If He wanted us all to be alike, He'd have made us that way.

Children raise up parents to be protectors of truth. Parents do not want new morality, situation ethics, or unrestrained license for their children. They want standards and values that are absolute and enduring. Truth comes from God's Word.

Parents, your job is difficult. You worry over your children's well-being and agonize over decisions you must make. You sometimes wish your children would get better grades or see different friends or be neater at home. Most likely your parents wished the same things about you! Cherish your children. You will not have them very long. Fall to your knees tonight and thank God for them. He has entrusted their early years to your care. Take that responsibility seriously.

Jesus Christ loved little children and said unless we become as little children, we cannot enter the Kingdom of God. Let us allow the little children to raise us up and teach us. We are all members of the family of faith and we all have a lot of learn.

*Read: II Timothy 1:1-5; Psalm 127:3-5; Proverbs 17:6*

# LYDIA AND THE SLAVE GIRL

*One who heard us was a woman named Lydia, ... a seller of purple goods, who was a worshiper of God. The Lord opened her heart to give heed to what was said by Paul (Acts 16:14).*

Acts 16 tells of two women who are examples of religion: Lydia, a model of healthy religion, and a slave girl, a model of sick religion. Like people, religions can get sick. Many things are paraded as religion that really are pathetic aberrations. We have only to recall tragedies caused by fanatical cult leaders to know their communes were founded on deadly distortions and lies. In less extreme cases, it is not always easy to be sure when sickness begins in a religion. Sometimes the illness is so gradual that we do not recognize the problem until symptoms are severe. It is like a cold or cancer. When exactly do they start? Where do they come from? Sickness is insidious, and so it is helpful to contrast the signs of healthy religion in Lydia and the symptoms of sick religion in the slave girl.

Lydia was a successful businesswoman who was open to ideas in Paul's preaching. Upon her conversion, she brought her whole household to be baptized, then invited Paul and his friends to stay at her home. Lydia demonstrated kindness and concern. She understood that we cannot worship God unless we have a good relationship with people. "If any one says, 'I love God,' and hates his brother, he is a liar; for he who does not love his brother whom he has seen, cannot love God whom he has not seen" (I John 4:20). Lydia shows us that healthy religion is meant to unite, not disunite; to reconcile people with God and others, not repel them; to build bridges, not barriers.

The slave girl was a pest and a nuisance who annoyed Paul and upset people. Though correct in theology, her strident manner did more harm than good for the cause of Christ. Notice, the Bible never mentions her name or what happened to her. Her religion was sick. She was useless to the Kingdom.

Strive today for a vital, vigorous, healthy faith in Jesus. Love Him with all your heart, soul, mind, and strength and your religion will be so healthy you will live through eternity.

*Read: Acts 16:11-24; James 1:26-27; I John 1:6-7*

102

## UNLEASHING GOD'S POWER

*"Rise, take up your pallet, and walk." And at once the man was
healed, and he took up his pallet and walked (John 5:8-9).*

Jesus once encountered a man in Jerusalem who had been
ill for thirty-eight years. Thirty-eight years is a long time!
Anyone would assume the poor invalid would want more than
anything to be cured of his infirmity. That is why Jesus's
question seems puzzling. "Do you want to be healed?" (John
5:6). Why wouldn't he? The fact is, some sick people do not
want to be healed, though they may not admit it or even realize
it. Notice, the sick man did not answer, "Yes, yes, I want to be
healed!" He launched into a sob story about having no one to
put him in the pool of Bethzatha when the waters were
troubled. Jesus's question seemed to catch him off guard. He
might not have been sure if he wanted to be healed. After all,
for thirty-eight years, he'd had a built-in excuse not to work or
take any responsibilities. Healing would change everything!
God knows today not all people want to be healed, and He
cannot do much for them. Healing miracles are beyond our
human comprehension. We do not know why God heals some
people and not others. It is not because more fervent prayers
are said for one individual than another, or because God plays
favorites and loves one more than another, or because God
heals only saints, for God does not pay us back according to
our sins. Just one thing seems sure: people whom God wants
to heal are healed faster and better if they want to be healed.
Jesus healed the man by the pool, but Jesus did not compel
him to respond or do the walking for him. He directed the man
to rise, pick up his bed, and do his own walking. That is a
great lesson for us today. We cannot know if God plans to heal
a specific malady or problem we have, but when we want to be
healed enough to do our part, then God's power is unleashed in
our lives. It might be the power of renewed health or it might
be the power of patient endurance. That depends upon the
providence of God. But the unleashing of God's power
depends upon us.

*Read: John 5:1-18; Mark 6:53-56; Psalm 147:1-6*

## SCATTER THE SEED

*"The kingdom of God is as if a man should scatter seed upon the ground, and should sleep and rise night and day, and the seed should sprout and grow, he knows not how. The earth produces of itself, first the blade, then the ear, then the full grain in the ear. But when the grain is ripe, at once he puts in the sickle, because the harvest has come" (Mark 4:26-29).*

Everything is easier when we know what is expected of us. That is why Jesus gave so many clear instructions on how God wants us to live. God intends for His people and His Church to grow. In the process of growth, there are certain things God must do and certain things He expects of us. So often we foul things up by trying to do God's part and not doing our own. Trying to do God's will without God's timing and power leaves us depleted and fearful, without faith, hope, and love.

Jesus helps us understand God's part and our responsibility through the parable of the farmer sowing seed. Jesus explains we are not required to make the seed or get the seed; God makes it and gives it to us. The seed is the Word of God. The Word of God is given to us and our responsibility is to scatter the Word of God all over the world. That means we have to get up, get out, and let go! Nothing grows in the hand. The seed must be cast out to be multiplied. There is a chance the seed might be lost, yet we plant in the hope it will produce good fruit. We allow the rain to replenish, the snow to cover, the wind to blow, and the hot days and cold nights to pass, trusting God to bring forth a bountiful harvest. We know not how growth comes, but we believe God's will shall be done.

When you give someone a special gift, you justifiably feel upset and insulted if it is stashed away in a drawer. You want it to be used, enjoyed, and valued. God has given you the most precious gift in all the world: His Holy Word. Use it. Enjoy it. Value it. Let it take root in your heart, then get up, get out, and let it go! Scatter the Word so other people can learn of God's love through Jesus Christ. Do not foul things up trying to play God. Today, just do your job and scatter the seed.

*Read: Mark 4:1-29; Ecclesiastes 11:6; Proverbs 11:18*

## TO TRIUMPH OVER TOUGH TIMES

*And he left there and went to the region of Judea and beyond the Jordan, and crowds gathered to him again; and again, as his custom was, he taught them (Mark 10:1).*

We should be grateful for Mark 10, for it shows Jesus having a tough day, as we do sometimes. Jesus was taking a trip He did not want to take, knowing it would lead to His death. He had a confrontation with Pharisees over the issue of divorce. When approached by mothers who wanted Him to touch their children, He had to scold His disciples for being overprotective. He met the rich young ruler and did not instantly win him to eternal life. Jesus's experiences give insight on how we can triumph over tough times. Mark tells us Jesus looked around, began to talk, and started to walk.

**Jesus looked around.** When everything goes wrong, most of us just want to lie low and hide. If we look around at all, we look for someone to blame for our troubles. Instead, we ought to look around to see what we can learn from tough times. God is not trying to punish us. He is trying to teach us something.

**Jesus talked.** We would rather clam up and vow, "Never again!" Keeping silent only aggravates the problem. It is far better to talk, not to complain or moan, but to speak about Jesus. Focusing on Jesus always gives courage and hope.

**Jesus walked.** Some people give up, on their families, jobs, even life itself. Nothing can be that tough. Quitting is the worst thing we can do. Even if it hurts, keep walking. At times we might only be able to hobble as a cripple or crawl as a baby, but the Christian keeps going! It does not matter how we walk in life; it matters with whom we walk. Walk with Jesus.

"The hand of the Lord is mighty" (Joshua 4:24). Take Jesus's mighty hand and walk today where Jesus walks. God will take care of you. He walks with you not only in the bright days, but in the dark nights as well. He is with you in the pleasant times and the tough times. Believing you are close to God through faith in Jesus Christ and knowing you are His own will strengthen you to triumph over tough times.

*Read: Mark 10:1-32; II Timothy 1:7; Psalm 29:11*

# PHILIPS AND ANDREWS

*Jesus said to Philip, "How are we to buy bread, so that these people may eat?" This he said to test him, for he himself knew what he would do. Philip answered him, "Two hundred denarii would not buy enough bread for each of them to get a little." One of his disciples, Andrew, Simon Peter's brother, said to Him, "There is a lad here who has five barley loaves and two fish; but what are they among so many?" (John 6:5-9).*

In John's account of the feeding of the 5,000, Jesus said to Philip, "We have a lot of people here who are hungry. We must feed them." Philip had an opportunity to participate in a miracle, but he missed it, thinking the task was unachievable. It was Andrew who said, "Lord, I have a lad with five barley loaves and two fish. I don't know if it will help, but here they are." Andrew brought what he had and the miracle began.

There are Philips and Andrews in every church. Philips respond negatively to each challenge. Immediately they find reasons why a new idea cannot be done. "It's impossible! It'll never work. Costs too much money! We never did it that way before!" They are good people, but their pessimism drains them of creativity and vitality. They usually do not accomplish a great deal in life. Thank God for Andrews! Andrews look for potential. They bring all they have to Jesus and say, "Here, Lord, this is what I can offer. Do with it as you wish."

Are you a Philip or an Andrew? God calls us to help in the making of miracles, in big and small ways. Consider all the people who contributed to that lunch. There was the farmer who planted the seed; the harvester who collected the grain; the baker who cooked the bread; the fisherman who caught the fish; the father who paid for the food; the mother who packed the sack lunch; the young lad who carried it. A lot of people went into that lunch, and that lunch went into a lot of people! Philip doubted the Lord could do anything with those meager resources. Andrew trusted in the power of God.

"Is anything too hard for the Lord?" (Genesis 18:14). Of course not! Be an Andrew and help to make miracles happen.

*Read: John 6:1-14; Jeremiah 32:27; Luke 1:37*

# WHAT TO GIVE UP

*Do not neglect to do good and to share what you have, for such sacrifices are pleasing to God (Hebrews 13:16).*

How much do we truly give up for the sake of Jesus Christ? All too often when it comes to giving, we prefer to give things out rather than give things up. We do not seem to mind giving out our astute advice, our informed opinions, and our penetrating insights on every possible subject. We gladly hand out those incomparable treasures with the confident expectation that they will benefit all who are wise enough to listen. But giving up is a different matter! We live in a society in which we do not like to talk about giving, and especially about giving up. It is always, "Gimme!" and "Get me!" We are people who, even in our best moments, scheme to get more. If only we concentrated instead on how much to give! We seldom realize that every time we give up something valuable to us in the name of Jesus Christ, we find love, joy, and peace.

Money, talent, time -- those are important to give up, but there is more. Maybe we are embroiled in a silly argument with someone; let's give up our pride and the need to win. Maybe we are in a painful estrangement but we do not want to make the first move toward reconciliation; let's give up our stubbornness. Maybe our problems are making us grumpy and inconsiderate; let's give up unkind words and unsmiling faces. Maybe we are so busy with our jobs and families that we never look around to see if someone needs help; let's give up our schedules to do something for somebody, even if it is somebody we do not know well and something we do not especially enjoy doing. Maybe we are tired at the end of the day and want to relax; let's give up our leisure to listen to a lonely friend, visit someone in a nursing home, or do a chore for a neighbor. No matter how much we give up, we will never give up as much for Jesus Christ as He gave up for us. Jesus Christ gave up His life on the Cross for our salvation.

Today, be willing to give up something for Jesus. Do good, share what you have, and you will know joy in pleasing God.

*Read: John 3:16-17; Romans 8:32; Proverbs 11:4*

# LETTING OUT THE ANCHORS

*Light dawns for the righteous (Psalm 97:11).*

Paul and a boatload of people found themselves in the midst of a raging storm in the midnight darkness. They were about to be shipwrecked and everyone was terrified. Everyone except Paul. Paul decided to call a prayer meeting! But first, fearing they might crash against the jagged rocks, "they let out four anchors from the stern" (Acts 27:29). I see the four anchors as symbols of four necessary prerequisites to prayer.

**Affirmation.** Paul affirmed the presence of God even in the furious tempest. Emmanuel, God with us. God travels every road and sails every sea. We need never be afraid.

**Duty.** Paul knew they could not expect God to save them unless they cooperated by getting rid of the ship's cargo. Prayer should never be a substitute for action. We cannot expect God to do the impossible unless we do the possible.

**Confidence.** Paul was undaunted, believing the outcome was in the Lord's loving hands. We, too, should trust God to do what is best, despite dark and threatening circumstances.

**Readiness.** Paul encouraged people to take nourishment and strengthen themselves to prepare for God's instructions. God is more eager to answer than we are to ask, so we should not go to prayer unless we are ready for His response.

After letting out the anchors, the people "prayed for day to come" (v. 29). They prayed for light. Isn't that what we still pray for today? We pray for the resplendent light of the one true Light of the world, Jesus Christ. Tomorrow, look at the dawn. God does not send the whole big ball of sun at once. It comes slowly, gradually. It takes time for the sun to appear completely on the horizon. That is how God answers prayer. He sends just a little light, then a little more, and a little more, for He knows we cannot take all the light too quickly. As we seek Him, we begin to find the power and promises of prayer.

If you are in the midst of a raging storm in the midnight darkness right now, let out the four anchors and pray for the light of God's love, and His light soon will dawn for you.

*Read: Acts 27:9-44; John 8:12; Daniel 2:20-22*

# SOUL MAGNIFICATION

*"My soul magnifies the Lord, and my spirit rejoices in God my Savior" (Luke 1:46-47).*

The Magnificat, the beautiful song of Mary recorded in Luke 1:46-55, has been an inspiration to countless people for nearly 2,000 years. Soul magnification -- that is God's will for you! God wants to magnify your soul so you fulfill the magnificent destiny He planned when He created you. Here is what you can do to today allow God to magnify your soul.

**Know Holy Spirit promises.** Jesus said, "Behold, I send the promise of my Father upon you" (Luke 24:49). Know and believe God's Holy Spirit is in you and will be with you forever, guiding you into all the truth.

**Flow with Holy Spirit plans.** God has a purpose for you, but He never said it would be easy to find. It is a fearful thing to be in the hands of the living Lord, but if you do not run risks and attempt the impossible, you never will discover His plan for your life. Go with the flow and follow His leading.

**Go to Holy Spirit people.** Seek the guidance of Holy Spirit people whose Christianity is sincere, people accustomed to God's mysterious ways. "Where two or three are gathered in my name, there am I in the midst of them" (Matthew 18:20). God's power is unleashed when Christians assemble together.

**Show Holy Spirit praise.** "Praise the Lord! Praise, O servants of the Lord, praise the name of the Lord!" (Psalm 113:1). Do not come to God only with requests. Since He is in charge, you do not have to tell Him incessantly of your needs. Just report for duty and praise Him for His kindness, mercy, and might. Praise Him for choosing you to be part of His eternal family and for the great things He has in store for you.

The key to soul magnification is in keeping your human spirit in tune with God's Holy Spirit. Then you will be able to rise above difficult situations and respond, not react, to the mean spirit of others; to focus on God and not fool with things that do not matter; to become more loving and forgiving. When God magnifies your soul, your life will be an inspiration.

*Read: Luke 1:39-56; John 14:25-26; Psalm 34:1-3*

# THE ART OF ENCOURAGING ONESELF

*When David and his men came to the city, they found it burned with fire, and their wives and sons and daughters taken captive... David was greatly distressed; for the people spoke of stoning him... But David strengthened himself in the Lord his God (I Samuel 30:3,6).*

Courage is not a luxury but a necessity of life, for all other spiritual gifts rely upon it. Most of us allow circumstances and people to control our level of courage. When things are fine and people are supportive, courage increases; when things go wrong and people are thoughtless or cruel, courage decreases. What do you do when no one says an encouraging word? Some people look for courage in a bottle or in pills, by putting other people down, or by quitting jobs, relationships, churches, even life itself. David knew the correct way to keep his courage up. He strengthened himself in the Lord his God.

When David led his weary army home, they found their town destroyed. The warriors blamed him and threatened his life. But David did not allow people to determine his courage. He found courage in the Lord. David believed he was special to God. He had a personal, intimate relationship with the Lord and knew nothing would separate him from God's love. He did not fear, for he knew the Lord was with him. David could look beyond bad situations to see the power of God. That is the secret of courage: to strengthen oneself in the Lord.

It is easy to get discouraged, feel down and out, think we have struck out, and fear the lights have gone out on us. The fact is, if we are despondent, we have no one to blame but ourselves, for God gives us power to strengthen ourselves by looking unto Jesus. Courage is a spiritual gift. We have all the courage we need to meet any obstacle, if we believe it and choose to strengthen ourselves in the Lord. No matter how many times we fail or how low we sink, no matter what blackness we are going through, we can live courageously through Christ, who strengthens us and gives us victory in life and in death. And that is an encouraging word for you today!

*Read: I Samuel 30:1-6; Isaiah 41:10; Psalm 28:8*

# GETTING OUR ATTENTION

*"Stop and consider the wondrous works of God" (Job 37:14).*

When God needs to get someone to do something, He often performs wondrous works that attract attention in a big way.

Moses discovered this the day God called him to lead the people out of Egypt. Off he went to the fields as usual, toting his lunch bucket, to tend his daddy-in-law's sheep, when suddenly the Lord appeared to him in a burning bush. "Moses hid his face, for he was afraid to look at God" (Exodus 3:6).

Peter experienced God's power after an unsuccessful night of fishing. When he followed Jesus's instructions to cast the nets again, he caught so many fish that the nets broke. "He was astonished, and all that were with him, at the catch of fish which they had taken" (Luke 5:9). Peter paid attention!

With Paul, when he was still called Saul, God put a little lightning in his life on the Damascus Turnpike, temporarily blinding him. "I saw on the way a light from heaven, brighter than the sun, shining round me and those who journeyed with me" (Acts 26:13). His dramatic conversion changed history.

The Ten Commandments, the resurrection, Pentecost -- the Lord certainly is masterful at orchestrating momentous, meaningful, marvelous events with phenomenal finesse!

What does it take for the Lord to get your attention? I hope you learn important lessons from the many wondrous works of God revealed to people throughout the Bible. If you look carefully, you probably will find God is working some wonders in your life as well, if only you have eyes to see. How thrilling! It means you have a calling, a mission, a special job to do for the glory and honor of the Kingdom. You need not have qualms about it, for through His Holy Spirit, God will equip you with the courage, strength, wisdom, and enthusiasm you need to complete that job, no matter what obstacles you face. "Work, for I am with you, says the Lord of hosts... My Spirit abides among you; fear not" (Haggai 2:4-5). If something wondrous happens today, pay attention. Stop and consider what the Lord might be telling you to do, then do it!

*Read: Exodus 3:1-12; Luke 5:1-11; Acts 26:9-18*

# IF JESUS STOPPED BY TODAY

*Let no one disregard you (Titus 2:15).*

If Jesus stopped by today, what do you think He would say to you? Do you think He would examine your sins, failures, and limitations, then harshly criticize you? In His ministry, Jesus never embarrassed anyone, no matter how wrong an individual was. From the woman at the well to the thief on the cross, Jesus treated people with respect. He saved His righteous rebuke for the Pharisees, Sadducees, and scribes who, in the name of religion, made people feel continuously guilty, denying them the dignity of self-worth. Jesus offered forgiveness and love. He never told people what they were; they already knew that. He told them what they could become.

Dignity in humanity is rare today. We are the crown of God's creation, but sometimes we treat ourselves and other people like garbage. We put ourselves down and think, "I can't do that. I'm not good enough." We apologize for our honest emotions and dwell on our silly mistakes. So many problems in churches, homes, and society develop because we do not respect one another. How disappointed our Creator must be! God honors humanity by calling us the salt of the earth, the light of the world, living stones, a chosen race, a royal priesthood, a holy nation, His own people. Let us try to believe what God says of us and find dignity in our humanity through Him. He values us. We are important to Him. We are His possession and He holds us in His loving hands. We should not disregard ourselves or anyone else, but rather regard one another as unique individuals created by our heavenly Father.

If Jesus stopped by today, He would not criticize or embarrass or disparage you. He would speak to you with love, patience, kindness, compassion, understanding, and respect, exactly as He wishes you to speak to people you meet. Try to regard yourself and everyone else with the innate dignity God created us to have. Use Jesus Christ as your model, for if Jesus stopped by today, we surely would find Him to be everything we ever hoped for, and much, much more.

*Read:  John 4:7-30;  Luke  23:39-43;  Matthew 5:13-16;  I Peter 2:9-10*

## PERFORMING CHRISTIAN SURGERY

*"If your right eye causes you to sin, pluck it out and throw it away; it is better that you lose one of your members than that your whole body be thrown into hell. And if your right hand causes you to sin, cut it off and throw it away; it is better that you lose one of your members than that your whole body go into hell" (Matthew 5:29-30).*

Strong words!  Now, I do not think God expects anybody, even the biggest sinner, to gouge out an eye and cut off a hand, but Jesus's vivid metaphorical language is an important warning to us that it is better to go through life maimed and half-blind than to have the whole body thrown into the pit of destruction.  To get into the Kingdom, we must remove sinful practices that separate us from God.  There is only one way to do it: radical, expensive, painful surgery.  Christian surgery!

**Pluck out the habits.**  Each of us knows the harmful, destructive habits that need to go.  Maybe we think we cannot live without them, but we can if we pluck them out at the root.

**Cut out the hungers.**  Unhealthy hungers -- physical, emotional, sexual, ego, financial, power -- can destroy us and everyone around us unless we cut them out with precision.

**Get rid of the hurts.**  We are not to hang on to hurts or use them as excuses.  Even if we have made big mistakes, even if we were neglected or abused or abandoned, even if we carry ugly scars inside from a painful past, we do not have to stumble through life beaten and lost.  We have the power to get rid of the hurts, to let go of those bad memories and look ahead.

It is not easy to admit we need an operation, but the hardest part about Christian surgery is that we have to perform the surgery on ourselves, without anesthetic.  Thank God, the Lord has compassion and we are not alone.  The head surgeon and chief of staff, Jesus Christ, is our friend.  He will help us through surgery and convalescence.  Oh, we might have some relapses, spike a fever, or feel weak for a while, but if we stick with it, our recovery is assured.  After performing Christian surgery, we soon will enjoy healthy new life in Christ.

*Read:  Mark 2:15-17;  Psalm 145:8-9;  II Corinthians 5:17*

# A FINE LINE

*"God anointed Jesus of Nazareth with the Holy Spirit and with power; ... he went about doing good and healing all that were oppressed by the devil, for God was with him" (Acts 10:38).*

Christians are called to help suffering people, people with desperate needs, people in confusion and pain, people who do not know God. Not all of us realize, though, there is a fine line between helping people and hurting them. It is difficult to render assistance without killing independence, and concerned friends, preachers, parents, psychiatrists, and government officials need to remember that. The goal in helping people is to make them stronger, not weaker and less resourceful.

Jesus knew how to help people. Throughout His ministry, He talked to anybody and everybody, any hour of the day and night. Jesus knew the best way to help people is to allow them to help themselves. He had the ability to communicate compassion without permissiveness. That is the toughest dilemma in trying to help people who are making sinful choices. It is not easy to show love, yet let people know they are doing wrong. Most of us go one way or another. Either we piously and sternly preach at them (people get the message, but there is no love along with it), or we act so loving that we allow people to think their selfish actions are morally acceptable.

Jesus loved sinners and hated sin. Mark writes, "He saw a great throng, and he had compassion on them, because they were like sheep without a shepherd; and he began to teach them many things" (Mark 6:34). Jesus taught people right and wrong so they could lead holier lives. We, too, are to be compassionate, yet teach clearly the unchanging principles of Christianity. We can do it only in the power of the Holy Spirit.

Jesus wisely and lovingly intervened in the lives of people and led them to God. When you try to help suffering people, point them to Jesus Christ, the only Savior. Never hesitate to go about doing good. Just be wise and loving. Remember, there is a fine line between helping people and hurting them. Make sure you are right with God so you do not cross the line.

*Read: Mark 6:30-44; Matthew 4:23-24; Psalm 121*

# WALKING IN LOVE

*Walk in love, as Christ loved us (Ephesians 5:2).*

Some people rush through life, swiftly scurrying here and there, dashing from one thing to another, moving rapidly yet never getting anywhere. Other people creep along with no energy, no drive, no motivation; they end up nowhere, too. Paul describes a better way to live: walking in love. Remember three beautiful, biblical facts about walking in love.

**We never walk alone.** No matter how lonely we feel, God walks with us, not on any merit of our own, but out of His goodness and grace. "Whither shall I go from thy Spirit? Or whither shall I flee from thy presence? If I ascend to heaven, thou art there! If I make my bed in Sheol, thou art there!" (Psalm 139:7-8). God's Holy Spirit is our friend. When we acknowledge Him, He directs our way. When we ask for help, He gives it. All we ever need -- power, wisdom, answers to life's questions -- we already have if we believe He is with us.

**We walk safest when we do not know where we are going.** When we think we know where we are going, we are in trouble, for our egos make us oblivious to everything but our own desires. When we do not know where we are going, we learn to live on the edge of expectancy, trusting in God's constant care. "Blessed are all who take refuge in him" (Psalm 2:12). True security comes when we abandon ourselves to Him, even when we cannot understand where He is taking us.

**Whatever happens, keep walking and never quit.** Our era is developing quitters, dissatisfied, angry people who think life is not worth living. Sadly, many people lose heart not because of the hurtful things evil people do, but because of disappointment in good people from whom they expected kindness. God wants us to persevere. "Stand firm in your faith, be courageous, be strong" (I Corinthians 16:13). With God beside us, we can march confidently into the future.

Jesus walked in love through this world. "Walk in the same way in which he walked" (I John 2:6). Walking in love is inexpressibly beautiful. Try it. You will love it.

*Read: Ephesians 5:1-20; Philippians 1:27; Colossians 2:6-7*

# THE ABIDING PRESENCE

*Do you not know that your body is a temple of the Holy Spirit within you, which you have from God? (I Corinthians 6:19).*

Our bodies are temples of God's Holy Spirit. God's Spirit abides in us, but that biblical truth is one many people find mysterious and difficult to understand. Jesus compared Holy Spirit to the wind. Like the wind, Holy Spirit blows where He wills. All of us ought to be very careful of anyone who claims to know the only course charted by the Holy Spirit. We cannot control Him, dictate to Him, command Him, or put Him into a little box. He is our Master! We can never be absolutely sure how or when or where He will work in our lives. That is what is so exciting about being a Christian. God alone knows the great things His Holy Spirit has in store for us.

Some people, though, are worried, not excited, about God's Spirit dwelling within them, for they live with the fear that they have committed the unpardonable sin. Jesus said, "Truly, I say to you, all sins will be forgiven the sons of men, and whatever blasphemies they utter; but whoever blasphemes against the Holy Spirit never has forgiveness, but is guilty of an eternal sin" (Mark 3:28-29). I have known people to be tormented and terrorized because they have done something they interpret as the unpardonable sin. They feel doomed. Let me reassure you if you are suffering with this secret burden. If you are concerned that you have committed the unpardonable sin, then you have not! As long as you are conscious of sin, as long as you are aware of God's presence within you, as long as you are trying to follow His leading, you have not blasphemed the Holy Spirit. Blasphemers of the Holy Spirit are not conscious of sin. They do not take sin seriously or wish to repent. They reject the Holy Spirit, who is the only avenue to God's saving grace.

Though God's Holy Spirit is undefinable, unpredictable, and uncontrollable, we have no need to fear Him, for He lives and dwells within us to help us, not hurt us, to guide us and comfort us and lead us into all the truth. Today, thank God for His abiding presence, who shall be with you forever.

*Read: John 14:15-26; II Timothy 1:14; I John 4:13*

## SPIRITUAL MAINTENANCE

*Let love be genuine; hate what is evil, hold fast to what is good; love one another with brotherly affection; outdo one another in showing honor. Never flag in zeal, be aglow with the Spirit, serve the Lord. Rejoice in your hope, be patient in tribulation, be constant in prayer (Romans 12:9-11).*

Our cars need maintenance. Our homes need maintenance. Our health needs maintenance. Yet many of us seem to think that spiritually, we can coast along without effort or exertion and automatically live happily ever after in Heaven. That is not how it works. Our spiritual lives need maintenance and discipline. The Bible tells us to present our bodies as living sacrifices to God, sacrificing the body and renewing the mind. Unfortunately, we usually like to do that in reverse, sacrificing the mind and renewing the body. Most of the time we prefer eating and sleeping to thinking and reading. It is only when we devote ourselves to spiritual maintenance that God can lead us to fulfillment. We are on a pilgrimage. We have a lifelong opportunity and responsibility to develop spiritually until we live the way Christ Himself lived, but we have to work at it!

Today, try to maintain the Spirit of God within you. How?

**Be genuine.** Be real, not hypocritical or phony. Paul tells us to love genuinely, to hate what is evil (not evil people, but evil itself) and hold fast to what is good, and to honor one another. We can all be honest and sincere if we so desire.

**Be enthusiastic.** Be excited about God. Smile more! Live with a spiritual glow that makes people glad to see you. Be alive to the now and make the most of every experience.

**Be joyful.** God loves you, so whatever happens, do not let your valleys and hurts destroy your confidence in His care. Be patient in tribulation, constant in prayer, and aglow with joy.

Take a look at your spiritual condition today. Is your car tuned up better than your faith? Is your home immaculate while your church attendance is spotty? Is your body operating efficiently while your mind lies vacant? Do not neglect spiritual maintenance, for your eternal future depends upon it.

*Read: Romans 12:1-13; Colossians 1:21-23; Proverbs 13:4*

# UNTYING THE INSTRUMENT

*"You will find a colt tied, on which no one has ever sat; untie it
and bring it" (Mark 11:2).*

We cannot comprehend Scripture in its fullness and power
without using our God-given, Spirit-inspired imaginations.
Often we read over words too swiftly. Picture the scene when
Jesus instructed two disciples to bring Him a colt in preparation
for His triumphal entry into Jerusalem on Palm Sunday. Those
disciples were fishermen, not farmers, more used to the sea
than the barnyard. They had to go down narrow streets on a
busy Sunday to get a donkey upon which nobody had ever sat,
a donkey that had never been away from its mama, and bring
that balky, untrained, scared, homesick animal across town to
Jesus. I am sure they were sweating and straining. I hope they
were working together and not screaming at each other! It was
quite a struggle to get that animal to Jesus, but they did it.
They obeyed, because the colt was the instrument that God in
Jesus Christ chose to ride upon on that special day.

God works mightily in our world when we are willing to
run the risk of releasing the instruments He chooses to use.
Jesus has chosen an instrument to be His Body on earth: the
Church. Jesus is the Head and we individually are members of
the Body. Sometimes we do not allow Jesus to control the
Church, to hold the reins, to lead the Church to her destiny.
Sometimes we cannot understand what God is doing among us.
God does not reveal in advance His program of providence,
and we have no need to know it. Our job as disciples is to
untie the instrument that so easily gets tied up in bureaucracy,
feuds, divisions; to put on the Spirit of Christ; to tell people
God loves them, Christ has redeemed them, and Holy Spirit has
great things in store for them; to turn away anger and criticism;
to view problems as possibilities; to believe that Jesus will lead
and direct the Church in His own time and in His own way.

Jesus said the gates of hell would not prevail against His
Church. When we untie His instrument, hand Him the reins,
and let Him reign, we quit playing church. We are the Church.

*Read: Mark 11:1-10; Acts 20:28; Exodus 15:18*

## ONE LITTLE WORD

*Come to him, to that living stone, rejected by men but in God's sight chosen and precious (I Peter 2:4).*

If you say just one little word, you can bring the biggest message in all the world to people you know and even to people you do not know. What is the biggest message in all the world? The message of the Gospel: Jesus Christ is the Son of God and the Savior of the world, and whosoever believes in Him shall be saved. What is the one little word? "Come."

Evangelism is a mysterious process. It is God and God alone who converts, but God works through His followers to bring people to a moment of confrontation with Jesus Christ. Though many people, including parents, teachers, and preachers, cultivate the way, it is usually one person who leads to the final step. Evangelism is part of our job as Christians, but often we are too timid to try it. We think it requires us to grab total strangers and shriek, "Brother, are you saved?" We feel unprepared to present deep theological explanations for every Scriptural doctrine a person might question.

There is another way. Simply say, "Come." Invite people to see Jesus Christ for themselves. That is what Andrew did. "He first found his brother Simon, and said to him, 'We have found the Messiah' (which means Christ). He brought him to Jesus" (John 1:41-42). Andrew is my favorite disciple. He was open, pleasant, and happy. He took things in stride and allowed the Lord to work with him. Later in Jesus's ministry, it was Andrew who saw the boy with the fishes and loaves Jesus used to feed the five thousand. It was Andrew who introduced some curious Greeks to Jesus. Andrew sought opportunities, thought possibilities, and brought people to Jesus.

Anyone can use the Andrew method of evangelism. Even you! Wouldn't you like to share the Good News of the Gospel and help to bring another person to the new life you have found in Christ? You can, and it is not as difficult as you might think. Just say, "Come. Come with me and see the Christ. Come." That one little word can have great big results. Say it today.

*Read: John 1:35-42; John 6:8-11; John 12:20-22*

# MY GOODNESS!

*Depart from evil, and do good; so shall you abide for ever (Psalm 37:27).*

Often when an unexpected event occurs, we exclaim, "My goodness!" or "For goodness sake!" We do not think much about those expressions, but maybe we should. As Christians, we ought to be vitally concerned about goodness and ask ourselves daily, "Has my goodness in God's sight increased or decreased today? What do people see in me: goodness or grouchiness? Is goodness growing or waning within me?"

Unfortunately, many people are more eager to achieve greatness than goodness. How we love to be honored and revered! We like to imagine that when we die, multitudes of admirers will extol our grand achievements and outstanding virtues. The desire to be great is a natural part of our humanity. Most of us, though, will never be considered great except by those who love us. We should not feel too sad about that, for greatness is not as great as we tend to think. When the disciples questioned Jesus about greatness in the Kingdom, He called a little child over and said, "Truly, I say to you, unless you turn and become like children, you will never enter the kingdom of heaven. Whoever humbles himself like this child, he is the greatest in the kingdom of heaven" (Matthew 18:3-4).

Goodness truly is more important in life than greatness. The Bible does not command us to be great, but to be good, to do good, and to love goodness. Jesus even said, "Love your enemies, do good to those who hate you, bless those who curse you, pray for those who abuse you" (Luke 6:27-28). That is not easy, but we grow in goodness when we commit ourselves to becoming more like Jesus Christ, the Son of God and the only perfect Person who ever lived.

Quit worrying about greatness and just try to be good.

"For goodness sake!" Yes, do everything for the sake of goodness. That is how to please God.

"My goodness!" Yes, think about your goodness. After all, you are the only one who can do anything about it.

*Read: Romans 12:9-21; Proverbs 22:1; I Thessalonians 5:15*

# GUILT TRIPS

*"What is my guilt?" (I Samuel 20:1).*

There are two forms of guilt: real guilt and conditioned guilt.

Real guilt comes when, in thought, word, or deed, we do something that violates the teachings and commands of the Lord. We deliberately disobey God. That is sin, and sin results in real guilt. Real guilt needs to be forgiven, and it can be forgiven; that is why Jesus Christ came to die. "If we confess our sins, he is faithful and just, and will forgive our sins and cleanse us from all unrighteousness" (I John 1:9). Real guilt is a spiritual problem and the only solution is forgiveness.

Many people, though, are tyrannized and dominated by conditioned guilt. Conditioned guilt is placed upon us by some person who, consciously, unconsciously, or through ignorance, sends us on a guilt trip. Usually it comes from a preacher or teacher or some other creature who means well, but is poorly informed and often guilt-driven as well. Tragically, some people run their lives on conditioned guilt. They do things, or do not do things, just to avoid guilt trips. Some couples eat two Thanksgiving dinners every November so neither side of the family can make them feel guilty. Some people let everybody push them around to avoid offending anyone. Some attend church only because they know if they sleep in, they will feel guilty later in the day. Some go through life saying, "I'm sorry, I'm sorry, I'm sorry," for things that are not even their responsibility or fault; their lives become a miserable cycle of apologies and remorse. No Christian should live like that, and no Christian has to live like that, because guilt, both real and conditioned, can be overcome.

Do not let guilt trips trip you up. Analyze your situation logically. Ask yourself, "What is my guilt?" Learn to recognize the difference between real and conditioned guilt. Real guilt -- face it, confess your sin, and pray for forgiveness, knowing God is "good and forgiving, abounding in steadfast love" (Psalm 86:5). Conditioned guilt trips -- just pack them away and forget them. You will travel better without them.

*Read: Hebrews 10:11-25; I Peter 3:13-16; Psalm 51:10*

# THE HEART OF THE GOSPEL

*"For God so loved the world that He gave His only Son, that whoever believes in Him should not perish but have eternal life. For God sent the Son into the world, not to condemn the world, but that the world might be saved through Him" (John 3:16-17).*

That is the heart of the Gospel. Most of us can recite John 3:16-17 from memory. We know the verses well -- possibly too well, for familiarity can diminish our appreciation and gratitude for these priceless words about the Lord. Think for moment, what if God did not love this world? What if God thought He made a mistake in creating us? What if he had not sent His Son to die for the sinful, selfish, hopeless people on earth? There would be no Christmas, Good Friday, Easter, or Pentecost; no Holy Spirit leading us; no Church; no New Testament; no forgiveness or redemption; no authority on right and wrong; no Christian literature, music, hospitals, or universities; no reservation in Heaven; no assurance at the graveside. We would be people to be pitied.

But Jesus did come, and not just for a few, but for whoever has the courage to believe. "Believe in the Lord Jesus, and you will be saved" (Acts 16:31). Believers do not know and understand all spiritual mysteries. They just believe, on the evidence they have, that God's love sent Jesus Christ into the world; Jesus lived in the flesh nearly 2,000 years ago and His Holy Spirit abides in us and in His Church today; because of Jesus, we live in the power of the resurrection; this world is not the end, and we shall meet our loved ones in Christ on the other side. Whoever believes has salvation and eternal life.

"Man believes with his heart" (Romans 10:10). What effect does John 3:16-17, the heart of the Gospel, have on your heart? Does it leave your heart cold or set your heart on fire with love for the Lord?

Take time today to meditate anew on John 3:16-17. "For God so loved the world." That includes you.

*Read: I Corinthians 15:12-19; Romans 1:1-6; Jeremiah 31:33*

# CONSTANT PRAYER

*Rejoice always, pray constantly, give thanks in all circumstances (I Thessalonians 5:16-18).*

Rejoice always -- we try to do it. Give thanks -- we know that is the way to live. But to pray constantly, or as the King James Version puts it, "pray without ceasing," is hard to understand. We can imagine we are destined to go through life on our knees with our hands tightly clasped and our eyes closed in self-imposed blindness! No, that is not what God, who loves life, wants us to do. Paul is not talking about a posture. He is talking about a principle. The point is that we are to be people who, twenty-four hours a day, seven days a week, three hundred and sixty-five days a year, are open, receptive, and responsive to God, doing everything in our power to keep the line of communication between God and ourselves open.

We pray constantly when we believe God is with us all the time, trust in His love and care, and know He is working for good in our lives, whatever is happening. Constant prayer does not require us to pour out lengthy, impassioned, eloquent dissertations to the Lord every minute. Far better are simple, short conversations, thanking Him for His many blessings, praising Him for the beauty of the day, giving Him credit for nice surprises, and asking for guidance when we are not sure what to do. That is constant prayer.

Notice that Paul lists constant prayer between rejoicing and thanksgiving. Prayer is like the center pole of a great tent; the side poles cannot stand up without the essential center pole. It is only when we pray constantly, realizing God's presence, recognizing His providence, and relying on His power, that we can rejoice always and give thanks in all circumstances. So pray constantly. Pray without ceasing! "This is the will of God in Christ Jesus for you" (I Thessalonians 5:18).

*Read: Romans 12:12; Colossians 4:2; Psalm 86:1-7*

# THE DIVINE TRAP

*Keep me from the trap which they have laid for me (Psalm 141:9).*

Paul and Barnabas almost were pushed into a trap in Lystra that any Christian can fall into today: the divine trap, the sin of trying to play god. Paul healed a man who was crippled since birth. The crowds were so impressed with his power that they shouted, "The gods have come down to us in the likeness of men!" (Acts 14:11). Christians, who live by faith, expect miracles, and attempt great things, are always vulnerable to the divine trap and must not let people force them into it. The adulation of others easily can lead us to deify ourselves rather than our Creator. In Genesis 3, evil entered the world when Adam and Eve wanted to be divine. The serpent tempted Eve to eat the fruit of the tree by saying, "God knows that when you eat of it your eyes will be opened, and you will be like God" (Genesis 3:5). We each have within us that original sin. When we claim to know all the answers, when we manipulate people, when we lie, cheat, and steal, when we selfishly think we have a right to create new truths and do whatever we want, that is playing god. From that sin comes every evil on earth.

The divine trap is dangerous. Some people try to avoid it by acting sub-human; they adopt degrading habits and clothing to make people think they are worse than they really are. Others try to protest and explain themselves; Paul tried this and it did not work. I think to stay out of the divine trap, we need three things: friends to keep us honest, tribulations to keep us humble, and commitment to keep us focused on our true goal of serving God. Be careful if people deify you; it is flattering, but you will find that those who want to worship you will be the first to turn against you later. Be careful whom you deify; we have one God and He commands us to have no others.

Stay out of the divine trap. Jesus said, "You are from below, I am from above; you are of this world, I am not of this world" (John 8:23). God created us, respects us, loves us, and redeems us through Jesus Christ, but we are human, not divine.

*Read: Acts 14:8-18; Genesis 3; I Corinthians 8:5-6*

# A BIBLICAL RECIPE

*"You shall eat and be full, and you shall bless the Lord your God" (Deuteronomy 8:10).*

I am not much of a chef, but I have found in the pages of God's Word a marvelous recipe for happiness, one that turns out great every time. You can cook it up whenever you want if you keep your home well-stocked with the vital ingredients.

**2 cups of thankfulness.** Begin with thankfulness. Think about the wonderful things you have: your country, family, friends, church. Thank God for His blessings. Thank Him also for some of the things you do not have. This moment, do you have a pain in the third toe of your left foot? If not, Hallelujah!

**1/2 cup of contentment.** Next comes contentment in all circumstances. Do not complain, whine, and contrive to amass more things. Be satisfied in every state with what you have.

**1 tablespoon of availability.** Add availability to God and other people. We each have three gifts to offer: money (the cheapest and easiest to surrender), talent (that is a little tougher), and time (the most precious of all). Put your gifts to work and show the love of God in everything you do.

**1/2 teaspoon of generosity.** Mix in generosity. Generosity is the amount we give beyond what we think we can afford. Give till it hurts; it will hurt so much, you will feel tremendous!

**A dash of originality.** As a distinctive, unique creation of the Lord, live for His glory in your own imaginative style.

**Joy and enthusiasm.** Top the recipe off with these zesty ingredients to keep it from falling flat. Pour on as much as you like; you cannot spoil the recipe one bit. Then just put the fire of love under it and wait for the spectacular, delicious results.

"O taste and see that the Lord is good! Happy is the man who takes refuge in him!" (Psalm 34:8). What's cooking at your house today? If you want to feast on happiness, try this biblical recipe. It never fails and it is perfect for any occasion, even better than chocolate cake with seafoam icing! Once people get a taste of it, they will beg for your recipe. Pass it along. The more you share it, the happier you will be.

*Read: Philippians 4:4-12; Genesis 1:29-31; Psalm 145:13-16*

# KING JESUS

*"Blessed is the King who comes in the name of the Lord!"*
*(Luke 19:38).*

Crown Him with many crowns!  We worship the King, Jesus Christ, King of kings and Lord of lords.  Jesus is King!

**Jesus is King of creation.**  This is our Father's world. God, one God in three Persons, the Holy Trinity, formed everybody and everything for His glory.  Together with the Father and Holy Spirit, Jesus created all things material and spiritual.  "In him all things were created, in heaven and on earth, visible and invisible, whether thrones or dominions or principalities or authorities -- all things were created through him and for him" (Colossians 1:16).  Jesus is King of creation.

**Jesus is King of revelation.**  Jesus reveals God to us.  "I and the Father are one" (John 10:30).  When we see Jesus, we see God.  "He is the image of the invisible God" (Colossians 1:15).  Jesus also reveals humanity as God intended it to be. When we look to Jesus, listen to Jesus, love like Jesus, forgive like Jesus, we achieve wholeness.  Jesus is King of revelation.

**Jesus is King of inspiration.**  Jesus motivates us to change, to start over, to be more generous, loving, and joyful. In Jesus, "we have redemption, the forgiveness of sins" (v. 14); we find new life, power, and hope.  Jesus inspires us with holy nudges, ecclesiastical pushes.  If we have the courage to obey them, we discover our destiny.  Jesus is King of inspiration.

**Jesus is King of reconciliation.**  Jesus came to reconcile us with the Father.  "In him all the fulness of God was pleased to dwell, and through him to reconcile to himself all things, whether on earth or in heaven, making peace by the blood of the cross" (v. 19-20).  The Church has a mandate to be the reconciling agent of God in the world today.  We worship the King when we reach out in love to help reconcile people to God and one another.  Jesus is King of reconciliation.

Blessed is the King who comes in the name of the Lord! Worship the King.  Crown Him with many crowns and He will crown you with many blessings in this world and in eternity.

*Read: Colossians 1:9-20; Luke 1:31-33; Jeremiah 23:5-6*

# LIVING SUCCESSFULLY WITH SUCCESS

*"O Lord, let thy ear be attentive to the prayer of thy servant, and to the prayer of thy servants who delight to fear thy name; and give success to thy servant today" (Nehemiah 1:11).*

Success is not a bad word unless we are successful in bad things. God created us to bear fruit and make a difference for good in the world. In the Old Testament, both Joseph and David achieved great success because the Lord was with them. Yet success can be misused. To become successful and remain successful in God's sight, remember to do three things.

**Give thanks to God.** "O give thanks to the God of heaven, for his steadfast love endures for ever" (Psalm 136:26). Without God, we can do nothing; our success comes from Him. A person who does not give thanks is not successful to God.

**Think about your success.** Success makes us vulnerable to losing our heads, getting swelled heads, and living in fear of people who are after our heads! The way to stay level-headed is to use our heads and manage our lives in a positive, God-pleasing way. "Set your minds on things that are above, not on things that are on earth" (Colossians 3:2). Success is not defined by money or trophies. Success comes when a mind puts a body into motion to accomplish things that are needed: healing a hurt, assisting a worthy cause. We should think daily about what we are doing. If we are building up the Kingdom, we are successful; if we are tearing it down, we are failures.

**Keep selfishness out of your success.** It is human nature to want other people to be successful up to a point, but not be more successful than we are. Often we try to look good at someone else's expense. The Bible tells us, "Do nothing from selfishness or conceit, but in humility count others better than yourselves" (Philippians 2:3). An egotistical, self-indulgent attitude makes us failures to the Lord, no matter what we accomplish and no matter how venerated we are by the world.

Genuine success cannot be measured by anyone on earth, but only by the Lord God in Heaven. Remember this biblical truth and you will live successfully with success.

*Read: Genesis 39:1-3; I Samuel 18:12-16; Proverbs 15:3*

127

## CHRISTIAN CITIZENSHIP

*So then you are no longer strangers and sojourners, but you are fellow citizens with the saints and members of the household of God, built upon the foundation of the apostles and prophets, Christ Jesus himself being the cornerstone (Ephesians 2:19-20).*

Paul divides people into two groups: citizens of this world and citizens of Heaven. Citizens of this world are enemies of the Cross. Citizens of Heaven are disciples trying to follow Jesus Christ. Where is your citizenship? It is not difficult to determine. Ask yourself five questions at the end of every day.

1. "Today did I control my appetites, drives, and desires or did they control me?" The hardest person you ever have to say No to is the person closest to you -- yourself! But unless you deny yourself daily, you cannot follow Jesus Christ.

2. "Did I live today as an optimist or a pessimist?" A citizen of Heaven rejoices in knowing Jesus Christ already has won, no matter what the score appears to be on any given day.

3. "Do I have a sense of shame over some things I said and did today?" Citizens of the world glory in sin; they cannot be embarrassed. To be a citizen of Heaven, you must be ashamed when you sin and pray, "Lord, forgive me."

4. "Did I invest my resources wisely today?" Did you give a little love, hope, forgiveness, and encouragement, or were you just thinking about what you could grab for yourself?

5. "Has my confidence been in me or in the Lord?" Even if people called you foolish, did you stand firm in your faith?

Paul wrote, "The wisdom of this world is folly with God" (I Corinthians 3:19). What could be greater folly than choosing citizenship in this world when the riches of Heaven are freely offered through Jesus Christ? If we are Christians, this world is not our home. We are traveling with a passport that lists us as resident aliens, strangers, sojourners, fellow citizens with the saints and members of the household of God. Wherever you go and whatever you do, be sure to keep your passport up-to-date and guard your citizenship in the Kingdom with your life.

*Read: Philippians 3:17-4:1; John 18:36; Psalm 26:8-12*

128

## TONGUES OF FIRE

*There appeared to them tongues as of fire, distributed and resting on each one of them. And they were all filled with the Holy Spirit (Acts 2:3-4).*

There are many mysteries in the Bible and we cannot understand everything about God, yet He has chosen to reveal Himself in various ways to people who genuinely seek Him. One of God's means of revelation is symbolism. Consider the way God introduced the descent, presence, and power of His Spirit into the world on Pentecost: through flaming tongues of fire. God could have used any symbol He wanted. He could have used an all-seeing eye to show His omnipresence. He could have used a listening ear, for God hears everything we say. He could have used a mighty hand to demonstrate His omnipotence. Why tongues? What can we learn about the nature of the Holy Spirit from this symbolic image?

Think about the functions of the tongue. The tongue is the most sensitive tool for **touching**. Holy Spirit touches our lives to bring new birth, new vitality, a fresh start. The tongue is the tool for **tasting**. Holy Spirit gives us the ability to be discerning and discriminating, to tell right from wrong, truth from falsehood. We do not have to digest everything that comes our way! The tongue is the tool for **telling**. Holy Spirit, we are promised, will lead us into all the truth. He is waiting for us to listen to all the marvelous things He wants to tell us.

How wise God is! The tongues of fire give deep insight into the mysterious nature of the Holy Spirit, but the insight comes only if we are willing to use everything we have -- mind, imagination, emotions -- to study, meditate, and brood upon the Word of God. "The Lord is with you, while you are with him. If you seek him, he will be found by you, but if you forsake him, he will forsake you" (II Chronicles 15:2). If we do not read the Bible regularly, if we pass over words hurriedly, if we do not think and wrestle, we will not grow in spiritual understanding, but if we diligently seek Him, He will richly reward us. We will begin to know God, and ourselves.

*Read: Acts 2:1-21; Joel 2:28-29; Galatians 3:10-14*

# LETTING THE LORD HELP YOU

*"The Lord your God is a merciful God; he will not fail you"*
*(Deuteronomy 4:31).*

Perhaps you have a problem today. Most of us do. Though we tend to think our problems are unique, we have only to hear Job's lament of four thousand years ago that "Man that is born of a woman is of few days, and full of trouble" (Job 14:1) to realize problems have always been part of the human condition. Maybe you are wondering what to do about a worrisome situation. God wants to help! He cares about every aspect of your life, your big dilemmas and even little difficulties you think He has not noticed. He will help you if you let Him, but there are things you have to give Him first.

**Fears.** Give the Lord your fears. We all have fears, and God knows that. Do not try to rationalize, deny, or suppress your fears. Honestly admit and express them to your Heavenly Father. Tell the Lord exactly what is frightening you.

**Attention.** Give the Lord your attention. Be specific with your concerns and concentrate as you ask for His guidance. Expect God to hear your request, then seek to find His answer.

**Intensity.** Give the Lord your intensity. Never take the silence of God as an insult. God answers all prayers: Yes, No, or Wait. Do not worry if He does not appear to respond. He might be holding off until the time and conditions are right.

**Trust.** Give the Lord your trust. Just trust Him with the problem and do not try to tell Him what to do. Use those simple, two-word prayers of trust, "Help me" and "Thank you."

**Humility.** Give the Lord your humility. Stop thinking you are the center of the universe! Keep a sense of humor and do not be quick to take offense. Be grateful for all you have.

Do not stand in the way of what your merciful God wants to do in your life. Let the Lord help you by giving Him your Fears, Attention, Intensity, Trust, Humility: that is **FAITH**! Put your faith in the perfect power and steadfast love of God. Invite Jesus Christ into your heart and you will be able to do all things through Him who strengthens you. He will not fail you.

*Read: I Corinthians 2:1-5; II Corinthians 1:3-4; Psalm 112:4*

# IF YOUR CHILD IS LOST

*"This my son was dead, and is alive again; he was lost, and is found" (Luke 15:24).*

Any parent can lose a child, physically, spiritually, or emotionally. It is tragic and devastating, perhaps life's greatest sorrow. Jesus offers help with this painful heartbreak through the actions of the father in the parable of the prodigal son.

**Do not waste time regretting your decisions.** The younger son did an ugly thing, asking for his inheritance early. The answer should have been No. The father's stupidity led to trouble, but he never publicly discussed his poor decision. Think and pray before you make decisions, but afterward, do not second-guess yourself or you will destroy your confidence.

**If your child is lost, never, ever chase him.** The father's life was shattered, but he did not pursue his wayward son. Chasing does not work. It only drives the child to run faster and farther, postponing the critical moment of truth.

**Wait!** The son in the far country did not change until he ended up in the pigsty. A lost child must "come to himself." He has to grow up, stop blaming other people, and assume personal responsibility for his life and destiny. That takes time.

**Run to your child at the first sign of repentance.** Seeing his son approach from a distance, the jubilant father ran to embrace the boy. When a lost child returns, forgive the pain caused. Sincerely welcome the prodigal home.

**Celebrate with the glad, and do not commiserate with the sad.** The father threw a party. When your child is found, rejoice! But until that great homecoming, do not let a lost child pull you down, too. Do not compound the tragedy by allowing stress, hurt, and worry to fracture the rest of your family. Cling together and draw strength and solace from one another.

If your child is lost, you know indescribable suffering. Do not give up, for the last chapter is yet to be written.

*Read: Luke 15:11-32; Psalm 138:3; Isaiah 58:9*

## RECLAIMING THE GOLDEN RULE

*"Whatever you wish that men would do to you, do so to them"*
*(Matthew 7:12).*

The Golden Rule: what a wise, wonderful motto to follow, and how often we fall short of it! In this age of anger, paranoia, and suspicion, our society's slogan seems to be, "Do it to other people before they can do it to you." We tend to expect the worst from people, probably because we act badly so frequently ourselves. The Bible says, "Let no one seek his own good, but the good of his neighbor" (I Corinthians 10:24), yet all of us by nature are selfish. We take care of ourselves first. We hide behind dishonesty and injustice and hurt one another with intimidation, blackmail, and gossip. We love to remind people of their mistakes and forget our own. We are far from the Golden Rule with our sinful, self-centered behavior.

Each of us can reclaim the Golden Rule if we firmly resolve to do so. We can be remade into the life Jesus intended us to have when He gave us the Golden Rule. We do it through repentance. Repentance is a complete change of heart and mind. We come to repentance when we realize the gravity of our sin before a holy God and feel deeply saddened by our willful disobedience. Paul speaks of being "grieved into repenting... For godly grief produces a repentance that leads to salvation" (II Corinthians 7:9-10). Repentance is a personal decision to turn away from sin and turn to God. No one can force that decision upon another individual. We cannot make anyone else over and it is foolish to try, but if we allow God to make us over, eventually the change in us will have an effect on those around us. As we grow to be like Christ, we become more loving, giving, honest, kind, caring, and joyful. We discover that "doing unto others as we would have them do unto us" is not simply a wise, wonderful motto, but a delightful way of life and the closest thing to Heaven on earth.

Today, reclaim the Golden Rule and offer yourself as living proof that the Golden Rule is the greatest rule to follow and Jesus Christ is the greatest Master to serve and adore.

*Read: Luke 3:3-17; Zechariah 8:16-17; II Chronicles 7:14*

## THE RANSOM FOR YOUR LIFE

*You were ransomed from the futile ways inherited from your fathers, not with perishable things such as silver or gold, but with the precious blood of Christ, like that of a lamb without blemish or spot (I Peter 1:18-19).*

Our lives have been bought with the most expensive price tag in all the world. Though we have sinned, though we have disobeyed, God has forgiven us by allowing His only begotten Son to die on the Cross to pay the price for our sin. Some of us like to think we are redeemed because of who we are; maybe our ancestors sailed over on the Mayflower, we have a famous last name, or we were born into a solid religious tradition. Others think we are redeemed because of what we do; we hold prominent, prestigious positions. That is not the teaching of the Bible. We are all redeemed, each one of us, the same way. We are redeemed because God our Father loves us so much that He allowed His Son, the greatest Person who ever lived and the only Person who never sinned, to die for us.

I never had the experience of having my life saved by another person, but I know of someone who did: a little boy named Charles. Charles lived at St. Paul's orphanage near Crafton, Pennsylvania. One beautiful summer afternoon, Charles and other kids from the orphanage went swimming. Nearby was a young clergyman with his youth group. Just as the pastor was packing to leave, he heard screams. Charles was drowning. The pastor dove in the water. He ruined his clothes, he lost his pocket watch, but he saved Charles's life. Charles never forgot that pastor. That pastor was my father.

I do not know if anyone ever risked everything to save your earthly life, but I can tell you this: Jesus Christ died for you. Have you ever pondered the message of the Cross and what it means to be ransomed by the precious blood and broken body of God's Son? The ransom for your life has been paid. What is your response to God's amazing grace? "Love so amazing, so divine, demands my soul, my life, my all." Have you surrendered your spirit, your life, your all, to Jesus Christ?

*Read: Psalm 49:7; I Timothy 2:5-6; Revelation 5:9-10*

# WHAT TO LOOK FOR IN A PERSON

*"The Lord sees not as man sees; man looks on the outward appearance, but the Lord looks on the heart" (I Samuel 16:7).*

When Samuel was sent by God to find a successor for Saul from among the sons of Jesse, he looked on the first boy and thought, "Surely the Lord's anointed is before him" (I Samuel 16:6), but God said, "Do not look on his appearance or on the height of his stature" (v. 7). Six more sons passed before Samuel, but it was the shepherd boy, David, who was chosen.

Samuel made an evaluation based on outward appearance. We often make the same mistake. We have physical standards (height, hair, muscles, curves), material standards (how much, how little, how expensive), numerical standards (homes, bank accounts, titles, age). God does not use these standards. "The Lord weighs the heart" (Proverbs 21:2). God looks to see what people do with the Holy Spirit within them, and He wants us to look at people as He does. It is not hard if we are observant. Listen to people's words. "What comes out of the mouth proceeds from the heart" (Matthew 15:18); evaluate what is said and how it is spoken, whether it builds up or tears down. Look at the eyes. "Your eye is the lamp of your body; when your eye is sound, your whole body is full of light; but when it is not sound, your body is full of darkness" (Luke 11:34); people who keep both eyes on God can look you straight in the eye, too. Watch the hands and feet. "The body is ... meant ... for the Lord" (I Corinthians 6:13); when hands are working for God and feet are walking by faith, a big heart is revealed.

Big hearts come in bodies of all shapes, sizes, and ages. Nobody should feel unworthy of being called by God. At the same time, we must not feel superior to anyone; that shows we judge by earthly standards. David's brothers felt superior, but it was David whom the Lord regarded as "a man after his own heart" (I Samuel 13:14). David had a big heart for God. When God called, he obeyed. That is what God looks for in a person. Remember to look at people as God does, and remember also that God is looking at you.

*Read: I Samuel 16:1-13; Mark 7:14-23; Psalm 44:20-21*

# A BAD MAN'S GOOD EXAMPLE

*"The master commended the dishonest steward for his shrewdness; for the sons of this world are more shrewd in dealing with their own generation than the sons of light" (Luke 16:8).*

The parable of the dishonest steward causes perplexity in many Christians. I think the message is simply this: sometimes the children of darkness are wiser, in their own time and way and to their own people, than the children of light, in their own time and way and to their own people. People who are not religious might be more clever and ingenious than people who are. Christians can learn good lessons from bad people.

From the dishonest steward, we can learn how to solve problems. The steward did not cry, worry, or even pray over his dilemma. He came up with a plan by himself and had confidence in his ability to accomplish it. So often Christians talk, debate, and solve nothing. Learn from a bad man's good example to solve problems quickly, creatively, and efficiently.

From the dishonest steward, we can learn how best to invest worldly possessions. The steward used his position and power to make friends who would help him later when he had nowhere to go. We should not squander resources on fleeting pleasures, but invest them wisely with the future in mind.

From the dishonest steward, we can learn it is easy very for good people to serve bad gods. The steward held a responsible, trusted position until he grew too lazy or proud or greedy. Even good people are tempted to be unfaithful to God, but only those who stay faithful will be commended by Jesus Christ.

Never imagine that Jesus is praising dishonesty in this parable. All Scripture instructs us to be godly and righteous. Dishonest people eventually will get the reward they deserve. Jesus is just showing us that even godless people can teach us valuable lessons. We like to think of ourselves as beautiful, bright children of light, but we still have a lot to learn. Be keenly interested in everyone around you, for the person from whom we cannot learn something has not yet been born.

*Read: Luke 16:1-13; II Samuel 23:6-7; I John 3:7-10*

# SECOND-MILE CHRISTIANITY

*"If any one forces you to go one mile, go with him two miles"*
*(Matthew 5:41).*

In the time of Jesus, Rome occupied Palestine and Roman law prevailed. One Roman law stated a Roman could, any hour of the day or night, compel any Jew to carry his baggage for one mile. All the Roman had to do was to speak and the Jew had to obey. Naturally, this one-mile rule played havoc with people's lives and led to resentment in people forced to do what they did not want to do. Surely, then, the disciples were puzzled by Jesus's command to go an extra mile. Does Jesus like to see people bossed around and humiliated? Of course not! Jesus always is trying to help us. He knows if we develop a second-mile philosophy, the first mile will go much easier and everyone will be better off. Imagine what the world would be like if we all went the second mile, willingly, with a smile. The Kingdom of Heaven would be a reality on earth.

It is not easy, but each of us should try to practice second-mile Christianity daily. We are so comical: no matter how many interruptions we had yesterday, we actually think we will not have any today. It never works out that way! Unexpected emergencies force us to alter our plans. We should not fret about these first-mile demands, but recognize them as opportunities to experience God's leading. We tend to think when we are doing exactly what we want to do, God's in His Heaven and all's right with the world. That is not true. Sometimes God's will is done best when we are forced to do things we do not want to do, but choose to do with the second-mile philosophy. It is then that God pulls untapped potential out of us and we learn to be more creative, patient, and loving.

Realize every day you will be forced by somebody to go a mile. Do not be offended. Remember, Jesus Christ went many second miles for you. He went all the way to the Cross so you might live. In gratitude, accept second-mile Christianity and go the extra mile. It makes the first mile wonderful, and you will be a great blessing to everyone, even yourself.

*Read: Matthew 5:38-48; Philippians 2:12-18; Ephesians 6:5-9*

# PROMISES FOR THE TOUGH TIMES

*He has granted to us his precious and very great promises (II Peter 1:4).*

We often talk about claiming the promises of God. If tough times come today, try claiming these biblical promises.

**"In the world you have tribulation"** (John 16:33). That's right, God promises we will have troubles. We like to concentrate on Jesus's promises of love, joy, peace, and forgiveness, but we also must accept this promise. Christian discipline does not prevent problems. Through the grace of God, though, we find strength to overcome adversity. When we expect tough times, they lose their power to throw us.

**"And it came to pass"** (Luke 2:1, KJV). Usually we gloss over these words, but they remind us that even the worst crises and trials we confront have come to pass. They will end.

**"Be of good cheer, I have overcome the world"** (John 16:33). With God, we can face anything. He is victor, now and always, and His will shall be done.

**"According to your faith be it unto you"** (Matthew 9:29, KJV). It is our faith that enables us to hang on, and God has placed within each one of us all the faith we will ever need.

**"All things work together for good to them that love God, to them who are the called according to his purpose"** (Romans 8:28, KJV). All things, even the tough times. We may not understand His providence now, but we will someday.

**"He who endures to the end will be saved"** (Matthew 24:13). We are not called to be successful, wealthy, or brilliant, but to endure, with unwavering loyalty to Christ.

**"Lo, I am with you alway, even unto the end of the world"** (Matthew 28:20, KJV). We are not alone, no matter how lost and forsaken we feel. God is with us every moment.

These are some of God's promises. There are many more in the Bible. Search for them. Memorize them. When tough times come, believe His precious and very great promises with all your heart. Remember, though, the Word of God cannot help you much in life if you do not know what it says.

*Read: Joshua 21:45; Romans 4:13-22; II Corinthians 7:1*

137

# A BLESSING OR A BLIGHT

*Fret not yourself because of the wicked, be not envious of wrongdoers! For they will soon fade like the grass, and wither like the green herb. Trust in the Lord, and do good (Psalm 37:1-3)*

It is important for all of us to consider daily what we are contributing to God's wonderful world. Whether we realize it or not, we contribute something to life every moment. By what we say or do not say, what we do or do not do, we are adding or subtracting, helping or hurting, bringing good or causing harm. In short, each of us is either a blessing or a blight. To be sure we are being the blessing God intends us to be, we must look at the nature of our contributions carefully and honestly.

Jesus has given us a standard that enables us to evaluate our contributions: His life. Jesus went about doing good and His earthly ministry is a model for us. We contribute good in the world when we, like Jesus, have Christian eyes, Christian ears, and Christian tongues. Christian eyes see what Jesus sees, not what we want to see. Christian ears sometimes hear what we do not want to hear. Christian tongues say kind words we might not want to say, and do not say biting words we would love to express. Through every incident in His life, Jesus shows us how to be a blessing. Our responsibility is to keep our eyes, ears, and tongues operating effectively and lovingly in all we see, hear, and say, for the honor of the Kingdom.

It is very hard to do good to people who wrong us. We tend to get anxious over the wicked and even a little envious of people who do bad things and seem to get away with it. The teaching of the Bible, though, is to do good to everyone, all the time. Paul wrote, "When reviled, we bless; when persecuted, we endure; when slandered, we try to conciliate" (I Corinthians 4:12-13). Recognizing God's unfailing love and goodness to us should motivate us to trust in the Lord and do good.

We are richly blessed by God's grace. Never should we take blessings for granted or think we deserve them. We are blessed for a reason, and that is to be a blessing, not a blight.

*Read: Genesis 12:1-3; Acts 10:36-38; Romans 12:14-21*

# HARMONY IN THE HOME

*May the God of steadfastness and encouragement grant you to live in such harmony with one another, in accord with Christ Jesus, that together you may with one voice glorify the God and Father of our Lord Jesus Christ (Romans 15:5-6).*

Family problems are interrelated.  When one person in the home has a problem, all in the family have a problem.  When one is in a bad mood, all are miserable.  Frequently the most stressful days are special occasions when we are supposed to be joyful: birthdays, anniversaries, holidays.  Some people wonder how they will survive the pressure of those times.  Christmas is torture for many families; depression, alcoholism, and marital warfare are worse then.  Clement Moore's famous ballad could read, "Every creature was stirring, each one acting like a louse!"  What do we need to keep harmony in the home?

**Honesty.**  So much suffering could be avoided if we quit playing games and simply told the truth.  Dishonesty ultimately damages relationships.  Have the courage to be honest.

**Thoughtfulness.**  Reacting from the gut, blurting out hurtful comments -- that is a sure route to disaster.  Brutal, savage words can wound for a lifetime.  Respond thoughtfully and consider other people's feelings as much as your own.

**Obedience.**  God tries to give us answers to our problems through His Word, prayer, meditation, dreams, and preachers, but we must be receptive and obedient to His leading.

**Patience.**  Quarrels, suspicions, estrangements, and tensions seem relentless and interminable, but we must wait patiently for God to work things out in the fullness of His time.

Harmony in the home comes best when all individuals join the "household of faith" (Galatians 6:10) by making Jesus Christ their Master and Lord.  The love of Christ brings unity to believers, who delight to sing choruses of praise to their gracious Redeemer.  In worshipping Him, we experience the mystery and beauty of His design for humanity, for we sing and live in perfect harmony as together we with one voice glorify the God and Father of our Lord Jesus Christ.

*Read: I Chronicles 16:8-11; Colossians 3:12-14; Proverbs 19:11*

# PERSISTENCE AND INSISTENCE
# BRING ASSISTANCE

*"Ask, and it will be given you; seek, and you will find; knock, and it will be opened to you. For every one who asks receives, and he who seeks finds, and to him who knocks it will be opened" (Matthew 7:7-8).*

A startling notion to consider is that Jesus approves of people who are pests! Jesus likes people who persist and insist until they get assistance with problems. Many New Testament parables and stories describe persistent, insistent people.

To teach His disciples about prayer, Jesus told the parable of a man who received an unexpected visitor during the night. He walked to a neighbor's house to borrow food for his guest, but the sleepy neighbor was less than thrilled. "Get away! Can't you see I'm in bed? My wife is asleep. The kids are asleep. The chickens are asleep. I'm not getting up!" The desperate man kept pounding on the door and eventually his neighbor dragged himself out of bed to provide the bread.

A widow made a nuisance of herself before a judge. He could not take the nagging. He vindicated her because he knew if he did not get rid of her, she would wear him out!

The Greek woman who hounded Jesus until He healed her sick daughter, the blind man who cried for help, the paralytic whose friends lowered him through a roof -- these and other healings came about through persistence and insistence.

Maybe you have a serious problem today: a frightening medical prognosis; a broken home; employment uncertainty; worries about the future. Do you believe God is willing to stop everything else just to listen to your anguished plea? Are you that persistent and insistent? You should be! God wants to listen. He wants to help. Do not give up if He does not appear to respond right away. Continue to trust the Lord, whatever happens. Keep asking, seeking, and knocking. Pray without ceasing. Believe He hears you and His answer is on the way. Your persistence and insistence will bring God's loving and faithful assistance in every situation you must face.

*Read: Luke 11:5-8; Luke 18:1-5; Matthew 15:21-28; Mark 10:46-52; Mark 2:1-5*

# Sweet Potato Casserole

1 large (29-ounce) can sweet
  potatoes
¾ stick margarine or butter
  (melted)
1¼ cups sugar
½ teaspoon cinnamon
½ teaspoon nutmeg
2 eggs

**Topping:**
¾ cup cornflake crumbs
½ cup chopped nuts,
  optional
½ cup brown sugar
¾ stick melted margarine

Warm potatoes in syrup and mash to a very smooth consistency.
Use a blender, food processor or mixer. Add other ingredients and mix
well. Place in 2-quart casserole dish. Bake, uncovered, 20 minutes at
400 degrees.

Mix together topping, spread on potatoes and brown for another 10
minutes. Serves 4 to 6.

...ently has the appropriate wardrobe

# REMEMBER SIN?

*For the wages of sin is death, but the free gift of God is eternal life in Christ Jesus our Lord (Romans 6:23).*

Sin. S-I-N. That is a succinct, one-syllable word, but many of us do not use it or even hear it much anymore. We do not like to talk about sin. We prefer to talk about maladjustment, chemical imbalance, psychosis, neurosis, childhood abuse or trauma, environmental conditioning, peer pressure, or sickness. The concept of sin seems rather old-fashioned and unpleasant, so we just try to forget it. According to the Bible, that is a deadly mistake. The Bible teaches that something is wrong with every human being. "The imagination of man's heart is evil from his youth" (Genesis 8:21). We all have within us the natural desire, the original sin, to be selfish, self-centered, and self-serving. We want to play God, but every time we try to control the universe and tell everybody else what to do, we bring more misery into this world. We create problems for ourselves, for God, for the country, and for all mankind.

Some people think they can refrain from sin through their own effort and will-power. Others just try to put it out of their minds or overlook it. The truth is, it is vitally important for us to remember sin. Only when we acknowledge that we are sinners in need of repentance can we receive forgiveness. "If we say we have no sin, we deceive ourselves, and the truth is not in us. If we confess our sins, he is faithful and just, and will forgive our sins and cleanse us from all unrighteousness. If we say we have not sinned, we make him a liar, and his word is not in us" (I John 1:8-10). To overcome sin's lethal bondage, we must ask for forgiveness of sins, those we have committed and those we desire to commit, and be born again by inviting Jesus, the Savior of sin, to come into our hearts and change us.

Do not ignore sin or excuse it by giving it some other name. Face it. Admit it. Confess it. "There is therefore now no condemnation for those who are in Christ Jesus" (Romans 8:1). Jesus came to the world to save people from their sin, and that includes you. Accept His free gift of eternal life today.

*Read: Psalm 53:1-3; Romans 3:10-26; Colossians 2:13-14*

# YOUR DAILY DUTY

*"Serve him with a whole heart and with a willing mind" (I Chronicles 28:9).*

Many of us are health conscious. We know good health requires careful daily attention. To keep our hearts strong and vigorous, we have to take care of them now. If we wait till arteries get clogged and the heart is weak, it might be too late. I think of good health habits as the D-E-R. D -- a balanced Diet. E -- sufficient Exercise. R -- proper Rest. If we follow the D-E-R, our hearts should function well; if not, our health will be poor. What is true with the physical heart is true of the spiritual heart as well. The spiritual heart God gave each of us can become hard, mean, rebellious, and selfish if we do not do our daily duty to protect and strengthen it. Again, we need the D-E-R. Here is the D-E-R for your spiritual heart.

**D -- Diet.** Feed your heart with God's Holy Spirit. Draw sustenance from Him every day through His Word, your conscience, other people, and the lessons of history and world events. We cannot get in touch with God's Holy Spirit with an 800-number or a letter, but if we listen, He will speak, guide us, and fill us with healthy nourishment for the soul.

**E -- Exercise.** Exercise by lifting up other people! That is the Christian exercise program. It is not sit-ups or jogging, but lifting up as many people as we can with encouragement and flexing our muscles to help them carry their burdens.

**R -- Rest.** Rest in the knowledge that each day of life is a precious gift of God. We cannot know how many days we have left, but we can learn to treasure every moment and live the way God wants us to live today. Put your cares and anxieties to rest by believing you are in the Lord's loving care.

You have the responsibility to stay spiritually robust, active, and vibrant so you can serve the Lord with a whole heart and a willing mind. Your prescription for good health is the D-E-R. Remember to follow instructions carefully. Fulfill your daily duty and stick with the regimen faithfully. Then you will be fit for the Kingdom of Heaven today and every day.

*Read: Hebrews 3:7-19; Ephesians 3:14-19; II Thessalonians 2:16-17*

# THE SUBJECT OF SUBJECTION

*Wives, be subject to your husbands, as to the Lord. For the husband is the head of the wife as Christ is the head of the church, his body, and is himself its Savior. As the church is subject to Christ, so let wives also be subject in everything to their husbands. Husbands, love your wives, as Christ loved the church and gave himself up for her (Ephesians 5:22-25).*

Have you ever read a verse of Scripture and thought, "I wish this were not in the Bible"? Some women have, about Ephesians 5:22: "Wives, be subject to your husbands, as to the Lord." Yet before women get too indignant, they ought to consider the rest of the passage. Men are hardly off the hook. See verse 25: "Husbands, love your wives, as Christ loved the Church." Think about it. Christ laid down His life and died for the Church. That sacrifice involves a lot more than being willing to miss a football game on television or dry the dishes!

The subject of subjection is difficult for us. By nature, we do not like to be controlled. We like to control. Paul helps by writing in verse 21, "Be subject to one another out of reverence for Christ." That is why we must do it: not because we want to, like it, or agree with it. We do it out of reverence for Christ.

The Bible teaches the "I am third" concept: God first, other people second, self third. The first commandment given to Moses was, "I am the Lord your God... You shall have no other gods before me" (Deuteronomy 5:6-7). When Jesus was asked for the greatest commandment, He said, "You shall love the Lord your God with all your heart, and with all your soul, and with all your mind. This is the great and first commandment. And a second is like it, You shall love your neighbor as yourself" (Matthew 22:37-39). God first, others second, self third. When we live by that principle, we learn life is found in giving, not getting; in caring, not conquering.

Do not let the subject of subjection scare you. You can be subject to one another, and enjoy it. And do not be afraid of any part of Scripture. The Bible was given by God to help us, not hurt us. God always blesses the reading of His Holy Word, even verses that at first might seem a little hard to take.

*Read: Ephesians 5:21-33; Colossians 3:18-24; I Corinthians 4:1*

# HOLY HAPPENINGS

*Has such a thing happened in your days? (Joel 1:2).*

When God wants to do something significant for people of all generations, He pulls out all the stops and creates a holy happening. A holy happening is a major production that takes place according to God's plan. He involves people in it, but He is in control and it cannot be stopped. He can do it anywhere, anytime, as we see throughout the Bible: the giving of the Ten Commandments, the resurrection of Jesus, the revelation of Holy Spirit and beginning of the Church at Pentecost, the conversion of Paul, the visions of John. Holy happenings are beyond human comprehension, definition, and explanation.

A holy happening may be going on now. Often we do not realize what God is doing until we see events in retrospect, for holy happenings are obscured by clouds, noise, confusion, fear, and trembling. Our finite minds cannot understand the vast mysteries of God. "My thoughts are not your thoughts, neither are your ways my ways, says the Lord. For as the heavens are higher than the earth, so are my ways higher than your ways and my thoughts than your thoughts" (Isaiah 55:8-9).

To recognize holy happenings, we must live with a sense of awe and wonder, never complaining that God does not provide visible, tangible proof of His presence. Real power is unseen. The real power of a home depends upon love and respect, not the size of the house. The real power of a plant is in the roots under the ground. The real power of electricity is in the current, not the cable. So it is with God. The real power of God is experienced not face-to-face, but through His many manifestations in the world. We need to accept this mystery and not be frightened when we feel lost in a foggy haze. God produces holy happenings to reassure us of His presence and power and love, not to terrify us. Remember, Scripture shows that peace always comes out of the confusion.

Holy happenings change history. Holy happenings change the world. A holy happening could change your life, so look around. One could be happening today.

*Read: II Samuel 22:7-20; Jeremiah 32:17-20; Psalm 104:1-4*

# IT'S A DIRTY JOB . . .

*"I am among you as one who serves" (Luke 22:27).*

. . . but somebody's got to do it. Usually we think the "somebody" who should do dirty jobs is "somebody else," not us. We are important and dignified! We hold responsible, well-paid positions. We are widely respected and distinguished and esteemed and prominent and . . . well, somebody else will just have to take care of those dirty, menial, degrading jobs.

Jesus Christ never expressed an attitude like that! He called His followers to be servants and demonstrated the level of service He expects through a startling example: by personally washing the feet of His disciples in the Upper Room the night before His crucifixion on the Cross. In biblical days, hosts normally provided a servant to wash the feet of guests who traveled along the dusty roads. Jesus did not pay anyone to perform that function, ask for volunteers, or suggest each disciple clean his own feet. He simply arose from the table, took off His outer garment, put on a towel, and filled a basin of water. Working from one end of the room to the other, Jesus humbly washed twenty-four feet. He even washed the feet of Judas Iscariot, knowing Judas would, within hours, betray him to the authorities seeking to kill Him. Can you imagine that scene? It is bad enough to clean our own dirty feet, but everybody else's? Picture the sores, the bunions, the corns, the odious infections our Lord must have touched! Why did Jesus Christ do such a dirty job? Why didn't He get somebody else?

"If I then, your Lord and Teacher, have washed your feet, you also ought to wash one another's feet. For I have given you an example, that you should do as I have done to you" (John 13:14-15). Could any words be more clear? Jesus expects us to serve God by serving people in every possible way, even people who might betray us, and even in jobs that are dirty and unpleasant. Look around today. People are in desperate need. You are called to serve them. Follow the example of Jesus Christ and help. Yes, it may be a dirty job, but somebody's got to do it. Jesus Christ is depending on you.

*Read: John 13:1-20; Joshua 22:5; Psalm 72:11*

# THREE WAYS TO LEAVE WORSHIP

*"Behold, I have set before you an open door" (Revelation 3:8).*

The parable of the Pharisee and the publican teaches that though we come to worship from different places, different homes, on different roads, with different emotions, we all leave one of three ways: as a Pharisee, a publican, or a passerby.

The Pharisee left worship thinking he was better than everyone else. "God, I thank thee that I am not like other men, extortioners, unjust, adulterers, or even like this tax collector. I fast twice a week, I give tithes of all that I get" (Luke 18:11-12). He imagined he was right with God because he led a good life. The publican left worship feeling dirty and unjust. He thought everyone else was better and cleaner than he was. He did not try to justify himself. He brought his unworthiness and sin to the Lord and prayed, "God, be merciful to me a sinner!" (v. 13). Then there is the passerby. Jesus did not talk about the passerby here, but every church has this type of worshiper: they are people who have no idea why they come to church, do not listen, are eager to depart, and later cannot remember a thing.

The Pharisee had eye problems: a good eye only on himself, a bad eye on everybody else, no eye on God. The publican saw pretty well: a good eye on God, a bad eye on himself, no eye on anyone else. A passerby has no eye on God and no eye on self; he might have an eye on some good-looking person he would like to meet, but basically the only eye he has is on the clock. He wastes his time and God's grace.

I wonder what we see about ourselves, other people, and God as we leave worship services. Just as we choose which door to go through, we choose the attitude with which we go. We can leave as a Pharisee, trying to earn through goodness what God alone can give through grace. We can just idly pass by, with no thought of commitment or faith. Or we can leave as a publican, freely accepting the grace of God in humility and gratitude. Be very careful with your choice. Some doors lead to death, but if you go through the open door Jesus sets before you, you are choosing the door to eternal life.

*Read: Luke 18:9-14; John 4:23-24; Hebrews 13:15-16*

## JESUS'S PRAYER FOR YOU

*"I do not pray for these only, but also for those who believe in me through their word" (John 17:20).*

On the night before He died, Jesus prayed for His disciples. Not only that. He prayed for you! Jesus still prays for you to your Heavenly Father, asking Him to help you in four ways.

**Jesus prays that God will grant you wholeness.** "Keep them in thy name, which thou hast given me, that they may be one, even as we are one" (John 17:11). Jesus prays for your wholeness, in relationships and within yourself. God desires unity for His children. Christianity is the only religion that speaks of God as a Father; the brotherhood of man is dependent upon the Fatherhood of God. Disliking ourselves or others is a theological problem that God does not want to happen.

**Jesus prays for you to have joy.** "These things I speak in the world, that they may have my joy fulfilled in themselves" (v. 13). Jesus wants you to be joyful, not superficially, but deeply joyful with peace that passes understanding, love that will not let you go, and faith that moves mountains. It is a joy that works at midnight, on dark days, and in rainy seasons. This joy comes one way: from obedience to the Word of God.

**Jesus prays that you will be kept from evil.** "I do not pray that thou shouldst take them out of the world, but that thou shouldst keep them from the evil one" (v. 15). Evil is a consequence of sin, which starts with human selfishness. Christ's victory on the Cross gives us strength to rise above selfishness, overcome temptation, and defeat the power of sin.

**Jesus prays for your sanctification.** "Sanctify them in the truth; thy word is truth" (v. 17). Jesus wants you to become more Christian every day by seeking the light of His revelation, living by biblical truth, and striving for personal holiness.

Perhaps at a difficult time in your life, you were touched to learn people were praying for your well-being. Their loving concern brought comfort and hope. Think what it means, then, that Christ Himself prays for you. Jesus's prayer will bring greater blessings than you can imagine, if you believe in Him.

*Read: John 17:9-21; Romans 8:31-34; Hebrews 7:25*

# OUR HIDDEN FAULTS

*Who can discern his errors? Clear thou me from hidden faults.
Keep back thy servant also from presumptuous sins; let them
not have dominion over me! Then I shall be blameless, and
innocent of great transgression. Let the words of my mouth
and the meditation of my heart be acceptable in thy sight, O
Lord, my rock and my redeemer (Psalm 19:12-14).*

Two things plague us: presumptuous sins and hidden faults.
Presumptuous sins are offenses we commit openly, blatantly,
disobediently. Hidden faults are flaws that God and other
people can see in us, but we cannot recognize in ourselves. We
all have hidden faults. They sneak out of us through our walk,
our talk, the way we sulk, and how we look. They gnaw at us
and make us moody, sullen, and difficult to live with. We
sense something is wrong, but do not know how to make it
right. Often we do nothing and just overlook or rationalize our
hidden faults; that is a choice we can make, but it means we
stay miserable. Sometimes we ask friends to point out our
faults to us; they probably can do it, but if we take this
approach, we likely will be short on friends before too long.

The best way to deal with hidden faults is to allow the
perfect, unchanging Word of God to be our only authority for
faith and practice. The Bible is given for reproof, correction,
and instruction for salvation. It is a two-edged sword that can
point to our sins and faults and cut them out of our lives. We
cannot discern our errors without the light of God's Word, "a
lamp shining in a dark place" (II Peter 1:19) that shows us how
to live. Do not let hidden faults make you miserable. Allow
God through His Word to clear you from them. Cherish the
Bible as a personal message from your Heavenly Father.

Following biblical precepts revives the soul and brings a
sense of rightness and joy to the heart. The words of your
mouth and the meditation of your heart will be acceptable in
the sight of the Lord if you know and obey Scriptural truth.
Faith, hope, love, and all the important things in this world and
the next are available to you today through God's Holy Word.

*Read: Psalm 19:7-14; Hebrews 4:12; II Timothy 3:14-17*

148

# RECOGNIZING GODLY AUTHORITY

*They went into Capernaum; and immediately on the sabbath he entered the synagogue and taught. And they were astonished at his teaching, for he taught them as one who had authority, and not as the scribes (Mark 1:21-22).*

We are all under authority, and there are many kinds: parental, governmental, legal, professional. These types of authority are given by people. There is also inherent or godly authority. God does not need people to give Him the privilege and power of authority. He takes it! To the Christian, godly authority is above every human authority. As Christians, we have the responsibility to get human authority to correspond to the principles of godly authority as revealed through Christ.

When Jesus taught in the Capernaum synagogue, people were astonished; when He healed a man with an unclean spirit, they were amazed! Through this experience, Jesus shows how to recognize that godly authority is gaining control in us.

**Teachings begin to gel.** Incredible teachings start to make sense. Finding life by giving it away? Loving enemies? Jesus's teachings begin to gel as we realize, they work!

**Evil spirits within yell.** The authority of God is the only force that frightens the power of evil. In the synagogue, the evil spirit yelled and convulsed, but then came out of the demoniac. If a civil war is raging within us, our struggle is evidence that godly authority is beginning to take control.

**Problems are made well.** Calamities and confusion mysteriously recede and miracles begin to happen. The authority of God makes the impossible possible.

**We go tell what we have seen.** We eagerly share our belief, though we cannot explain it. There are things we cannot understand, but on Judgment Day, God will not give an exam to test our knowledge. He will ask if we believe in the Cross.

Jesus said, "All authority in heaven and on earth has been given to me" (Matthew 28:18). Recognize Jesus Christ as your supreme authority. Submit joyfully to the authority of God and He will authorize you to do great things in His name.

*Read: Mark 1:21-28; Matthew 7:28-29; Luke 5:17-26*

# THE REAL WINNERS

*Indeed I count everything as loss because of the surpassing worth of knowing Christ Jesus my Lord. For his sake I have suffered the loss of all things, and count them as refuse, in order that I may gain Christ (Philippians 3:8).*

Our culture is obsessed with winning. Who is number one? Who is on top? Who got the gold, the silver, and the bronze? Who has the most hits? Who set the latest world record? Who signed the biggest contract? Hurrah for the winners! Too bad, all you losers. Too bad. Looks like you wasted your time.

Winning is exciting, but often we place far too much emphasis on competition. What difference does it all make in the Kingdom of God? Of what value are medals and trophies to Jesus Christ? The real winners in life generally do not make the front page of the newspaper, receive awards, or hear applause. Most of the time they are not even thanked or appreciated for what they do. Who are the real winners? Parents who are willing to take back-talk when, in love, they say No to their children to teach them discipline and responsibility. Teachers who prepare, care, and give their best, believing their efforts will result in some good in the lives of students. Honest workers who put in long hours to get the job done right. Ordinary people who share generously their time, talent, and treasure, not to be noticed or praised, but merely to be helpful. Christians who bring encouragement, love, joy, and peace to the world and give all the honor to God.

Society assigns excessive value to fame and fortune. Prominent celebrities who live luxuriously are envied, while Christians who work quietly and diligently for the sake of the Kingdom are considered foolish. Still, the real winners never quit. They have faith to believe, no matter what anyone else says, does, or thinks, their lives are going to make a difference for good in the world. Medals and trophies are fine in their place, but worldly acclaim loses out in comparison with the surpassing worth of knowing Christ Jesus as Lord. That is the secret of being a real winner, as any real winner will tell you.

*Read: Philippians 3:7-11; Matthew 16:24-27; Proverbs 29:23*

## EQUIPPED FOR COMPLETENESS

*All scripture is inspired by God and profitable for teaching, for reproof, for correction, and for training in righteousness, that the man of God may be complete, equipped for every good work (II Timothy 3:16-17).*

Whatever we need in life, we already have. That is because we have God's Holy Word, God's special revelation to all humanity and our only authoritative rule for faith and practice. The Bible is a lamp unto our feet and a light unto our path. Scripture teaches us what is important in this world as well as in the spiritual Kingdom of Heaven. God expects us to be productive and successful as we follow Him, and He equips us with His Holy Word to make our lives complete.

The Bible is the most precious thing in all the world, and it is discouraging that so few people, even church members, read it. God gave us inquisitive, questioning minds. Most of us read newspapers, magazines, and books. We support education, though we have different areas of interest. Some people like the "ic"s: mathematics, physics, statistics. Others prefer the "y"s: history, biography, philosophy, psychology. Often we are eager to learn about the "ic"s and the "y"s, while we disregard the greatest source of wisdom and guidance, God's Word. Of course, some people never learned about the Bible in childhood, and others have forgotten what they once knew. But many people ignore the Bible because they do not wish to be corrected; they would rather not know their sins and faults, as they have no desire to change their selfish behavior.

Neglect of God's Word is a perilous mistake. Only by strengthening ourselves in the Bible will we be in condition to face temptations, tempests, and troubles. Many people learn the hard way that if they wait until a devastating crisis disrupts their lives to turn to Scripture, it could be too late to find the help they need. Let us get rid of excuses and laziness and try from this day forward to commit ourselves to meaningful Bible study, always thankful that the blessed gift of God's Holy Word has equipped us for completeness in life.

*Read: Psalm 119:89-105; Mark 13:31; Proverbs 30:5-6*

# A HUMBLE WALK WITH GOD

*"He has showed you, O man, what is good; and what does the Lord require of you but to do justice, and to love kindness, and to walk humbly with your God?" (Micah 6:8).*

The Christian life is a life of action. We cannot call ourselves Christians if we sit around doing nothing. The Bible exhorts us to "walk in newness of life" (Romans 6:4); "walk by the Spirit" (Galatians 5:16); "walk in love" (Ephesians 5:2); "walk in the light" (I John 1:7). That is a lot of walking! Walking is a great way to keep fit, but it requires discipline. Walking with God requires so much discipline that many people think they cannot do it. There are the disciplines of Bible reading, prayer, worship, tithing, seeking the Kingdom. Not only that; we are required to "walk humbly" with our God, and humility is a quality difficult to understand and achieve.

Some people think of humility as a self-consciousness of defects and liabilities, a sense of insignificance, lack of spirit, abject timidity. That is far from the biblical meaning. Jesus was the most humble person who ever lived! Walking humbly in practical terms means being good at something but not bragging about it; not retaliating when an injustice is perpetrated; giving one's best no matter how many or how few people are watching; having money in our pockets and not spending it foolishly; doing a job as enthusiastically at the end as at the beginning; not feeling whipped when criticized; getting up again no matter how often we get knocked down; loving people who do not love us; forgiving people who do not forgive us. Humility is essential for Christians, for humility brings God's grace. "Clothe yourselves, all of you, with humility toward one another, for 'God opposes the proud, but gives grace to the humble'" (I Peter 5:5).

No one can force another to walk humbly with God. We can ignore the disciplines, sit around doing nothing, and forget humility, but that would be extremely foolish. When God shows what is required of us, we are wise to obey. Today, do what is good: do justice, love kindness, and take a humble walk with the best companion you will know, the Lord God.

*Read: Proverbs 11:2; Psalm 138:6; Isaiah 57:15*

# THE SPIRIT THAT LASTS

*Do not get drunk with wine, for that is debauchery; but be filled with the Spirit (Ephesians 5:18).*

Everyone wants more love, more joy, and more exhilaration, but the secular world and the Christian Church differ on how to get them. Many people try to find happiness with spirits of alcohol. They open their mouths, pour it in, and wait for good feelings to come. It works! I have seen people who are too bashful to stand in church with five hundred people and sing a hymn belt out "Melancholy Baby" all by themselves to entertain at a party. Talk gets loud; people become best friends with total strangers; shrill laughter resonates. There is just one catch: the mood does not last. Soon people learn that being filled with those spirits is expensive. It brings headaches, heartaches, and horrors.

"Who has woe? Who has sorrow? Who has strife? Who has complaining? Who has wounds without cause? Who has redness of eyes? Those who tarry long over wine, those who go to try mixed wine... At the last it bites like a serpent, and stings like an adder" (Proverbs 23:29-30,32). Some parents express relief that their kids use alcohol instead of "real drugs." The fact is, alcohol is the greatest drug problem in America and countless lives are damaged or destroyed because people, young and old, look for a few hours of happiness through intoxicating drink.

To find lasting satisfaction, try being filled with God's Holy Spirit. You will get the same benefits -- freedom, excitement, a song in the heart -- and they will not disappear the next day! When Holy Spirit came upon people at Pentecost, observers accused them of drunkenness. Peter explained they were not filled with wine, but with the Spirit of God. "The fruit of the Spirit is love, joy, peace, patience, kindness, goodness, faithfulness, gentleness, self-control" (Galatians 5:22-23). No other spirits can compare. Open your heart to God's Holy Spirit today. Other spirits will fail and disappoint you, even ruin you, but Holy Spirit will fill your heart with blessings of love, joy, and exhilaration that endure forever.

*Read: Ephesians 5:3-20; Isaiah 5:11-12; Proverbs 20:1*

# YOUR SECRET PLACE

*"When you pray, go into your room and shut the door and pray to your Father who is in secret; and your Father who sees in secret will reward you" (Matthew 6:6).*

Where is your secret place, the special place where you meet God one-on-one? We all need a private meeting place nobody else knows about to rendezvous with God and utter unto Him our deepest prayers and longings. It may be in a room, on a chair, or under a tree. Jesus found His secret place on a mountain. Peter found it on a rooftop. Everyone's secret place is different. The important thing is to have one and use it! It is in your secret place that you pray for the Lord's guidance in specific situations. You do not have to speak volumes, expecting Him to respond with an encyclopedic answer. Just put your plea before Him in short, sincere words, then attentively watch for His signals showing you what to do.

Spending time alone with God in your secret place can change your life if you remember to do two essential things. First, remember to take child-like faith with you into your secret place. In child-like faith, believe God is your loving heavenly Father, His answer will be the best answer for you, and He is always working for good in your life. Second, remember to keep anger, hate, and malice out of your secret place. Check your heart and make sure to check all those negatives outside your prayer life, for hostile, spiteful, surly attitudes block intimate communication with the Lord and prevent us from recognizing His love and leading day by day.

The Psalmist speaks of a secret place with God. "He that dwelleth in the secret place of the Most High shall abide under the shadow of the Almighty" (Psalm 91:1, KJV). Abiding under the shadow of the Almighty -- that sounds like a wonderful place to live! Realize what a privilege it is to be able to meet with God, your Creator, Master, and Lord, in a secret place, knowing He is interested in you and will answer your prayers. Treasure your moments with God in your secret place and exciting things will begin to happen there.

*Read: Matthew 6:6-15; Mark 6:46; Acts 10:9*

## WAITING BY THE MAILBOX

*"Does he thank the servant because he did what was commanded?" (Luke 17:9)*

If you are waiting for God to send you a thank-you note for all the work you have done for Him, for all the money you have given, and for serving on all those committees at church, you are going to be waiting for a long, long time. God does not send thank-you notes. Nowhere in Scripture does God write, "Thank you for being my servant." Polite rules of etiquette are a human invention, not a divine attribute. That is difficult for us. We like to be patted on the back; we need strokes; we feed on praise. How else can we know self-confidence and pride?

Well, God does not owe us thank-you notes, gratitude, or anything else. We are His servants and He expects us to do our duty. To illustrate, Jesus told the parable of a master and servant. The servant worked hard in the field all day, but when he came home, the master did not say, "Hey, relax, sit down, take your shoes off. We'll call out for pizza tonight!" No, the servant still had a job to do. The master was absolutely right in expecting the servant to ask, "What can I get you for dinner? I'll make you a tasty, delicious meal and wait upon you, and when you are finished with me, then I will sit down to eat." The message is that we are servants twenty-four hours a day, seven days a week. Dedicated servants do not keep their eyes on the clock. Servants labor until the work is done, whatever it requires in effort, sacrifice, and personal suffering. If we need to hear other people telling us how brilliant and wonderful we are all the time, we are not true servants of Jesus Christ. Justifiable self-confidence and pride come not from hearing human praise, but from cheerfully doing our duty for Christ.

Does the Master thank His servants for doing what is commanded? No, He does not, so do not waste time waiting by the mailbox for a glowing thank-you note from God. Just keep busy loving the Lord and doing your duty today and every day. His good and faithful servants do not get thank-you notes, but they do receive heavenly satisfaction.

*Read: Luke 17:7-10; John 12:26; James 1:22*

# OUR BOUTS WITH DOUBT

*Then he said to Thomas, "Put your finger here, and see my hands; and put out your hand, and place it in my side; do not be faithless, but believing." Thomas answered him, "My Lord and my God!" Jesus said to him, "Have you believed because you have seen me? Blessed are those who have not seen and yet believe" (John 20:27-29).*

A bout with doubt is agonizing and miserable, yet periods of doubt can work to strengthen our faith if we know how to clout our bouts with doubt. If not, those bouts with doubt can knock us out of the Kingdom, temporarily or permanently.

After Easter, Thomas doubted the resurrection of Christ, the sanity of his friends, and his own wisdom in following Jesus. The name Thomas means "twin," and I think we all can consider Thomas our twin, for we, too, experience bouts with doubt. Thomas teaches us how to overcome them.

**Stay, don't stray.** Thomas unnecessarily suffered for eight days because he strayed from his friends on Easter night. When we doubt, we need Christian fellowship more than ever. The presence of God is found in the presence of God's people.

**Talk, don't balk.** Thomas's friends kept communicating with him. When stuck in a bout with doubt, we should talk, ask questions, and listen, even if we do not feel like it.

**Try, don't cry.** Despite the uncertainty, we can wipe away our teardrops by remembering we have the God-given power to choose a mental attitude of belief. If we try, we can believe we will find direction and discover our doubts to be wrong.

**Hear, don't peer.** Thomas wanted visual proof, but faith comes by hearing. We believe first, then sense God's presence.

We all have a clear choice to make: we can be faithless or believing. The faithless person is "like a wave of the sea that is driven and tossed by the wind" (James 1:6). The believer is "like Mount Zion, which cannot be moved, but abides for ever" (Psalm 125:1). It is faith that overcomes doubt. God has given us the gift of faith, but we decide whether to accept it or reject it. Accept the gift of faith and clout your bouts with doubt so you will not be knocked out of the Kingdom!

*Read: John 20:19-31; Romans 10:17; Psalm 125*

# WHAT MAKES DAD CRY

*If I have prophetic powers, and understand all mysteries and all knowledge, and if I have all faith ... but have not love, I am nothing (I Corinthians 13:2).*

It is tough to be a dad. Often there is an awkwardness between fathers and children. It happens sometimes because dads are afraid to reveal their emotions. We have a crazy notion in our culture that men should not cry. That makes it hard for men to show love. Usually men are not good communicators at home. They are fine at the office, on the golf course, and at parties, but at home, they do not say much to the people they love the most. Though they provide for their kids, they hesitate to get actively involved in the role God expects them to fulfill as dads. They prefer to have teachers and preachers guide their children, but no professional can replace a loving father, no matter how ill-prepared and inexperienced that dad may feel.

I had a great dad. I saw him cry when I was twelve years old, and I remember it as if it were yesterday. He stood at the foot of the casket of his mother, my grandma. Some men were about to close the casket. I heard sobbing and turned around. It was my dad. My mother held him in her arms as he wept uncontrollably. I learned a lot about my dad that day. It was a painful moment, but I always have been glad it happened. I cry easily, and I do not apologize for that. I am free to shed my tears because I had a great dad who was not ashamed to cry.

These are stressful times for families. I think we would be better off if dads cried a little more at home. Wives, children, encourage the sharing of deep emotions. You will never know closeness without the freedom to be honest. Men, do not be afraid to lose control over what makes you cry. That wordless communication might save you and your family heartache, trouble, and regret. Jesus cried openly. His tears revealed His deep love for all people. Let your tears reveal your deep love for your family. You might have power, understanding, knowledge, faith, and many things, but if you have not love, you are nothing. Whatever you do, do not miss love.

*Read: Luke 19:41-42; John 11:32-35; Proverbs 15:17*

# WORDS OF PEACE

*"Thou dost keep him in perfect peace, whose mind is stayed on thee, because he trusts in thee" (Isaiah 26:3).*

Many of us, if we are honest, would have to admit we are not entirely eager to come face-to-face with Jesus Christ. At least, not yet. We are a bit frightened by that moment of confrontation. We feel guilty about the many occasions when we mistreated God, other people, and ourselves, and we wish we had a little more time to dream up reasons to justify our actions. We are not quite sure what Jesus thinks of us. We wonder, "What will Jesus say to me? What will He do?" We do not realize that right now, Jesus is looking at us with love and mercy, even if we are having a difficult time looking at Him. Jesus has four words to say to us: "Peace be with you." Peace. Peace is what Jesus wants to give us this very moment.

How can we know that? Because those are the words Jesus spoke to His disciples when He came face-to-face with them after the resurrection. "Jesus came and stood among them and said to them, 'Peace be with you.' When he had said this, he showed them his hands and his side. Then the disciples were glad when they saw the Lord. Jesus said to them again, 'Peace be with you'" (John 20:19-21). Those men had forsaken Jesus at the Cross. Jesus had every right to be angry, but He did not criticize or condemn. He loved them. He forgave them. He offered them peace, not once, but twice! Their moment of confrontation with Jesus Christ was not an experience of terror or punishment, but one of unconditional love and acceptance.

"Peace be with you." How beautiful are those words, and what reassurance they bring! Peace is available, no matter what we have done, no matter how we have forsaken, denied, and betrayed Jesus, no matter how troubled and hopeless we are right now. Jesus offers peace to anyone who will take it. Accept the peace of Jesus Christ, and to show your gratitude for this gracious gift, share His words of peace with everyone. Give peace away and you will have even more of it.

Keep your mind stayed on Jesus Christ, trust Him completely, and you will find perfect peace today and forever.

*Read: John 20:19-31; Philippians 4:7; Psalm 119:165*

# CHURCH KEYS

*For no foundation can any one lay than that which is laid, which is Jesus Christ (I Corinthians 3:11).*

As Christians, we are members of the Church of Jesus Christ. We have the responsibility of keeping His Church alive and vital in the world today. God has given us the keys to the Kingdom, spiritual keys we must accept, understand, and believe in order to keep His Church open, free, and secure.

**The key of a personal confession of faith.** The Church is built upon people who come together with the personal confession of faith in Jesus Christ as the Son of God, the living Lord and Savior, and the Redeemer of the world.

**The key of individual revelation from the Father.** We believe in divine revelation to the individual. Mysteriously, God speaks by the power of His Holy Word and Holy Spirit. When seemingly out of nowhere we get ideas for exciting, Christ-honoring ventures, that is God at work in our lives.

**The key of absolute accountability.** The Church is accountable to God. We are not a society of people trying to please one another. We are here to serve. On Judgment Day, when no one will be absent, all will be asked two questions: "Why did you do it?" and the bigger question, "Why didn't you do it?" Our answer then depends upon our actions now.

**The key of faithful obedience to Jesus Christ.** "If you love me, you will keep my commandments" (John 14:15). Keeping the commands of Jesus proves our love for Him. We in the Church must obey Him faithfully in every detail.

These spiritual keys are the chief tenets of the Christian Church. Insidious philosophies have challenged Christianity in all ages of human history. "False prophets also arose among the people, just as there will be false teachers among you, who will secretly bring in destructive heresies" (II Peter 2:1). We easily can be misled unless we believe and hold fast to the truth that Jesus is Lord. Today, let us accept the keys to the Kingdom and devote our lives to keeping the Church of Jesus Christ open, free, and secure until He comes again in glory.

*Read: Matthew 16:13-20; II Timothy 2:19; Colossians 1:15-20*

159

# THE PRACTICE OF PRACTICING

*Set the believers an example in speech and conduct, in love, in faith, in purity... Practice these duties, devote yourself to them, so that all may see your progress (I Timothy 4:12,15).*

It is a basic principle: often we have to practice what we want to believe in order to believe it. Scientifically-minded people like to demand proof before they make decisions, but that is not the way it works in the spiritual world. In the Kingdom, "We walk by faith, not by sight" (II Corinthians 5:7). We cannot experience Jesus in a dynamic way until first we believe He is alive and He wants us to trust Him as Lord.

Belief takes practice! We do not object to the practice of practicing in other areas. We realize we have to practice cooking to be connoisseurs in the kitchen. We have to mess up wood with saws and hammers to gain skill in carpentry. It takes practice to excel. So it is in faith. How can we expect to grow in faith without effort or participation on our part?

Jesus said it is not enough to hear His words. We have to do them! Doing Jesus's words takes practice, for they are very difficult to obey, yet our response to Jesus's words determines whether we are wise or foolish and whether we stand or fall in crises. "Every one then who hears these words of mine and does them will be like a wise man who built his house upon the rock; and the rain fell, and the floods came, and the winds blew and beat upon that house, but it did not fall, because it had been founded on the rock. And every one who hears these words of mine and does not do them will be like a foolish man who built his house upon the sand; and the rain fell, and the floods came, and the winds blew and beat against that house, and it fell; and great was the fall of it" (Matthew 7:24-27). If you want to be wise and stand firm through the fierce storms of life, make the decision to hear and do the words of Jesus Christ.

Accept the principle that you have to practice what you believe to become a believer. Devote yourself to the practice of practicing belief in Jesus daily, and soon your speech and conduct will set an example in love, faith, and purity for all.

*Read: Hebrews 11:1-6; Psalm 111:10; Proverbs 3:5*

# LET YOUR LOVE GROW

*May the Lord make you increase and abound in love to one another and to all men (I Thessalonians 3:12).*

Christian agape love is very different from any other kind of love. Agape love comes not from the feelings or emotions but from the will, and is higher than romantic love, love for country, and love for family. Christian agape love cannot be achieved by human power alone. It comes from the Lord.

Christians are to be "rooted and grounded in love" (Ephesians 3:17), and God wants agape love to grow within us daily. God brings the miracle of growth, but there are things you can do to help Him reap a bountiful harvest of love through you. Love begins to grow as you become aware of the seed of agape love God plants in you. Jesus would not command us to love if we were unable to do it. He places love within us, and we must not trample, ignore, or misuse His gracious gift. For the plant to mature, it needs Son-light, the light of Christ shining forth from the Word of God. Do not be afraid to expose love to the other elements as well. Rain, heat, snow, gales -- those forces either destroy the plant of love or enable it to thrive. Unless love can weather the storms, the dark days, the starless nights, the winds of adversity, it will not survive. Finally, though it is not easy, be patient and afford love time and space. Agape love does not grow overnight. If you crowd or smother the plant, you kill it.

Agape love is demanding, but it is the goal of the Christian life. Be sure to examine your heart and mind frequently to see if love is developing. Love should be growing all the time, not remaining static or diminishing. If you are still angry at the people who infuriated you in the past, if you do not have more appreciation for yourself and others than you used to, if you continue to give the same amount of time and money in Jesus's name as you did years ago, your love is stagnant.

"Make love your aim" (I Corinthians 14:1). Today, aim for agape love and let your love grow!

*Read: Ephesians 3:14-21; John 15:12-17; I Corinthians 13*

# LOOKING AT A MIRACLE

*"He delivers and rescues, he works signs and wonders in heaven and on earth" (Daniel 6:27).*

A miracle is something that defies human abilities and baffles human understanding. We see miracles every day. Life is a miracle. You are a miracle! We see people being born and people being reborn in the Spirit. We see hurting people who somehow cope and sick people made well. Yet though we all see miracles, we react to miracles differently. When Jesus healed a blind man, people looked at that miracle in four ways.

**Frustration.** The blind man's neighbors were baffled and flabbergasted, unable to figure it out. Some even doubted the man before them was indeed the man blind since birth. They took him to the temple and asked the religious leaders to interpret what they should have seen with their own eyes.

**Anger.** The Pharisees were furious. Jesus healed on the Sabbath, and they believed God would not do such a thing! The Pharisees had the audacity to tell the world what God could and could not do. That kind of religiosity put Jesus on the Cross. God can do anything, anytime, anywhere He wants.

**Fear.** The blind man's parents should have fallen to their knees and thanked God for the healing, but they caved in. Fearing the Pharisees, they refused to vouch for their son. I frequently have seen parents panic when kids "get religion," and I find their reaction pathetic. Coming to Christ is the greatest moment in a person's life. That leap of faith should bring joy, not fear, to loved ones who claim to be Christian.

**Faith.** The blind man knew how to look at a miracle: he believed and worshipped Jesus Christ. "Once I was blind, but now I can see" (John 9:25). In spite of everyone else's reactions, he was filled with faith, happiness, and gratitude.

The Lord still delivers and rescues. He still works signs and wonders. We rob ourselves of miracles when we doubt His power to perform them. Jesus did not do mighty works in His hometown because of the people's unbelief. Believe! Look at miracles through the eyes of faith and praise God!

*Read: John 9:1-39; Mark 6:1-6; Psalm 72:18-19*

# HOW TO SERVE A KING

*King of kings and Lord of lords (Revelation 19:16).*

We call Jesus the King of kings and we talk about the Kingdom of Heaven, but America is a democracy and we really do not understand much about kings and kingdoms. We are accustomed to electing our leaders for a short time and granting them limited power. Kings have their positions by birth, rule for life, and exercise unlimited power. So how exactly do we serve the King of kings and Lord of lords, Jesus Christ?

**Accept Jesus's authority.** We serve Jesus not only by giving Him our time, talents, and tithes, but by accepting His authority. A divided kingdom cannot stand. If Jesus is not the number one authority in our lives, He is no authority in our lives. We accept His authority when we obey His Word.

**Fight with faith, not fists.** Jesus's Kingdom is not of this world. The weapons of the world are fists, guns, lies, fear, prejudice, threats. We cannot use the weapons of the world for the sake of the Kingdom; they do not work. The weapons a Christian uses are faith, hope, love, and truth. In the name of Jesus, Christians fight with faith and overcome evil with good.

**Trust the truth.** We show trust in the Word of God when we live it. Some of the teachings of Jesus do not appear logical, but they work! Jesus Christ tells the truth and the truth sets us free. The truth of God's Holy Word will never fail.

**Conduct yourself with courage.** We should never compromise our convictions to gain popularity, but rather, take a bold stand for Jesus Christ, do right, and fight injustice.

The Kingdom of God is not a democracy, but think about the King whom you serve. He created you. He loves you. He died for you. He has a plan for your destiny. He wants the best for you. He will never leave you nor forsake you. He will help you through every day of your life and welcome you into your eternal home. What a privilege to serve such a King!

"To the King of ages, immortal, invisible, the only God, be honor and glory for ever and ever. Amen" (I Timothy 1:17).

Serve your King today.

*Read: John 18:33-40; I Timothy 6:11-16; John 8:31-32*

# THE HARDEST THING TO DO

*So David prevailed (I Samuel 17:50).*

The hardest thing in the world to do is to be yourself. We live in a time when people try to be like everyone else. We face tremendous peer pressure at all ages and it is difficult to protect our precious, God-given individuality. David, "the anointed of the God of Jacob, the sweet psalmist of Israel" (II Samuel 23:1), probably came as close as anyone save Jesus to finding complete fulfillment. He faced three forces that could have kept him from becoming the unique, wonderful person God intended him to be. We face the same three forces today.

**Giants.** David's giant was the huge Philistine, Goliath, but we, too, contend with giants: cruel people who threaten and intimidate us and put us down; nasty people who try to make us feel small and weak and insignificant. Giants can crush our spirits unless we, like David, believe we are on God's side.

**Sauls.** Big Saul lovingly tried to be helpful by offering little David his military armor, which worked so well for him; unfortunately, it did not work for David. We, too, have people who love us and want to help. They are trying to direct our lives and they have the future all figured out! The problem is, it might not be the future God has planned for us. Like David, we must quickly put off anything we believe is not of the Lord.

**Sin.** David's sin with Bathsheba led to tragic consequences for many people, including himself. Sin always finds us out and damages us. Only by admitting our sin and repenting, as David did, can we be restored to fellowship with God.

Giants, Sauls, sin -- we all face these obstacles, and unless we overcome them, they will diminish severely our potential to find fulfillment in life. The great message in the story of David is that with God's help, David prevailed over all the obstacles. We, too, can prevail, for God will help anyone who believes and trusts in Him. Today, make sure you are not controlled by giants, Sauls, sin, or anything else besides the Spirit of God. Allow God to take charge of your life and you will have the power to do the hardest thing in the world: be yourself.

*Read: I Samuel 17:31-51; I Samuel 11:2-12:15; I Kings 2:1-4*

# YOU'RE IN THE WILL

*May you be strengthened with all power, according to his glorious might, for all endurance and patience with joy, giving thanks to the Father, who has qualified us to share in the inheritance of the saints in light (Colossians 1:11-12).*

Every wage-earning adult ought to have a will. A will is a legal document that enables us to distribute our possessions as we wish after we die. Some people hesitate to make out a will, fearing that even thinking about it could cause premature death. That is superstition. It is best to be prepared. Many people are secretive about who is named in their wills. Big surprises often stun those gathered at the reading, leaving family and friends honored and elated, or disappointed and angry.

You are in a will. God's will. If you confess Jesus Christ as Lord of your life, you are in God's will. Congratulations!

Paul writes, "For all who are led by the Spirit of God are sons of God. ...you have received the spirit of sonship. When we cry 'Abba! Father!' it is the Spirit himself bearing witness with our spirit that we are children of God, and if children, then heirs, heirs of God and fellow heirs of Christ" (Romans 8:14-17). Being heirs of God and fellow heirs with Christ means we have an inheritance that will never fade away, an inheritance nobody can take away from us, an inheritance that will not spoil or perish. It means our salvation has begun for us here on earth and will find its completion in Heaven. It means we have a guaranteed reservation in the house of many mansions and our reservation will be honored no matter what hour of the day or night we arrive. We are not in the will on any merit of our own, but through the love, sacrifice, work, life, death, and resurrection of Jesus Christ. If we belong to the Christian household of faith, we can count on being in the will, though we will not fully understand it until we get to the other side.

"Come, O blessed of my Father, inherit the kingdom prepared for you" (Matthew 25:34). You are included in the will of God. I hope you are honored and elated. You should be! God's will truly is the only will that matters.

*Read: I Peter 1:3-9; Hebrews 9:15-22; John 14:1-3*

## RECOGNIZING A CHRISTIAN EXPERIENCE

*After these sayings he took with him Peter and John and James, and went up on the mountain to pray. And as he was praying, the appearance of his countenance was altered, and his raiment became dazzling white. And behold, two men talked with him, Moses and Elijah (Luke 9:28-30).*

Have you ever experienced a mysterious, life-changing, faith-strengthening confrontation with Jesus? Peter, James, and John did when they witnessed the Transfiguration of Christ. There we see how to recognize a Christian experience.

**We cannot plan for it.** The three disciples went up the mountain unaware they would come down changed, transformed. Christian experiences occur at the least expected moment and place, almost as an accident or interruption. We can hope for them and expect them, but not plan for them.

**We cannot explain it.** Jesus's face shone; His raiment turned white; Moses and Elijah appeared; there was a cloud; a voice said, "This is my Son, my Chosen; listen to him!" (v. 35). The Transfiguration affirmed Jesus as the ultimate revelation of God and the fulfillment of Old Testament prophecy. Christian experiences are mystical and spooky. If we can completely explain an experience, it probably is not a Christian experience.

**We want to remember it.** Yearning to memorialize and prolong the glorious occasion, Peter said, "Master, it is well that we are here; let us make three booths, one for you and one for Moses and one for Elijah" (v. 33). When we have a Christian experience, we know we will never forget it.

**We will be hesitant at first to talk about it**. The disciples kept silent until later. After a Christian experience, we need time to think. God does not give Christian experiences so we can brag about them. He gives us those mighty, mysterious experiences to teach us to listen to Him. When we do, He is able to bring us to the next experience He has planned for us.

Christian experiences do not grow out of our wishes or even our prayers. They come when we have the courage to listen to Jesus and follow Him. Listen and follow today!

*Read: Luke 9:28-36; II Peter 1:16-18; Luke 3:21-22*

# HOW TO FIND YOUR LIFE

*"Whoever would save his life will lose it, and whoever loses his life for my sake will find it" (Matthew 16:25).*

God is the Creator of all things, and all things He creates, He creates good. He created you. He created me. "In him we live and move and have our being" (Acts 17:28). He created us as individuals. Each of us embodies a combination of abilities and limitations the like of which the world has never seen. He brought us to life at this time, at this place, for a reason.

God gives life, but He expects us to devote ourselves to finding our purpose in life. Granted, God could have made this information available to us in a more direct way. He could have tacked a little note to our diapers that read, "This is why I created you." He could have sent us away at age twelve to a nice camp and told us, "Here is the map for your destiny." He could have supplied an explicit vision proclaiming, "This is what I intend for you to do." But for most of us, there was no note on the diaper, no camp revelation, no astonishing vision.

So how do we find the meaning of life? First, through the Bible. "Thy word is a lamp to my feet and a light to my path" (Psalm 119:105). God gives us His Holy Word to enlighten us and guide us in the way we should go. Second, through the Word made flesh, Jesus Christ. We have the promise that if we become disciples of Jesus, He will lead us to an understanding of who we are. It is not easy to follow Jesus. It is probably the greatest challenge in all of life. To follow Jesus, we must make hard decisions and stick to them; run risks and go out not knowing where we are going; pick up crosses we may not want to carry; persevere through pain and confusion. It is difficult, but do not let that stop you! Discipleship is worth every hardship, for only in following Jesus will you discover the unique, magnificent destiny God has planned for you.

Find your life by giving your life to Jesus Christ. "I am the light of the world; he who follows me will not walk in darkness, but will have the light of life" (John 8:12). The light of life. Isn't that what you have been looking for all along?

*Read: Matthew 16:21-28; John 8:51; Isaiah 2:5*

# THE BASIN OF HOPE

*May the God of hope fill you with all joy and peace in believing, so that by the power of the Holy Spirit you may abound in hope (Romans 15:13).*

It is a principle of life that to know hope, one must first know hopelessness. Before we can have our basin of hope filled and overflowing, we must know the basin is empty. Hopelessness is hell. Tragedies beset us and we wonder where God is and why He has forsaken us. "My God, my God, why? Where are you?" Since the beginning of time, people have grappled with the reality of suffering. Some renounce God when they find no answers for their questions. Christians have questions, too, but Christians also have the knowledge that millions of people for nearly 2,000 years have endured extreme suffering, yet found peace and joy in Christ. Jesus Christ has overcome the world and He gives victory if we believe in Him.

If you have reached the bottom of your basin of hope, do not quit! The only way to go is up. God never leaves you nor forsakes you. He is present, though you may not recognize Him. Once you believe, even a little, that God is with you, new hope begins to fill the basin. Whatever your trial may be, God knows, cares, and wants to help. If you lean upon Him, He will enable you to triumph over tragedy. Even in death, we have hope. Paul wrote, "We would not have you ignorant ... concerning those who are asleep, that you may not grieve as others do who have no hope. For since we believe that Jesus died and rose again, even so, through Jesus, God will bring with him those who have fallen asleep... So we shall always be with the Lord" (I Thessalonians 4:13-14,17). I believe when we die, the first voice we hear in Heaven will be Jesus Christ calling us by name. We can never be separated from His love.

Hope is "a sure and steadfast anchor of the soul" (Hebrews 6:19). If you have triumphed over hopelessness and your basin is filled and overflowing, throw out an anchor to hurting souls and bring them to the God of hope. Help people suffering the hopelessness of hell to find the hope of Heaven in Jesus Christ.

*Read: I Thessalonians 4:13-18; Romans 5:1-5; Romans 12:12*

# WISE WORSHIP

*Going into the house they saw the child with Mary his mother, and they fell down and worshiped him (Matthew 2:11).*

As a pastor, I am interested in what happens in worship services. I sometimes try to form a mental image of those wise men falling down to worship baby Jesus. There are many questions about the wise men: how many there were, who they were, how long it took them to get to the manger. Tradition says there were three, but that is because of the three gifts. They may have been magi, kings, or astrologers. Some Bible scholars say they traveled for two years to see Christ. Can't you picture those distinguished men, though, kneeling before little Jesus? I wonder about that worship service: if it was on a Sabbath day, if they sang and prayed, if they sat in silence or shouted praise, if it took sixty minutes, ninety minutes, or (as some people would prefer) fifteen minutes. Matthew simply tells us they fell down and worshipped the Child.

Diversity in the structure of worship services is increasing. It used to be no matter what church you entered, you could be sure of the menu: hymns, prayers, sermon, offering. Times have changed. All sorts of things are happening, some good, some not so good; some impressive, some oppressive. When I see church bulletins, the contrast amazes me: some have four pages on the order of worship and some have none. Worship is taking varied types of expression. The least innovation upsets some people, while others think any variation is just fine.

Amid the changes, remember one unchanging fact. Wise worship is not merely a weekly observance. It is a way of life, something we are to do daily. Wise worship is trusting God even when we do not like what happens, believing in Him when our instincts tell us not to, honoring Him for who He is, thanking Him for blessings, being willing to change, giving gifts out of gratitude, seeking the Lord while He may be found, calling on Him while He is near, and loving Him with all the heart, soul, mind, and strength. Like the wise men of old, fall down and worship Christ, not just on Sunday, but every day.

*Read: Matthew 2:1-12; Psalm 106:19-23; Revelation 22:1-9*

## ABRAHAM, THE FRIEND OF GOD

*"Look toward heaven, and number the stars, if you are able to number them." Then he said to him, "So shall your descendants be." And he believed the Lord; and he reckoned it to him as righteousness (Genesis 15:5-6).*

Abraham is a model of faith for all generations.

There he was, old enough for Social Security, with a wife, Sarah, almost his age. Suddenly he got the idea God was calling him to a covenant relationship and the establishment of a new nation. "Sarah, pack the suitcases. We're leaving home to go to a land God will show us, and we're going to be a great nation!" Sarah didn't know if the Reuben sandwich was backing up on him, if she should consult the local psychiatrist, or if he was in the third stage of senility, but being an obedient wife, she said, "Okay, Abe, I'm with you." After a while, they got a message that Sarah would have a baby. Could a couple so old possibly have a child? They sure could; Isaac was born! Later, God said, "Abraham, go up into the hills of Moriah. Take your boy, Isaac. Take some wood and a knife. I want you to offer your son as a burnt offering." Off they went. Isaac said, "Hey, dad, where is the sacrifice?" "The Lord will provide, son, the Lord will provide." The Lord did provide. As Abraham was ready to bring the knife down on Isaac, the Lord said, "Stop! Look in the thicket." A ram took the place of Isaac. Abraham passed the test of faith and the Lord blessed him mightily.

Abraham, "the friend of God" (James 2:23) and "the father of us all" (Romans 4:16), went out not knowing where he was going, walking not by sight but by faith. "In hope he believed against hope, that he should become the father of many nations; as he had been told... No distrust made him waver concerning the promise of God, but he grew strong in his faith as he gave glory to God, fully convinced that God was able to do what he had promised" (Romans 4:18,20-21). If you want to be the friend of God, follow Abraham's example by trusting in the promises of God and living in obedience to His will. Perhaps your life, too, will be a model of faith for all generations.

*Read: Genesis 12:1-9, 21:1-7, 22:1-19; Romans 4:13-25*

# SURPRISE!

*Now while he was serving as priest before God when his division was on duty, according to the custom of the priesthood, it fell to him by lot to enter the temple of the Lord and burn incense. And the whole multitude of the people were praying outside at the hour of incense. And there appeared to him an angel of the Lord standing on the right side of the altar of incense. And Zechariah was troubled when he saw him, and fear fell upon him (Luke 1:8-12).*

Some people like surprises. Others do not. Zechariah was a preacher who experienced a startling surprise in the middle of a worship service, and he did not seem to like it.

In biblical times the descendants of Aaron, Moses's brother, officiated as priests. In Judea there were 24,000 priests divided into sections of 1,000. They took turns fulfilling priestly functions in the temple at Jerusalem and determined who served by casting lots. When Zechariah drew the lot, it was a great day, a tremendous honor. But during the worship service, something happened that he did not anticipate or expect: he met the Lord! The angel Gabriel revealed that Elizabeth, his wife, would bear a son who would prepare the hearts of people for the coming Messiah. Yet instead of rejoicing and believing, Zechariah was frightened and doubtful. Because of his disbelief, God took away his voice for nine months.

All of us come to worship services with different levels of expectation. If God spoke to you in church someday, would you be just as shocked and overwhelmed as Zechariah? If only we went to church expecting to meet God! Of course, meeting God can be a frightening experience. We cannot be receptors of God's Holy Spirit without being filled with fear and trembling. But God expects us to rise above fear and, when mysterious things happen, believe what we see, hear, and feel is the Holy Spirit of God being born anew within us.

In your next worship service, you might experience the power and presence of God as you never have before. Try not to be surprised. Simply say, "Thank you, Lord!"

*Read: Luke 1:5-23; Habakkuk 2:20; Psalm 77:11-14*

171

# A RISK WORTH TAKING

*Let us then pursue what makes for peace and for mutual upbuilding (Romans 14:19).*

We all like to think we are good communicators. Actually, most of us are not. Poor communication is a problem throughout the world. Nation cannot speak with nation. Management cannot speak with labor. Parents, children, friends, neighbors, church members -- we all seem to have trouble opening up and talking honestly. The reason many marriages end in divorce is not that couples are not in love, but that they cannot communicate their love to one another.

Communication is scary and a big risk. It only can succeed when people are courageous enough to say things they may not want to say to other people who are courageous enough to hear things they may not want to hear. It must be done kindly and politely, without fear of retaliation, recrimination, or desertion. It is difficult to get the words out, and when it is over, there frequently is hurt, shock, anger, denial, and pain. Cynics say, "That's just plain dumb. It's masochistic, putting yourself through so much needless torture." It could seem that way, except for one thing: it works! Heart-to-heart communication makes relationships more caring, joyous, and stable than they ever were before. I have seen it happen time and time again.

If somebody you love begins to share deep concerns with you, do the responsible, loving thing. Keep quiet! Let that brave individual speak and tell you everything. You might not like what you hear, but you have reached a crucial moment of honesty. You now have an opportunity to get to the heart of a problem and move on. Just embrace that person and say, "I love you, and nothing will separate us." God will help you get over the pain. And if you feel led to speak to someone you love about matters of importance to you, be bold and do it.

To enjoy relationships that grow healthier and happier and stronger all the time, pursue what makes for peace and for mutual upbuilding through honest, loving communication. Yes, it is scary and a big risk, but it is a risk worth taking.

*Read: Proverbs 17:1; John 15:12-17; Colossians 3:12-25*

# A TRILOGY FOR PRAYER

*Hear my cry, O God, listen to my prayer; from the end of the earth I call to thee, when my heart is faint (Psalm 61:1-2).*

Prayer is the most powerful force the Spirit of God gives us to use, but prayer is so simple that it is difficult. To be effective, consider prayer a trilogy: pre-prayer time, prayer time, and post-prayer time. What we do before, during, and after prayer determines the power we know in prayer.

**Pre-prayer time.** Our prayer power depends upon what we believe about God before we go to prayer. If we picture God as an angry deity or a demanding boss, prayer will be frightening, inefficient, sheer drudgery. Jesus told us to look unto God as a Father who loves and understands us, wants us to be happy, healthy, and whole, and desires the best for us. He dwells in us, knows our needs, and wants us to succeed. Come to prayer believing the Lord is your loving Heavenly Father.

**Prayer time.** Use the ASK Method: Ask, Seek, Knock. Ask for help when you need it; be specific with your concerns. Seek, determined that you will find; be tenacious, serious, and intense. Knock, knowing it will be opened; acknowledge your total dependence on the Lord and trust Him to help you. When you come believing, you soon will be receiving.

**Post-prayer time.** Expect an answer. Believe the answer is on the way. It may not be the answer you want or anticipate, but God will answer your prayer. Whatever answer He gives ultimately will be the best answer for you and everyone else.

Probably none of us will live up to our potential prayer power, but we should keep trying. The more we use our prayer potential, the more power we will have. Our prayer lives grow deeper and stronger when we practice the whole trilogy of prayer. Be willing to experiment. Prayer is not a packaged product. Prayer is a process, a pilgrimage. Call unto God. He will hear your cry, listen to your prayer, and strengthen you when your heart is faint. Today, pray as you never prayed before. Tomorrow, do it again. Do it every day. That is a way you will come to know the power of God in prayer.

*Read: Luke 11:1-13; Psalm 17:6-7; Proverbs 15:29*

# PRUNING AND PICKING

*"I am the true vine, and my Father is the vinedresser. Every branch of mine that bears no fruit, he takes away, and every branch that does bear fruit he prunes, that it may bear more fruit" (John 15:1-2).*

Christians are called "to lead a life worthy of the Lord, fully pleasing to him, bearing fruit in every good work and increasing in the knowledge of God" (Colossians 1:10). Bearing good fruit glorifies our heavenly Father. Jesus said, "You did not choose me, but I chose you and appointed you that you should go and bear fruit and that your fruit should abide" (John 15:16). To produce abiding fruit, we need to abide in Jesus by allowing His Word to abide in us. When His Word enters our minds and hearts, Jesus abides in us. I must warn you, though: as God's Word takes control and we begin to see the world through His eyes, two things will happen.

**We are going to get pruned.** God prunes us through His Holy Word. We come to see ourselves as we really are, and the truth stings and jolts us. "Ouch! That's me the writer is talking about!" God is not trying to wound us, but to help us grow stronger. Unless He prunes us back and cuts out the dead wood, we never will be as productive as we were meant to be. Branches that do not produce are taken away. Those that are productive are pruned so they can bear more fruit.

**We are going to get picked on and picked at.** Not only will God prune us, but people will pick on us and pick at us. People will make fun of us, put us down, and try to make us waver in faith. The Psalmist wrote, "Many are my persecutors and my adversaries, but I do not swerve from thy testimonies" (Psalm 119:157). Despite the picking, we must never swerve from God, for apart from Jesus Christ we can do nothing.

Pruning and picking are painful, but God uses them to bring forth the harvest. "Let us not grow weary in well-doing, for in due season we shall reap, if we do not lose heart" (Galatians 6:9). Trust the vinedresser. He created you to produce good fruit and He will enable you to do it if you do not lose heart.

*Read: John 15:1-11; Isaiah 5:1-7; Matthew 3:10*

# A WINNING SITUATION

*"It is more blessed to give than to receive" (Acts 20:35).*

Can you think of many situations in life in which everyone involved comes out a winner? I know of one: the act of giving. God intends that we share our time, talents, and treasures generously and cheerfully. When we do, wishing we could give even more, everybody is blessed. Everybody wins!

**Recipients.** The needs of people are met through our gifts. More importantly, recipients experience a new understanding of love and hope. Sometimes people who are struggling think nobody cares. When we help, their faith in humanity grows and they begin to thank God for gifts they receive. "Every good endowment and every perfect gift is from above, coming down from the Father" (James 1:17). Many needy people do not believe that biblical truth until they experience God's love the through practical, caring, generosity of Christians.

**Givers.** I do not know why, but when we give, we feel great. I guess it is because we are born to give. If we give happily, we live happily. Generous giving means we are putting a deed to our creed and showing that our profession of faith works. Never should we feel superior to others if we are richly blessed. "What have you that you did not receive? If then you received it, why do you boast as if it were not a gift?" (I Corinthians 4:7). We are given our blessings to share. This responsibility is not a hardship, but a delight. It is a joy to know we are helping God build His Kingdom on earth by giving hope to hurting people whom we may not even know.

**God.** God is blessed. People, both recipients and givers, find themselves thanking God for the opportunity to know and show His love in action. "It is good to give thanks to the Lord, to sing praises to thy name, O Most High; to declare thy steadfast love in the morning, and thy faithfulness by night" (Psalm 92:1-2). We glorify God both when we give gifts and when we thank Him for gifts we receive in His name.

God loves cheerful givers. Stinginess is for losers. Be a cheerful, generous giver and create a winning situation today.

*Read: II Corinthians 9:6-15; Matthew 6:1-4; Proverbs 28:27*

# ON BEING A FRIEND

*"Greater love has no man than this, that a man lay down his life for his friends. You are my friends if you do what I command you. No longer do I call you servants, for the servant does not know what his master is doing; but I have called you friends, for all that I have heard from my Father I have made known to you" (John 15:13-15).*

Friendship is so special and rare that many people miss it. They settle for superficial acquaintanceships devoid of forthright communication and love. It is a shame, because all of us have the potential to develop and enjoy enduring friendships if we learn from Jesus what it takes to be a friend.

Friendship begins by obeying the commands of Christ. To be the friend of Jesus and others, keep His commands to love and forgive. We have the power to love anybody and forgive anything. When we love and forgive, friendship flourishes.

The greatest love we can show is in laying down our lives for someone else. Most of us will never be required to die for another, but to be a friend we must be ready to suffer "little deaths": laying down our plans for people and not manipulating them in the name of love; laying down our calendars and watches to wait when they are late or slow; laying down our masks to be real; laying down our megaphones and not betraying secrets and confidences. These sacrifices are insignificant compared with the joys of true friendship.

Do not blame the world if you have trouble finding friends. Having friends and not having friends are choices. You decide which it will be. If you do harm, hold grudges, and expect people to cater to you, I doubt you will have many friends. To be a friend, live like Jesus: be loving, forgiving, and self-sacrificing. Your best friend, Jesus Christ, will help you make friends if you pray, "Lord, help me today to be a friend of yours, a friend of everybody, and a friend to myself."

With the courage to obey God's commands and the strength to lay down your life for others, you will forge those special, rare friendships that begin on earth and last throughout eternity.

*Read: John 15:8-17; Psalm 25:14; Proverbs 17:17*

## HOW TO LOOK AT THE WORLD

*"A disciple is not above his teacher, nor a servant above his master; it is enough for the disciple to be like his teacher, and the servant to be like his master" (Matthew 10:24-25).*

Basic psychology tells us we eventually become like whatever we look at. We turn into whatever we concentrate on. If we look at naughty, vulgar, obscene books and movies, we become dirty old men or women. If we look at a tangled mess, in the home, office, or wherever we are, we become messy. The same principle is true in the realm of theology. If we look at Jesus Christ as our teacher and master, we become like Him. We begin to look at the world through His eyes. Jesus said, "I did not come to judge the world but to save the world" (John 12:47). Jesus Christ wants the world to be saved, but many people judge the world as an abominable place that ought to be condemned. Jesus Christ loves all humanity, but many people judge that humanity is worthless, except for themselves and a select group of their favorite companions.

To look at the world as Jesus did is to look upon people as individuals who can be changed and transformed by God's love. Jesus, our teacher and master, expects us to look at everyone with kindness, love, and forgiveness. When scribes and Pharisees planned to stone an adulterous woman, Jesus said, "Let him who is without sin among you be the first to throw a stone at her" (John 8:7). The people left, and Jesus said to her, "Neither do I condemn you; go, and do not sin again" (v. 11). His example teaches us to be gracious to people who make mistakes; to be tender and understanding; to see people's potential, not their past; to offer hope of a new start. Jesus always loved and helped people, as He expects us to do.

How do you look at the world today? Do you think it should be condemned, or do you want to see it saved? If you view other people as stupid, simple, silly, shiftless, and sinful, you may be right, but love them anyway! Be a true disciple and servant of Jesus Christ and look at the world as He does, not with harsh condemnation, but with unending love.

*Read: John 8:2-11; Luke 6:37-38; Psalm 34:22*

# THE REBEL WITHIN

*"If you will not hearken to the voice of the Lord, but rebel against the commandment of the Lord, then the hand of the Lord will be against you" (I Samuel 12:15).*

If you are in the habit of talking to yourself, be careful with the advice and suggestions you give, for there is a voice within that can get you into trouble. It is the voice of the rebel, the old Adam. That voice will tell you to be disobedient to Jesus, to be unfaithful to His commands, to go ahead and do whatever you feel like doing. The rebel whispers, "Don't take Jesus seriously. He's not coming back for a while. Live for yourself!" If you have ever been someplace you should not have been, doing something you should not have done, all the while hoping no one in the world would ever find out, it is because you listened too much to the voice of the rebel within.

"The voice of the Lord is powerful" (Psalm 29:4), but the voice of evil is strong as well. Underestimating its power can lead to ruin. Peter warns, "Your adversary the devil prowls around like a roaring lion, seeking some one to devour" (I Peter 5:8). It does not matter how long we have been redeemed by the blood of Jesus Christ and sanctified by His Holy Spirit; the roaring lion stalks us to the grave. That does not mean we must be devoured by it. "The reason the Son of God appeared was to destroy the works of the devil" (I John 3:8). God gives victory over that rebellious voice through Christ. In His earthly ministry, Jesus demonstrated authority over demons, and unclean spirits recognized Him as the Son of God even when the Jews did not. By believing in Jesus, depending upon His Holy Spirit, and being obedient to His Word rather than our desires, we can overcome evil and say with conviction, "Satan, get behind me. I do not march to you. I listen to the Lord!"

If you enjoy talking to yourself, go ahead and do it. You might be the most stimulating conversationalist you know! Just make sure you realize there are different voices inside you, and be very careful to follow, obey, and hearken to the voice of the Lord, and not to the voice of the rebel within.

*Read: Psalm 29; Luke 4:31-37; John 12:31-32*

## CAPTAIN BEST FAITH

*When Jesus heard this he marveled at him, and turned and said to the multitude that followed him, "I tell you, not even in Israel have I found such faith" (Luke 7:9).*

Only twice in the Bible is Jesus described as being amazed, surprised, filled with marvel. First, He marveled at the disbelief of family and friends in Nazareth, His hometown. Later, He marveled at the belief of a Roman centurion, a man who was not a professed disciple. Faith at its worst and faith at its best: both caused Jesus to marvel.

Since most of us tend to lose or not use our faith, we can learn from the centurion. I call him Captain Best Faith. A Roman living with Jews, unwanted, resented, different in race and religion, Captain Best Faith endured horrible conditions, yet he made the decision to do right and treat people with love. When a servant fell ill, he sent a humble message to Jesus asking for help. "Lord, do not trouble yourself, for I am not worthy to have you come under my roof; ... say the word, and let my servant be healed" (Luke 7:6-7). Captain Best Faith accepted the power of Jesus's word, believing Jesus had the authority of God behind Him and would do what was best.

Do we live up to the faith of the centurion? It is easy to let bad situations tempt us to be indifferent. Often we are too proud to ask for help. At times we doubt the power of God's Word and question Him when things turn out differently than we would like. That is closer to worst faith than best faith.

The centurion was captain of his own faith, but he had no more faith in his life than the people of Nazareth did or than we do now. We all have faith, for faith is a gift of God's grace. The difference is that some people use it for the best, and some people do not use it, which makes it the worst. We do not need to pray for more faith, because God has given us all the faith we ever will need. Rather, we should pray fervently, "Lord, help me to use my faith," then use it and make it the best.

Jesus watches everything we say and do, today and every day. I wonder if He marvels at the kind of faith He finds in us.

*Read: Luke 7:1-10; Mark 6:1-6; Hebrews 3:12*

# THE PREACHING PROFESSION

*Preach the word (II Timothy 4:2).*

People often like to tell me I'm in a great profession because I only have to work one day a week. I usually respond, "That's right, and only one hour that day!" Sometimes the humor escapes me, though, when one twelve-hour day runs into another and another. At times, too, people's reactions to my profession are a little hard to take. Preachers are respected by many people, but shunned by others like the flu.

Preaching is the power God has blessed from the beginning of time for salvation. People cannot be helped spiritually without it. "How are men to call upon him in whom they have not believed? And how are they to believe in him of whom they have never heard? And how are they to hear without a preacher?" (Romans 10:14). Preaching the message of redemption brings hope, release, and new life to the poor, not only people poor in material possessions, but people with a poor quality of life, a poor self-image, a poor attitude, or a poor concept of God, Jesus Christ, His Holy Spirit, and the Church.

The preaching profession is powerful. The preaching profession is important. And I do not mean to shock you, but you are called to be part of it. That's right! In God's eyes, all of us, no matter how we earn our living, are called to be preachers of His Word. Jesus tells disciples, "Go into all the world and preach the gospel to the whole creation" (Mark 16:15). We are "ambassadors for Christ, God making his appeal through us" (II Corinthians 5:20). Your pulpit might be different from mine, but if you confess Jesus as Lord and Savior, God commissions you to be a preacher in the Body of Christ and counts on you to spread the Good News of the Gospel through your words, actions, compassion, and love.

"As for you, go and proclaim the kingdom of God" (Luke 9:60). Welcome to the preaching profession! When you take your commission as a preacher of the Word seriously, you find you have to give more than one hour of one day of each week. You have to give your life. Don't worry, though. It's worth it.

*Read: I Corinthians 9:16-23; Matthew 24:14; Luke 24:44-53*

# CATCH THAT VISION

*I will take my stand to watch, and station myself on the tower, and look forth to see what he will say to me, and what I will answer concerning my complaint. And the Lord answered me: "Write the vision; make it plain upon tablets, so he may run who reads it. For still the vision awaits its time; it hastens to the end -- it will not lie. If it seem slow, wait for it; it will surely come, it will not delay" (Habakkuk 2:1-3).*

God communicates with people through His Word, messengers, prophecy, dreams, and visions. Visions are like dreams except we have them when we are awake. A vision is God's way of showing us through the eye, either the physical eye or the insight of the inner eye, what He wants us to do. A vision from God cannot be bought, sought, or taught. It can only be caught! Habakkuk, who prophesied during the time of Jeremiah, helps us understand how to catch a vision from God.

**Wait and watch.** Visions do not depend upon physical ability or mental ability or even spiritual ability, but rather, upon availability. If you do not have a vision yet, wait upon the Lord and watch for His message. It may be coming today.

**Weigh it.** When you think God has sent you a vision, ask questions to be certain it is of the Lord. Does the vision glorify God, help other people, and bring fulfillment to the talents and gifts God has given you? Is it in complete accord with biblical principles? God cannot lie. If you get a vision that is contrary to Scriptural truth, you can be assured it is not sent from God.

**Write it.** I am not sure why, but when we write a vision down, we become more committed to it. Tell people what you have seen. Explain it to them. Do not keep it a secret.

**Work it.** Give it action! A vision without action is absolutely worthless. When you have a vision and combine it with energetic action, you can help to change the world.

If you have received a vision from God, work it and make it a reality. If a vision comes to you today, weigh it, write it, and be faithful to it. If it has not come yet, wait and watch. Always be ready to catch that vision, for it will surely come.

*Read: Numbers 12:6; Joel 2:28-29; Acts 2:17-18*

## SECRETS OF CONTENTMENT

*I have learned, in whatever state I am, to be content (Philippians 4:11).*

Ever find yourself longing for "the good old days"? Many of us imagine contentment was easier to attain in the past, but history shows that people of all eras have faced enormous obstacles to inner tranquillity. When Paul wrote to the church at Philippi, he was jailed in a Roman prison. Paul's secrets of contentment can help us learn to be calm, serene, and more confident in coping with difficulties.

**Rejoice at all times.** Paul is not telling us to rejoice because we are sick, depressed, grieving, or persecuted. We rejoice because the Almighty Lord is with us and we are not going through those hard trials alone. God is closer than hands and feet, always guarding, protecting, loving, and leading us.

**Pray for all things.** Some people think because God knows everything, He should just solve our dilemmas and heartaches before we even ask. Yet prayer shows we recognize God's presence, and recognizing His presence helps Him to help us. Parents realize that pushing well-meaning advice on children before they ask for help results in disaster. Once children ask, parents can freely give the necessary assistance.

**Be gentle.** We cannot find contentment if we are angry, vengeful, and surly. Instead, we should live with meekness.

**Think about good things.** No one would suspect it from the news, but millions of people are not in jail, on drugs, or in hospitals. Think about what is pure, beautiful, and excellent.

**Be thankful.** We should not moan and gripe over what we lack, but be grateful every day for our countless blessings.

You can learn to be content in whatever state you are today. Contentment is not an unattainable goal and the secrets of contentment really are no secret. They are right in the Bible for anyone to see and use in life. Why long for the good old days when you can enjoy great new days today and tomorrow? Contentment is born in the mind, so make up your mind this moment to be content and simply rejoice in God's grace.

*Read: Philippians 4:4-13; I Timothy 6:6-8; Luke 11:11-13*

# THE BIGGEST HEARTBREAK

*"O my son  Absalom, my son, my son Absalom!  Would I had
died instead of you, O Absalom, my son, my son!" (II Samuel
18:33).*

In over thirty-five years of ministry, I have counseled many
men who experienced business crises, social disgrace, and
divorce, but what seemed to break their hearts most is the
realization that they failed their children.  Even successful,
distinguished, prominent men live with broken hearts because
they feel like failures as a dad.  It happens all the time.  It
happened to David.  David had it all: money, intelligence,
power, prestige, influence, good looks.  Yet he was a failure
with his family, especially with his son, Absalom.  They had
trouble with competition; Absalom wanted to take over his
dad's empire.  They had trouble with communication; for two
years, they lived near one another in Jerusalem, but neither
took the initiative to say, "We've got a problem.  Let's fix it."
The result was a needless war in which thousands died,
Absalom was killed, and David's life was shattered.

Tragically, many fathers and children today still do not take
steps to heal broken relationships while there is time.  In every
estrangement, between family members, friends, or neighbors,
a moment can come when reconciliation is no longer possible.
Death claims one person, and the other struggles for years,
perhaps a lifetime, with guilt, sorrow, and regret.  Can't you
feel the terrible pain and anguish in David's mournful,
heartbroken cry over Absalom?  That is what happens when
estrangements persist.  The hurt lasts beyond the grave.

The Psalmist wrote, "My soul melts away for sorrow"
(Psalm 119:28).  If your soul is melting away because you are
separated from someone you love, if there is any broken
relationship in your life, do something about it now.  Make a
move toward reconciliation.  Maybe you think it is unfair you
should be the one to act first.  I offer no guarantee the other
individual will respond to you in love, but try it, please.  Try it.

Do not let that big, irreparable heartbreak happen to you.

*Read: II Samuel 18;  Proverbs 18:14;  I Peter 3:10-11*

## WRESTLING WITH THE LORD

*Jacob was left alone; and a man wrestled with him until the breaking of the day (Genesis 32:24).*

If you want to stay away from a confrontation with the living Lord, do not pray! Prayer is dangerous and powerful, for prayer can lead to a wrestling match with God. It happened to Jacob. Struggling with guilt and indecision, Jacob prayed for help beyond his own strength, and his prayer led to a frightening, life-changing encounter with the Lord.

The same thing could happen to any one of us. Like Jacob, we can survive and grow stronger from a wrestling match with God, but the skirmish is scary. The Lord usually comes when we are alone, tired, overworked, lost in darkness and gloom. He will not always identify Himself and we may not recognize Him as God. He may be disguised in an issue we do not want to face, a struggle with sin, or a person we dislike. We never know how, when, or in what form God will wrestle with us. He often responds to prayer in mystical, spooky ways.

Are you thinking you should give up prayer? Don't! Our loving God wants you to win the match! He wrestles with us not to destroy us, but to save us and make us winners. We win when we allow Him to change us; when we realize we are blessed to be a blessing; when we understand our lives are meant to help people; when we let God make a difference in us that all can see. Though Jacob left the wrestling match with his thigh out of joint, he also left with a new name, a new attitude, new life, and new love for his Creator. Later, God appeared to Jacob and said, "A nation and a company of nations shall come from you" (Genesis 35:11). Because Jacob had the courage to wrestle with God, he was blessed with a great destiny.

Some people wrestle all their lives instead of coming to a decision. Do not make that mistake. You have a part in the conversion God wants to see in you, for you have the power to decide when the wrestling match will end. It ends as soon as you allow God to make you a new person who can help transform the world with love. If you have been wrestling with the Lord, end the match before the breaking of another day.

*Read:  Genesis 32:22-32;  Genesis 35:9-15;  I Corinthians 5:17*

184

# THE BULL MOOSE PRINCIPLE

*"Prepare to meet your God" (Amos 4:12).*

Many of us are acquainted with the antics of the Alaskan bull moose. In the fall mating season, the males buck heads, clashing and grinding at one another's antlers in a fight for dominance. The one with the strongest, mightiest antlers wins. What we need to remember about the bull moose is that his antlers are grown and developed in the summer, before the fall mating season. Though the battle is fought in the fall, it really is won in the summer. When we translate the bull moose principle to the spiritual realm, it means that sustaining faith and strength to triumph over trials in life are best developed before they are needed. Preparation -- that is what counts.

Living in our comfortable world and secure neighborhoods, we often overlook the fact that Jesus Christ is coming again. He came once and many people missed Him, but nobody will miss Him next time! He will come suddenly and there will be a physical separation in our midst. Some people will be lifted up and others will wonder, "Where did they go?" It will be too late then to run to our Bibles. Those who are prepared will be with Jesus Christ forever. Those who are not will be excluded.

Incredibly, many people throughout history have claimed to know God's timetable. In anticipation, they sold belongings, gathered on mountains, and awaited His imminent arrival, only to be disappointed and embarrassed. The plain teaching of the Bible is that no one can predict the day or time of Jesus's return. He will come unexpectedly, as a thief in the night. "Watch therefore, for you do not know on what day your Lord is coming. But know this, that if the householder had known in what part of the night the thief was coming, he would have watched, and would not have let his house be broken into. Therefore you also must be ready; for the Son of man is coming at an hour you do not expect" (Matthew 24:42-44). Clearly, we must be watchful, ready, and alert every moment.

Are you prepared today to meet your God? Do not be bull-headed. Learn from the bull moose. Be prepared!

*Read: Matthew 24:36-44; Acts 1:6-11; Luke 12:40*

# YOUR WORDS ARE YOU

*He who guards his mouth preserves his life; he who opens wide his lips comes to ruin (Proverbs 13:3).*

If each of us today were to listen to our words as carefully as other people do, we might be in for a rude awakening. We like to recall the sweet, kind, loving things we say and ignore the thoughtless, nasty remarks that slip out. Other people do not. People around us listen all the time. They may know more about us than we do! Jesus said, "Out of the abundance of the heart the mouth speaks" (Matthew 12:34). Every time we open our mouths, we reveal the spiritual condition of the heart. It does not take long for people to figure out if we are happy or sad, positive or negative, grateful or grumbling, constructive or critical, sound or sick. Foolishly, we seldom take time to evaluate the true nature and effect of our words.

Listen to yourself today, not only to what you say but how you say it. That is you! What you say reveals your inner self. Be especially vigilant over words spoken carelessly: idle words, unguarded words, words you speak in private or in the presence of loved ones who will forgive you for anything. "I tell you, on the day of judgment men will render account for every careless word they utter; for by your words you will be justified, and by your words you will be condemned" (Matthew 12:36-37). Think about that. Your words control your destiny.

Get to know the spiritual condition of your heart by monitoring everything that comes out of your mouth. Consider it a spiritual cardiogram, and do not be astonished if you discover you have a spiritual heart deficiency. Most of us do. Thank God, there is a cure: God's Holy Word. When we study and obey His Word, Jesus begins to treat the sickness in our hearts, but the Master Physician can only heal us if we invite Him in and entrust our lives to His transforming care.

Is your spiritual heart in good shape today, or could you use a little help and healing from the Word of God? If you think you are doing just fine without the Word of God, you need more help and healing than you realize.

*Read: Matthew 12:33-37; James 3:5-12; Proverbs 10:11-14*

# OVERCOMING THE GREEN-EYED MONSTER

*If you have bitter jealousy and selfish ambition in your hearts, do not boast and be false to the truth. This wisdom is not such as comes down from above, but is earthly, unspiritual, devilish. For where jealousy and selfish ambition exist, there will be disorder and every vile practice (James 3:14-16).*

Jealousy is known as the green-eyed monster, and what a monster it is! We see it in people who rejoice in other people's sorrow and deplore other people's happiness. People reveal jealousy through their petty actions, snide facial expressions, mean words, and vulgar gossip. Jealousy comes from self-love, inferiority, and fear that someone else might get away with something or get something we think we should have. It strains relationships and divides groups, but does the greatest damage to the jealous person, eating away like a cancer. Saul's jealousy of David led to sickness, hatred, and insanity. "Jealousy is cruel as the grave" (Song of Solomon 8:6). Unfortunately, every human being is susceptible to jealousy.

Paul cites jealousy as a sign of spiritual immaturity. "While there is jealousy and strife among you, are you not of the flesh, and behaving like ordinary men?" (I Corinthians 3:3). Overcoming the green-eyed monster takes more than will-power, clenched fists, and tough skin. We find strength to conquer jealousy only through heavenly wisdom. Spiritual, godly wisdom is poured into us from above, bringing purity, peace, gentleness, openness, mercy, stability, and sincerity. Earthly jealousy simply cannot coexist with heavenly wisdom.

James tells us God will give wisdom to all who ask for it in faith. "If any of you lacks wisdom, let him ask God, who gives to all men generously and without reproaching, and it will be given him. But let him ask in faith, with no doubting, for he who doubts is like a wave of the sea that is driven and tossed by the wind" (James 1:5-6). If jealousy is eating away at you today, pray, "Please, Lord, give me your wisdom," and believe His wisdom will come. When the light of heavenly wisdom shines in you, the green-eyed monster will vanish.

*Read: James 3:13-18; I Samuel 18:8-30; Proverbs 27:4*

# FREEWAYS TO FAITH

*These are written that you may believe that Jesus is the Christ, the Son of God, and that believing you may have life in his name (John 20:31).*

There are three ways to come to faith.

**Seeing.** Some people want to see Jesus with their own eyes before they believe. After Jesus's resurrection, His own disciples hid in fear behind closed doors until Jesus appeared visibly among them. "Then the disciples were glad when they saw the Lord" (John 20:20). Today, people who want to see Jesus could have a long time to wait, because they will not see Him till He comes again or till they meet Him in Heaven. The seeing way to faith is jumpy, jerky, and time-consuming. The time to believe in Jesus is now! If we do not know Jesus here on earth, we will never recognize Him on the other side.

**Demanding.** Other people want Jesus to prove Himself by meeting criteria they set up. They demand a healing or some other experience. Thomas said, "Unless I see in his hands the print of the nails, and place my finger in the mark of the nails, and place my hand in his side, I will not believe" (v. 25). Demanding people are grumpy, glum, and negative. They rob themselves of the peace and power Jesus wants to give now.

**Believing.** Simple belief. Why be jumpy or grumpy when we can just be happy and believe? The Bible tells us to believe as a little child. How sad that children initially trust people, but must be taught to be suspicious and wary! Belief is more natural than unbelief. We simply can choose to believe God loves us, Jesus Christ has redeemed us, and Holy Spirit is alive in our lives and has great things in store for us. It is not complicated or difficult if we just trust God's Holy Word.

The three ways to faith are freeways. We are free to choose any way we want to take. If we rely on seeing or demanding, though, we may not travel far. Those freeways can be dead ends. Choose the believing freeway and use the Bible as your road map. You will never lose your way. Instead, you will find "the way, and the truth, and the life" (John 14:6).

*Read: John 20:19-31; Mark 10:15; I John 3:23*

## YOUR DARKEST MOMENTS

*"Fear not, for I have redeemed you; I have called you by name, you are mine. When you pass through the waters I will be with you; and through the rivers, they shall not overwhelm you; when you walk through fire you shall not be burned, and the flame shall not consume you. For I am the Lord your God"* (Isaiah 43:1-3).

Those dark, lonely hours before the dawn of a new day seem unending when we are hurting. In the silent shadows of the night, storms appear overwhelming; fiery trials, all-consuming. We cry, "Where is the Lord? Is He here? Why can't I recognize Jesus in my life?" That is what makes our darkest moments so painful. It is not the darkness of the sky. It is our inability to recognize the presence of Jesus Christ.

I wonder if we would recognize Jesus if He physically came down to earth today and passed us on the street. I wonder how we will recognize Him in eternity. Sometimes it is difficult to recognize the Lord, especially in our dark, lonely hours. We know He reveals Himself in His Holy Word and through creation, but Jesus tells us to look for His presence in people as well. "As you did it to one of the least of these my brethren, you did it to me" (Matthew 25:40). We learn to recognize Jesus when we spend our earthly lives trying to see Him in other people. Look for Jesus Christ in poor people who need to be fed and clothed, in lonesome people who need a kind word, in sick people who need comfort, in lost people who need direction. Look for Jesus Christ also in people who feed and clothe you, who give you a kind word, who comfort you and guide you. If we are not able to recognize Jesus Christ in people here on earth, we might never recognize Him at all.

Jesus is everywhere: in His Word, in creation, in other people, and in you. He tells His disciples, "Take heart, it is I; have no fear" (Mark 6:50). In dismal, difficult times, believe in His constant, benevolent presence. Once you trust Him, your darkest moments will begin to brighten, the light will break through, and the Son will shine in your life, for you are His.

*Read: Mark 6:45-51; Matthew 1:23; Psalm 124:8*

# THOSE LITTLE GREEN APPLES

*We are to grow up in every way (Ephesians 4:15).*

Christian faith requires a lifetime of growth. Growth, both physical and spiritual, is a mystery nobody fully understands.

I have apple trees at my home. When I look at the apples in June, they are small and green. They are young, undeveloped, unripe. If I were to pick them and eat them, they would be bitter and sour, full of acid. They are not very tasty that time of year. They need to grow. During July and August, the sun of the sky beats down upon them and the soaking rains pour. By autumn, the big red apples will be there. It takes the sun of the summer to bring those little green apples to maturity.

Sometimes followers of Jesus, especially those new to faith, realize somewhat fearfully they are not too joyful, not too strong, not too sure about things. It seems as though every believer has firmer faith, livelier hope, and greater love than they do. They wonder if they even belong with other Christians. If you ever have those doubts, it does not mean you are not a Christian. It may be simply that you are a little young, a little green, a little unripe, a little bitter and sour and full of acid. You need to change. To grow spiritually, let the Son, Jesus Christ, shine on you. Live in the light of the Son by following His commands to love and forgive. Let His blessings shower upon you and be thankful for everything He is doing to help you mature. Realize that the storms that pound you will deepen your roots and make you stronger.

It is God who gives growth, so turn to Him with trust. He will provide everything you need to come to completion. "How precious is thy steadfast love, O God! The children of men take refuge in the shadow of thy wings. They feast on the abundance of thy house, and thou givest them drink from the river of thy delight. For with thee is the fountain of life; in thy light do we see light" (Psalm 36:7-9). Feast on the abundance of the Lord, drink from the fountain of life, live in His light. God wants you to grow up in every way. He will help you do it if you depend upon Him to cultivate and nourish your spirit.

*Read: I Corinthians 3:7; Luke 6:43-44; II Peter 3:18*

# HELP FOR HESITANCY

*"Whoever seeks to gain his life will lose it, but whoever loses his life will preserve it" (Luke 17:33).*

The people who make a difference in life are those who do not hesitate to do things and go places when opportunities arise. Hesitancy can sabotage the future and keep us from finding fulfillment, joy, and peace. Nothing deters entrance into the Kingdom more than hesitancy. It haunts us and hurts us. Though in youth we sometimes do not have enough hesitancy, as we grow older we tend to have far too much.

Hesitancy often is born in the mind. We hesitate to act when we worry excessively about security, safety, even our sanity. We like to be assured things will work out and we will be comfortable. We cannot follow Jesus with that attitude! To be a disciple, we need to be a little reckless, bold, and, in the eyes of the world, even a bit foolish. Sometimes hesitancy develops in the home. The family is the greatest institution God created, and it is there we are to learn the intangibles of life. In some homes, though, people never learn to let go and thus cannot make a commitment to Christ. When Jesus called James and John by the Sea of Galilee, "immediately they left the boat and their father, and followed him" (Matthew 4:22). Immediately! Hesitancy would have cost them the honor of being among the first disciples of the Son of God.

Help for hesitancy comes in rising to Jesus's challenge to lose our lives for His sake and the Gospel. Christ is our model. Jesus was steadfast. He never looked back or hesitated in doing His Father's will. As He drew near the close of His ministry, we read that "his face was set toward Jerusalem" (Luke 9:53), though He knew a gruesome death awaited Him there. Do not let worries, your home environment, or anyone or anything keep you from the Kingdom. If today you are ruled by timidity, indecision, and hesitancy, your body is alive, but your spirit is dead. Live courageously! Accept the challenge to lose your life for Jesus Christ's sake and you will find not only the cure for hesitancy, but your destiny as well.

*Read: Luke 9:51-62; Psalm 46:1-3; Proverbs 28:1*

# WHY JESUS WEEPS

*When he drew near and saw the city he wept over it, saying "Would that even today you knew the things that make for peace! But now they are hid from your eyes" (Luke 19:41-42).*

Jesus wept over the people of Jerusalem, and He weeps over us today. Christians are called to "pursue what makes for peace" (Romans 14:19), yet throughout the world we see rage and destruction, while peace seems elusive and unattainable. People shout about peace, protest about peace, and argue about peace, but peace never comes from shouts, protests, and arguments. Peace comes from people who are at peace.

Before we can be at peace with others, we must be at peace with God through Christ. "For in him all the fulness of God was pleased to dwell, and through him to reconcile to himself all things, whether on earth or in heaven, making peace by the blood of his cross" (Colossians 1:19-20). We do not have the excuse of people who lived before Good Friday, Easter, the ascension, and Pentecost. They did not know Jesus had come to bring peace on earth, to die, rise, and ascend, and to send His Holy Spirit to be with us. We are post-Easter people! We are supposed to know the things that make for peace: peace comes when we accept our individual responsibility to make peace, not merely hope or pray for it; peace comes not from might, but from doing right, no matter what anyone else does or how evil the enemy is; peace comes when we do not wait for someone else to make the first move, but we make the first move.

"God ... through Christ reconciled us to himself and gave us the ministry of reconciliation" (II Corinthians 5:18). Let us dedicate ourselves to this vital ministry. Only the Gospel has the power to bring never-ending peace. When we do not energetically spread the Word, we allow the world to grow angrier, meaner, and closer to destruction, and Jesus weeps.

Time is running out. We who follow Jesus Christ, the Prince of Peace, have the answer to peace, and that is to live peace now. "The harvest of righteousness is sown in peace by those who make peace" (James 3:18). Sow peace today.

*Read: Luke 19:28-44; Matthew 5:9; Ephesians 2:14-18*

# DO NOT BE A TEMPTER

*"Temptations to sin are sure to come; but woe to him by whom they come! It would be better for him if a millstone were hung round his neck and he were cast into the sea, than that he should cause one of these little ones to sin" (Luke 17:1-2).*

God takes sin seriously, far more so than we do. When we sin individually, His heart is broken, He is disappointed, and He hopes we repent. But when we cause someone else to sin, God is not only broken-hearted and disappointed. He is angry! God gets angry at tempters. Most of us restrict too much our definition of tempters. We picture tempters as drug pushers, prostitutes, loan sharks, pornographers, shifty villains we can easily spot. We love to think these are the only tempters, but they are not. In God's sight, anyone who provokes another to anger is a tempter. Parents who demand too much of children and push them into the temptations of cheating and lying are tempters. A business manager who drives employees on with ridiculous incentives and cutthroat competition is a tempter. Anyone who injures the souls of "little ones" is a tempter.

Jesus loved "little ones." "See that you do not despise one of these little ones; for I tell you that in heaven their angels always behold the face of my Father who is in heaven" (Matthew 18:10). By "little ones," Jesus did not mean only people under five feet tall or small children. Jesus was talking about people little in strength, little in faith, little in knowledge of the ways of the world. The weak, the doubting, the innocent: those are people we are not to tempt. We are called to help them, not hurt them. "Let us no more pass judgment on one another, but rather decide never to put a stumbling block or hindrance in the way of a brother" (Romans 14:13).

Do not be a tempter and cause God to be angry with you. If you lead others astray, you will destroy yourself. "He who misleads the upright into an evil way will fall into his own pit" (Proverbs 28:10). Make sure all the big things and little things you do are loving and kind. Be thankful for the opportunity to lead people to Jesus, and lead them not into temptation.

*Read: Matthew 18:1-14; Mark 14:38; Proverbs 16:25-30*

# RIGHT ASSOCIATIONS WITH WRONG PEOPLE

*"And he arose and came to his father. But while he was yet at a distance, his father saw him and had compassion, and ran and embraced him and kissed him" (Luke 15:20).*

The story of the prodigal is perhaps the most famous of Jesus's parables, probably because so many of us have prodigals in our lives, people who defy the laws of God and man, do everything the hard way, and cause inexpressible anguish and worry. There are five ways to deal with prodigals.

**Forget them.** Pretend they are dead, obliterate their names and faces from memory, and live as though they never existed.

**Fear them.** Treat them as if they have leprosy and avoid them because of their embarrassing, scandalous behavior.

**Follow them.** Try to be like them. Sometimes they seem to have a great time, don't they? We all have a rebellious streak urging us to forget morality and do whatever we want.

**Fight them.** Get angry and try to teach them a lesson. The elder brother in the parable was furious when the prodigal returned. The story ends with the angry brother and his father outside in the field, missing the party. That is what happens when anger consumes us. We miss life's joy and happiness.

**Forgive them.** Forgiveness is the right, biblical association to have with people who go wrong but repent. It is difficult. Television shows solve problems in one hour, but in real life, forgiveness takes time. We must wait, sometimes for years, maybe for a lifetime. We must watch, always ready to run and welcome the prodigal back. We must ask God for help to forgive one who has hurt us badly. He will give us that power.

We cannot save prodigals, no matter how deeply we love them. Only they can decide to end the stupidity and suffering by admitting their mistakes and courageously rising up out of the pigsty to begin a new life. All we can control is our response to their choices. If there is a prodigal in your life who wants to come home, respond lovingly, with compassion, embraces, and kisses. That is forgiveness. Forgiveness is the right, Christian way to associate with people who go wrong.

*Read: Luke 15:11-32; Ephesians 4:31-32; Psalm 130:3-4*

# THE DOCTRINE OF THE LIGHT BULB

*"You are the light of the world. A city set on a hill cannot be hid. Nor do men light a lamp and put it under a bushel, but on a stand, and it gives light to all in the house. Let your light so shine before men, that they may see your good works and give glory to your Father who is in heaven" (Matthew 5:14-16).*

Jesus calls us the light of the world, and it is our responsibility to brighten this dark world by lighting up one another with His love. We are Jesus Christ's light bulbs!

For a light bulb to shine, there are four requirements.

1. The light bulb must be fitted into a socket. The socket for us is the Church. We need to find a church where we belong and fit; it's got to be a tight fit, with a little pressure, but we cannot have dynamic faith without Christian fellowship.

2. The socket must be connected to power. The power of a church comes from the working of the Holy Spirit. A church without the Spirit is dead. To be charged with excitement and electricity, a church must be empowered by God's Holy Spirit.

3. The light bulb must be turned on. We all came to Christ because someone, whose name we may not remember, turned us on to the Gospel message. Sadly, many people were once turned on, but became turned off by an insensitive, unkind, or indifferent church member. It is imperative that our lives turn people on, not off, to the glory of the Kingdom.

4. The light bulb must shine forth all the time; that is its job. Whatever happens, we are to shine as radiant examples of God's love, without embarrassment, fear, or trepidation, to transform the world by the light of Jesus Christ shining in us.

"Those who are wise shall shine like the brightness of the firmament; and those who turn many to righteousness, like the stars for ever and ever" (Daniel 12:3). Remember the doctrine of the light bulb as you let your light shine. This dark world needs people who are willing to be a focus of goodness. One shining light can brighten the lives of countless others. Shine today and light up the universe. Help Jesus to build a better world and a better tomorrow through His light ablaze in you.

*Read: Isaiah 60:1-3; John 1:1-5; Ephesians 5:8-14*

# TRUSTING OR TESTING

*We must not put the Lord to the test (I Corinthians 10:9).*

There are two ways to learn life's great lessons: the smart way, by trusting God, and the stupid way, by testing God. All of us are tempted to test God rather than trust Him. The temptations come in the office, home, church, and community. Many people think we are tempted in our weaknesses, but we are tempted in our strengths! Like Jesus, who met temptation in the wilderness after His baptism, we are tempted to abuse or misuse our God-given power, popularity, and possessions.

**Power.** "Command these stones to become loaves of bread" (Matthew 4:3). Jesus had the power to change things. He changed water into wine, sickness into health, the Cross into a crown. But Jesus refused to abuse His power for personal gain. Instead, He used His power to serve others.

**Popularity.** "Throw yourself down" (v. 6). Jesus refused to throw Himself from the pinnacle of the temple. Taking unnecessary risks to impress people is dumb. Any popularity we have in life should be dedicated to God's glory, not ours.

**Possessions.** "All these I will give you" (v. 9). Jesus was tempted with worldly kingdoms. Many people compromise their convictions to acquire possessions. That is worshipping materialism, not God. We are given possessions to share, not to store. Storing is greed, and greed leads to self-destruction.

Essentially there is just one temptation: the temptation to test God. We test Him by willfully misusing His gifts and defiantly demanding that He still love and protect us. Testing God is stupid. It leads to trouble and tragedy. Each of us must decide how we want to learn about life: by testing God or by trusting God. If you always have tried to figure things out for yourself and play by your own rules, you probably have made big mistakes and learned hard lessons in the past. There is a better way. Jesus said, "Learn from me" (Matthew 11:29). Trust God with your life from this moment on and be guided by His Holy Spirit. If you let Him, He will lead you into all the truth. That is the intelligent way to get your education.

*Read: Matthew 4:1-11; Psalm 31:14-24; Isaiah 12:2*

196

# THE STRENGTH TO BE GENTLE

*The fruit of the Spirit is love, joy, peace, patience, kindness, goodness, faithfulness, gentleness, self-control (Galatians 5:22-23).*

Christians treasure the fruit of the Spirit, but sometimes I think we feel a little embarrassed about gentleness. It is a word we do not like much. We think to succeed, we must be ruthless and tough. "Do what you have to do. Fight your way up! Be aggressive and assertive. It's the only way to get ahead." That is not New Testament, but some people live that way.

Jesus said it is the meek who will inherit the earth, not boisterous bullies, and He said of Himself, "I am gentle and lowly in heart" (Matthew 11:29). Gentleness requires a tremendous amount of inner strength and self-control. We wrongly equate gentleness with weakness, but only strong people can be gentle. Being gentle means having the opportunity and power to pin somebody to the wall, but showing kindness instead. It means having justice and the law on our side, but offering mercy. It means knowing something that could smear another person, but saying nothing. It means refraining from publicly embarrassing or demeaning anybody, even our worst enemy, even when that person is completely wrong. It means behaving politely toward everyone, not just people we hope to impress, not just people in church, but people with whom we live and work every day. It means being considered loving, forgiving, and honest by those closest to us.

Imagine what our world would be like if we all followed biblical advice "to speak evil of no one, to avoid quarreling, to be gentle, and to show perfect courtesy toward all men" (Titus 3:2). It is much easier to be inconsiderate and selfish. That is why gentleness requires strength. It is only with the help of God's Holy Spirit that we have the power to be gentle.

Peter wrote of "the imperishable jewel of a gentle and quiet spirit, which in God's sight is very precious" (I Peter 3:4). Ask God for the strength to be gentle and quiet in spirit so you can experience the deep joy of being very precious in God's sight.

*Read: Matthew 5:5; II Timothy 2:24-26; James 3:13-18*

197

## DEFEATING DIVISIVE DEMONS

*Be united in the same mind (I Corinthians 1:10).*

God created us to be different and each one of us is different, but God never intended our differences to create divisions among us. Yet in homes, businesses, communities, and nations, dissension occurs. Regrettably, even in the Church, the Body of Christ, divisive demons sometimes creep in, bringing calamitous disharmony and strife. Divisions develop when people worship the messenger instead of the message. They increase when people demand personal rights instead of doing right. They intensify when people, in anger, grow cross with one another and neglect to carry the Cross of Jesus Christ. Divisive demons especially multiply when individuals come to believe only other people are the problem.

God is not pleased with divisive demons, and God alone has power to defeat them. We cannot take on the malevolent force of evil with our minds, will-power, brute force, or anything else. God defeats divisive demons the same way He defeats every other enemy: through the Cross of Jesus Christ.

The Cross is difficult to understand. To people who are perishing, the Cross is foolishness, a complete stumbling block. To those who believe, it is the power and wisdom of God. For healing to occur in divided relationships, we, like Christ, must be willing to appear foolish. It seems foolish to follow Jesus's commands. Loving that nasty imbecile, forgiving some scoundrel, giving away our hard-earned money? Yes, such foolishness is necessary to restore harmony. We, like Christ, also must be willing to be stumbling blocks. Suffer pain and agony, allow people to trip over us, yell at us, and hurt us in their disbelief and frustration? Yes, Jesus Christ suffered on the Cross for us, and at times we will suffer as we follow Him.

Let us seek to honor the prayer of our Lord Jesus Christ that His believers be one, united in harmony and love. Only the message of the Cross, which is foolishness to some and a stumbling block to others, has the power to defeat divisive demons. Believe, trust, and live the Cross of Christ today.

*Read: I Corinthians 1:10-31; John 17:20-23; Psalm 133:1*

# SEIZE THE DAY

*"Choose this day whom you will serve" (Joshua 24:15).*

"It's a limited offer, folks! Time is short!"

Advertisers bombard us with those words daily, trying to pressure us into running out immediately to buy their products. Most of us learn to tune them out, ignore them. We know there is no hurry, no need to rush. We know we have plenty of time to think about it. There's always tomorrow, or some other day.

Maybe that is why it is so difficult for us to understand the New Testament teaching about the Kingdom of Heaven. The opportunity to enter the Kingdom of Heaven is a limited offer, and time is short! That is disturbing, but preachers are taught not just to comfort the disturbed, but to disturb the comfortable. If any of us begin to feel completely comfortable with our lives, if we think we've got it made and we see no need to try to change or mature in faith, I wonder if we are truly committed to Christ. Disciples of Jesus Christ must be willing to work diligently every day to grow a little bigger, to become a little better, to make this world a little brighter. It is not easy. It is not comfortable. Though God is very loving, very forgiving, and very patient, He demands absolute obedience to His words, even words we do not fully understand or like. To be obedient, most of us need to make some major changes in our lives, not in the future, not when it is convenient, but now. Today!

Seize the day! You do not have all the time in the world to make a decision for Jesus Christ. Decide this moment to make Jesus first in your life and to love Him with all your heart, soul, mind, and strength. Try to do all you can to make today a great day in the Kingdom for God, other people, and yourself. Be more giving, more kind, more helpful, more understanding, more forgiving. Serve the Lord gladly! That is the way to live life to the fullest and make each day count for Jesus.

Choose this day to serve Jesus Christ. Invite Him into your heart and make Him Lord of your life. Seize the opportunity to enter the Kingdom of Heaven -- today! It's a limited offer. Time is short. Tomorrow may be too late.

*Read: Joshua 24:14-28; Luke 13:22-30; Mark 13:32-33*

# THE LORD HAS NEED OF YOU

*We are God's fellow workers (I Corinthians 3:9).*

When Jesus Christ prepared for His triumphal entry into Jerusalem on Palm Sunday, He sent two disciples ahead to find the colt on which He would ride. "Go into the village opposite, where on entering you will find a colt tied, on which no one has ever yet sat; untie it and bring it here. If any one asks you, 'Why are you untying it?' you shall say this, 'The Lord has need of it'" (Luke 19:30-31). The Lord had need of a colt that day. Yet many people, created, loved, and valued by God, believe the Lord has no need of them. The painful sense of being unneeded, unappreciated, and unwanted is damaging to individuals, families, communities, and churches.

Christians have a message for the world: "God loves you; believe Him! Christ has redeemed you; accept Him! Holy Spirit has great things in store for you; follow Him!" We do not proclaim the rest of the message as often as we should: "The Lord has need of you!" Some people are just waiting to be asked to give time and talent to a project. Many are filled with creativity and abilities they do not even realize they possess. They will never have the opportunity to use their gifts to help in building the Kingdom unless they are invited to get involved in the cause of Christ. "Having gifts that differ according to the grace given to us, let us use them: if prophecy, in proportion to our faith; if service, in our serving; he who teaches, in his teaching; he who exhorts, in his exhortation; he who contributes, in liberality; he who gives aid, with zeal; he who does acts of mercy, with cheerfulness" (Romans 12:6-8). Believing we have important, urgent jobs to accomplish for the Lord is a sure cure for loneliness and depression. It is so simple and obvious that we frequently overlook it.

If you feel a little unneeded, unappreciated, and unwanted right now, remember that the Lord had need of a colt one day, so I'd say He certainly has need of each of us. As one of God's fellow workers in His Kingdom on earth, spread the word and tell somebody this day, "The Lord has need of you!"

*Read: Luke 19:28-40; Matthew 9:35-38; II Timothy 2:15*

# HOW TO BECOME A NEW PERSON

*Walk in newness of life (Romans 6:4).*

People who study such things claim in seven years, almost every cell in the human body is replaced. Your body is really only seven years old! It is called the Seven-Year Switch, and it happens to everyone. Many people wish the same process could happen with the spirit, that the spirit could become new, past mistakes could be forgotten and forgiven, and they could have a new beginning, a fresh start. The message of the Bible is that we can have spiritual rebirth! We can begin anew.

Now, we cannot change the spirit as we change the body or mind. We can change the body somewhat through exercise and diet, and we can change the mind through study and meditation, but it is God in Christ who changes the spirit. The secret is that we must be "in Christ." "If any one is in Christ, he is a new creation; the old has passed away, behold, the new has come" (II Corinthians 5:17). There is no other way.

To experience spiritual rebirth, we must invite Jesus in and be instructed by the message of His Holy Word. As His Word abides in us and we abide in His Word, new life begins to take hold and our attitudes gradually change. We start to see God as Jesus saw Him. We start to see ourselves as Jesus sees us. We start to see our enemies as Jesus saw His enemies. We start to see problems as Jesus saw problems. We start to face life as God wants us to. Eventually, like Paul, we can say, "I have been crucified with Christ; it is no longer I who live, but Christ who lives in me; and the life I now live in the flesh I live by faith in the Son of God, who loved me and gave himself for me" (Galatians 2:20). We come to have the mind of Christ and think like God, and deal with people, problems, pressures, and our own personalities in ways that glorify Him.

It takes seven years for your body to change. For your spirit to change, it takes a decision to invite Jesus into your heart, and you can do that now! Today would be a beautiful day to be born anew into God's Kingdom. Commit your life to Jesus Christ and walk in joyful, triumphant newness of life.

*Read: II Corinthians 5:16-21; Colossians 3:5-11; Romans 7:4-6*

# PATHS OF PROVIDENCE

*Lead me in the way everlasting! (Psalm 139:24).*

Many people have a difficult time recognizing God's providence in their lives. They cannot see how the Lord is leading them along paths that will bring them to their destiny. Though God constantly opens up new avenues of experience, they become confused and discouraged at every unfamiliar fork in the road. There are three reasons for the difficulty.

**Lack of knowledge.** "Some have no knowledge of God" (I Corinthians 15:34). Many people, either by choice or circumstance, are ignorant of God's Holy Word. They do not know Jesus Christ is the true light of the world, those who follow Him shall not walk in darkness, and the Bible is the true and eternal authority on which our lives are to be based.

**Lack of understanding.** Some people know the Word of God, but do not comprehend it. They "hear but never understand" (Matthew 13:14). They simply do not grasp the meaning of the Cross, the message of salvation, the need for forgiveness, or the presence of God's Holy Spirit within them.

**Lack of eyes to see.** Many people do not see that God is working for good in all their experiences. They equate God's providence with happiness, ease, prosperity, and above all, no problems! When a crisis hits, they accuse God, question His love, and plunge into self-pity. "The Almighty has dealt very bitterly with me... The Almighty has brought calamity upon me" (Ruth 1:20-21). Such bitterness against God can ruin us spiritually, for in our hurt we fail to see that God can use any situation to bring forth change, growth, and deepened faith.

It is sad when people cannot recognize God's providence, yet often it is their own fault. They do not try to know. They do not try to understand. They do not try to see. They think they have all the time in the world to figure things out. That attitude is perilous, because no one of us knows how much time we have left or when Jesus will come again in glory. If we want the Lord to lead us in the way everlasting, we must try to know, understand, and see His paths of providence today.

*Read: Jeremiah 10:23; Psalm 119:168-169; Isaiah 58:11*

# THE WORST NAME IN THE WORLD

*Keep Satan from gaining the advantage (II Corinthians 2:11).*

Some people deny Jesus as the Christ, but He can handle them; He says, "Father, forgive them; for they know not what they do" (Luke 23:34). Some people ignore Jesus, and He can handle them; He keeps working and never gives up on anyone. The people with whom Jesus has difficulty are those who call Him Lord and Savior, go to church, read the Bible, and bask in the blessing of His grace, but then challenge Him, dispute His Word, and declare He does not know what He is doing. He calls these people by the worst name in the world: Satan. Satan is "the enemy" (Matthew 13:39); "the prince of demons" (Matthew 12:24); "the father of lies" (John 8:44); "the deceiver of the whole world" (Revelation 12:9).

Peter was called the worst name in the world when he protested Jesus's forthcoming death. "Peter took him and began to rebuke him, saying, 'God forbid, Lord! This shall never happen to you.' But he turned and said to Peter, 'Get behind me, Satan! You are a hindrance to me; for you are not on the side of God, but of men.'" (Matthew 16:22-23). How devastating, how shattering, how humiliating, to be called the worst name in the world by the best Person who ever lived!

Jesus demands absolute obedience even in times of disaster, death, and depression. God's Word is eternally true and we are to believe Him. When He speaks and we argue, debate, and dispute, we become hindrances to His plan of salvation. Satan is a crafty, subtle threat who "disguises himself as an angel of light" (II Corinthians 11:14), yet the Bible promises, "Resist the devil and he will flee from you" (James 4:7). We overcome evil through faith in Christ, who proclaims, "The ruler of this world ... has no power over me" (John 14:30). No one wants to be called "Satan" by Jesus. We want to be His disciples, His friends, His good and faithful servants. We can be, if we are on the side of God, not men, and we trust Him completely.

Keep Satan from gaining the advantage over you so Jesus never has reason to call you the worst name in the world.

*Read: Matthew 16:13-28; Genesis 3:1; I Peter 5:8-9*

# DARE TO BE DIFFERENT

*In those days came John the Baptist (Matthew 3:1).*

John the Baptizer was different. He was really different. He looked different and he sounded different. He was bold. He was brash. He was outspoken. His clothing was different: camel hair and leather. Even his diet was different: locust bean and wild honey. He probably did not bathe often, and when he did, it was in the river. He was not theologically trained. I am not sure how much Bible he knew. But God used this individual who dared to be different to prepare the people of his day to meet Jesus Christ. People from all the region came to hear this different person speak. Many confessed their sins, repented, and were baptized in the river Jordan. Jesus Himself was baptized by John, and later said, "Among those born of women there has risen no one greater than John the Baptist" (Matthew 11:11).

Jesus dares all His followers to be different, but I do not think He intends us to switch to camel hair and leather clothes and a diet of locust bean and honey. John dared to be different in more important ways than that. He courageously spoke out against evil and wrong, even though his confrontation with Herod eventually led to his death. He showed people how to change, how to do right, how to live with integrity. John, "a burning and shining lamp" (John 5:35), pointed people to Christ, gladly sacrificing his own popularity in favor of the Lamb of God who came to take away the sin of the world.

Each of us today should ask ourselves, "Am I committed and courageous enough to dare to be different in my walk of faith? When was the last time I spoke out boldly against wrong? Have I been helping people to turn their lives around? Am I taking every opportunity to tell others about Christ?"

Our enthusiasm, dedication, and love for Jesus should be so remarkable, so extraordinary, and so inviting that people in these days ask, "What's your secret?" Be daring and tell them! This dark world will not see Jesus, who is the light, the fire, and the spirit of life, unless His disciples dare to be different.

*Read: Matthew 3; Mark 6:12-29; Isaiah 40:3-5*

# WHILE WAITING FOR YOUR BRIDGES

*Wait for the Lord; be strong, and let your heart take courage; yea, wait for the Lord! (Psalm 27:14).*

"Don't cross your bridge until you come to it." That familiar maxim holds some good theology. The Bible tells us not to be fearful. In the Sermon on the Mount, Jesus said, "Do not be anxious about tomorrow, for tomorrow will be anxious for itself. Let the day's own trouble be sufficient for the day" (Matthew 6:34). Paul wrote, "Have no anxiety about anything" (Philippians 4:6). Yet worry plagues all of us from time to time. Some people think sincere Christians never worry. That is not true. Worry comes to Christians just as it does to everyone else. Worry is as natural to humanity as breathing.

When we have some bridge looming before us and we do not know how we are going to get over it or where it is going to lead, there is only one thing to do: keep our hearts and minds on Jesus through prayer. Prayer is the most powerful force God makes available to us. In prayer, we have the privilege of carrying everything, our anxieties, requests, hopes, and fears, to God, who created us, loves us, and wants the best for us.

So often when we are upset and fretful, we take our worries to the wrong place. We love to talk about our problems incessantly with one another, but other people usually are not very concerned about our troubles; they are too wrapped up in their own. It is God to whom we should take our worries, for He is vitally concerned about every aspect, big and little, of our lives. "The eyes of the Lord are upon the righteous, and his ears are open to their prayer" (I Peter 3:12). If you have a scary, uncertain bridge ahead of you today, bring your anxiety to God in prayer, then thank Him for the answer you believe will come. Once you give your worry to the Lord, forget it. Just forget that bridge and concentrate instead on trusting Jesus Christ. He will take care of you. Right now, He is preparing the bridge for you to cross and He is preparing you to cross it. He loves you and He will clear the way for you to pass safely through this world to your home in the Kingdom of Heaven.

*Read: Philippians 4:4-7; Psalm 40:1-3; Isaiah 30:18*

# THE SECRET OF SENSITIVITY

*"When you give a dinner or a banquet, do not invite your friends or your brothers or your kinsmen or rich neighbors, lest they also invite you in return, and you be repaid. But when you give a feast, invite the poor, the maimed, the lame, the blind, and you will be blessed, because they cannot repay you. You will be repaid at the resurrection of the just" (Luke 14:12-14).*

One of Jesus's marvelous attributes was His sensitivity. Wherever He went, He recognized people who needed help.

**Jesus had eyes and ears that were open.** Whether it was little Zacchaeus up a tree, a bleeding woman tugging at the hem of His garment, or a thief dying on a cross beside Him, Jesus saw and heard hurting people wherever He went.

**Jesus had a heart that could be broken.** Jesus wept over Jerusalem because the people He loved were like sheep without a shepherd. Their spiritual blindness broke His heart.

**Jesus left unsaid words that could be spoken.** Jesus did not speak empty, idle words. Jesus acted! He helped, healed, and offered people solutions, assistance, and hope.

The Church is the Body of Jesus Christ in the world today. There are desperate needs everywhere, countless people who want to be saved from sin, homelessness, hunger, nakedness, imprisonment. The Church is to be the answer to these needs. Christians must be sensitive to hurting people so the Church can effectively help them. We must ask ourselves, do we have eyes and ears that are open? Are we willing to have our hearts broken? Can we leave some words unspoken? We cannot just close ourselves up in church with our friends and families, pray, read the Bible, and talk about what should be done. We must get in touch with pain in the world, even if we risk pain ourselves. Our help should be practical and concrete. "If a brother or sister is ill-clad and in lack of daily food, and one of you says to them, 'Go in peace, be warmed and filled,' without giving them the things needed for the body, what does it profit?" (James 2:15-16). Only through our sensitivity can desperate, suffering people be identified and saved.

The secret of sensitivity is simple: simply live like Jesus.

*Read: Colossians 1:18; Isaiah 58:6-9; Proverbs 21:13*

# LIVELY HOPE

*Blessed be the God and Father of our Lord Jesus Christ, which according to his abundant mercy hath begotten us again unto a lively hope by the resurrection of Jesus Christ from the dead, to an inheritance incorruptible, and undefiled, and that fadeth not away, reserved in heaven for you, who are kept by the power of God through faith unto salvation ready to be revealed in the last time (I Peter 1:3-5, KJV).*

A Christian should be a person with a lively hope. A lively hope is dynamic, vital, joyful hope that gives daily assurance of God's love and care. A lively hope assures us our sins are forgiven by God; even if family and friends do not let us forget the nasty, embarrassing things we say and do, God forgives and forgets our sins because of the sacrifice of His Son on the Cross. A lively hope assures us our names are written in the Lamb's Book of Life, in capital letters, underlined; we are precious children of the Father. A lively hope assures us we can stand at the open grave of a Christian loved one and be assured we will see our loved one again. Whoever believes in Jesus shall have life, and that life shall be forever. Those who die in Christ will be with Christ when we go to be with Him.

Never let anyone convince you that you are weak because of your Christian hope or faith is some kind of crutch you need to limp along through life. Lively hope is mysterious, to be sure, for it looks to the unseen spiritual world. "Hope that is seen is not hope. For who hopes for what he sees? But if we hope for what we do not see, we wait for it with patience" (Romans 8:24-25). Still, the lively hope of Christianity is not just a comforting idea or wishful thinking. It is based on the promises of the Creator of the universe! Christians claim the "hope of eternal life which God, who never lies, promised ages ago" (Titus 1:2). God's promises never fail. As Christians, we have no reason to doubt or fear. We have every reason to hope, for we have victory in life and in death through Christ.

Hope in any name other than the name of Jesus Christ is dead, so enliven your spirit by keeping a lively hope in Him.

*Read: Hebrews 11:1; Psalm 43:5; Joshua 21:45*

# GETTING TO KNOW GRACE

*"'Am I not allowed to do what I choose with what belongs to me?'" (Matthew 20:15).*

The parable of the vineyard owner paying his laborers is not easy to interpret, for it illustrates the doctrine of grace, a concept difficult to comprehend. God gives grace to all of us and we cannot live without it. Grace saves us, sanctifies us, seals us with Holy Spirit, and surprises us. Grace is unlimited, unmerited, uncontrollable, undefeatable. And it is unfair.

That's right. To us, grace often appears unfair. That is the point of the parable. All the workers, those who started early, those who joined at midday, and those who came later, received the same pay. To our minds, that seems unfair. Yet if we demand fairness and question God's dealings with us, we cannot enter the Kingdom. Faith means accepting the mystery of grace and believing God always knows best and does right.

The parable shows three ways people experience grace.

As **Senior Saints.** Senior Saints are faithful, dedicated, hard-working people who have been around the church for a long time. Sometimes, though, they become a little bitter. They think they are getting less than they deserve, though they are getting exactly what they agreed upon at the beginning.

As **Junior Joiners.** Junior Joiners come later, but find themselves treated equally with Senior Saints. They are very grateful, for they know they are getting more than they deserve.

As **Mid-Time People.** Mid-Time People simply come with confident trust in the Lord, respecting Him as a loving Master who will treat them well, whatever He does.

Whether we are Senior Saints, Junior Joiners, or Mid-Time People, Jesus honors us by calling us His friends. He died for the least of us so we might live in grace. Do not get hung up on fairness. That shows a limited human perspective. "The earth is the Lord's, and the fulness thereof, the world and those who dwell therein" (Psalm 24:1). The Lord is allowed to do what He chooses with what belongs to Him, so just thank God today for His constant kindness, goodness, and grace to you.

*Read: Matthew 20:1-16; John 15:12-17; Psalm 24*

# JUDAS AND JUDAS

*Judas (not Iscariot) (John 14:22).*

It must be terribly embarrassing to carry the same name as a person of infamy. Many people are unaware that there were two disciples among the twelve named Judas. It is Judas Iscariot who gets all the notorious publicity as the betrayer of Jesus Christ, but there was also Judas, not Iscariot, called Thaddaeus in the Gospels of Matthew and Mark.

How different these two men were!

People have debated the motives of Judas Iscariot for centuries. Perhaps it was simple greed that prompted him to turn Jesus over to the authorities for thirty pieces of silver. Maybe he acted out of disappointment; he hoped for a Messiah who would lead a great army and overthrow the Romans, yet Jesus came talking about love, forgiveness, and giving. Possibly Judas was trying to compel Jesus to call in the forces of Heaven to defeat His enemies. Most likely his motivation was a combination of factors we will never decipher here on earth, but one thing is sure: his actions arose out of faithlessness to Jesus and out of his own choice and self-will.

Judas, not Iscariot, is a little known man who is quoted only once in the New Testament, yet to his one question, Jesus gave all of us the explanation of how Jesus Christ and God come to live within us. "Judas (not Iscariot) said to him, 'Lord, how is it that you will manifest yourself to us, and not to the world?' Jesus answered him, 'If any man loves me, he will keep my word, and my Father will love him, and we will come to him and make our home with him. He who does not love me does not keep my words; and the word which you hear is not mine but the Father's who sent me'" (John 14:22-24). That is, if we know His commandments and keep them, then we love Him and He will be at home in us. This forgotten Judas asked Jesus a question whose answer will be remembered for all time.

Judas Iscariot chose to betray Jesus Christ. Judas, not Iscariot, chose to be faithful. Like people of all succeeding generations, we have the same option before us today.

*Read: John 14:18-24; Mark 14:43-46; Proverbs 25:19*

# GO TO YOUR NEIGHBORS

*"You shall love your neighbor as yourself." Love does no wrong to a neighbor; therefore love is the fulfilling of the law (Romans 13:9-10).*

Many of us claim to be born-again Christians. We pack into churches on Sunday, put big bucks in the offering plate, read Bibles, and pray, but we never think about sharing the Good News with our neighbors. We do not mind sharing other news. If we had a serious illness and God healed us through medicine or meditation or another wonderful cure, and if we knew a neighbor was diagnosed with the same disease, we would go and say, "I have found new health. Let me tell you about it!" If at the end of the street there was a pot of gold that could never be emptied, and the more people took from it, the more it was refilled, and if we knew somebody did not have enough, we would go and say, "I don't know you well, but I can tell you of a pot of gold that provides endless refreshment." Yet when it comes to the most important news, the offer of salvation through Jesus Christ, we go nowhere and say nothing.

Like the lawyer to whom Jesus told the parable of the Good Samaritan, we try to justify our indifference by asking, "And who is my neighbor?" (Luke 10:29). We look down on people. "I know that neighbor and I don't like him." "That woman threw garbage in my yard. She's not good enough to come to church." "I read about that scoundrel in the paper. Jesus wouldn't be interested in him!" Our condescending attitude violates Jesus's command to love people, whatever we think of them. Out of love, we should be eager to spread God's Word.

We all have neighbors who are struggling. Some might be heading for disaster. Others could be stuck in degrading sins. Christians claim to have the answer in Jesus Christ. Share it! Most people do not come to the Kingdom until they hear the Word from a caring, concerned Christian. Your neighbors are people God created and loves. Go to them and explain the Gospel message. Someone did that for you once, remember?

*Read: Luke 10:25-37; II Corinthians 4:5-6; Psalm 66:16*

# TARRYING TIMES

*And it came to pass, that he tarried many days in Joppa with one Simon a tanner (Acts 9:43, KJV).*

Tarrying times are times of waiting, times of indecision, times when we find ourselves in-between assignments and unsure of what God wants us to do next. Tarrying times come to all of us and usually we think they are wasted time. Peter's experience in Joppa shows we should value these times, for God uses tarrying times creatively to shift our focus and prepare us for new challenges. Peter tarried at Simon's house after the miracle of raising Dorcas from the dead. Before lunch one day, he went to the housetop to pray. There he had a spectacular vision that gave him new insight and soon united him with Cornelius, a devout centurion, to whom he said, "You yourselves know how unlawful it is for a Jew to associate with or to visit any one of another nation; but God has shown me that I should not call any man common or unclean... I perceive that God shows no partiality, but in every nation any one who fears him and does what is right is acceptable to him" (Acts 10:28,34-35). Thus the Gospel spread to the Gentile world.

If you find yourself in a tarrying time, pray for the Lord to give you a vision and the desire to do His will. When you are eager to serve Him, He will send a revelation. Of course, we will not receive His instructions on beautiful stationery with golden edges and the zip code for Heaven on the return address, nor can we telephone Him on an 800-number. God sends messages through symbols and signs, visions and dreams. To interpret God's unique communication system, we must understand the spirit of the total message of the Bible. People can use Scripture to say anything they want. Get into the Bible and brood over it to discern its meaning as a whole and discover God's personal message to you. Then comes the time for action! Implement God's revelation, go in that new direction, and allow for the next miracle He has planned.

Value your tarrying times, for God will use these times to bring forth great things for His Kingdom through you.

*Read: Acts 9:36-10:48; Lamentations 3:25-26; Psalm 130:5*

# WHEN IS A DISCIPLE A DISCIPLE?

*Jesus said to Simon, "Do not be afraid; henceforth you will be catching men." And when they had brought their boats to land, they left everything and followed him (Luke 5:10-11).*

Precise moments are difficult to define. The precise moment when life begins or death occurs is hard to pinpoint. All of us are called to be disciples and to make disciples of all nations, but for most of us, it is not easy to identify the precise moment when we became disciples. Jesus's calling of Simon Peter shows how to become disciples of Christ.

**Respond.** Disciples respond immediately and obediently to God. When Jesus stepped into Peter's boat, Peter was no longer captain of his ship. Jesus never says, "Please." He commands! We can ignore Him, but to be a disciple, we obey.

**Recognize.** Disciples recognize blessings and gifts from God. When Peter obeyed Jesus, the boat was filled with fish. Everything we have comes from the hand of the Lord. If we never give God credit or glory, we are not disciples.

**Realize.** Disciples realize their sin. We all sin, but some people do not know it. Peter fell at Jesus's knees when he realized his sin. We are disciples when we realize that though we deserve nothing, God loves us, forgives us, and redeems us.

**Rethink.** Disciples rethink their life's plan. Peter was able to change. If we think we have seen it all, heard it all, and done it all, we are not disciples. A disciple always asks God for direction in finding more opportunities to serve.

**Relinquish.** Disciples relinquish everything to follow Jesus. When Peter got to shore, he willingly gave up all he had. So must we, remembering God never takes things out of our lives without replacing them with something else.

**Reflect.** Disciples reflect Jesus in their lives and do not have to tell people of their Christianity. It is obvious!

Take a moment to consider your commitment to Jesus Christ. Have you done all you must do to be His disciple?

*Read: Luke 5:1-11; Matthew 28:16-20; Matthew 19:27-29*

## YOUR PERSONAL BATTLE

*"And I will pray the Father, and he will give you another Counselor, to be with you for ever, even the Spirit of truth, whom the world cannot receive, because it neither sees him nor knows him; you know him, for he dwells with you, and will be in you" (John 14:16-17).*

We all have inside us both God's Holy Spirit and our own human spirit. Holy Spirit convicts us of sin, convinces us of right and wrong, cleanses, and converts. Our human spirit gives us the desire to indulge ourselves, judge other people harshly, and live selfishly. Holy Spirit and human spirit fight for control; we have an internal battle raging daily. The outcome is crucial, for Holy Spirit is the means by which God pours His love into our hearts. God delights to give us His Holy Spirit. "If you then, who are evil, know how to give good gifts to your children, how much more will the heavenly Father give the Holy Spirit to those who ask Him!" (Luke 11:13). The Christian life enables us, through the reading of God's Word, meditation, and prayer, to keep our human spirit subservient to Holy Spirit and allow Holy Spirit to be our motivating force.

There are major differences between Holy Spirit and human spirit. Holy Spirit is a leader, counselor, comforter, helper; human spirit stubbornly resists help and ultimately hurts us. Holy Spirit operates in the faith factor; human spirit demands facts. Holy Spirit believes in truth; human spirit acts on feelings. Holy Spirit bears fruit of love, joy, peace, patience, kindness, goodness, faithfulness, gentleness, and self-control; human spirit brings hate, meanness, and fear.

Both spirits are inside us. Which one is winning your personal battle? The good news of Scripture is that we have the power to choose the victor, and God Himself wants to help. "With us is the Lord our God, to help us and to fight our battles" (II Chronicles 32:8). We can give in to our selfish human spirit or we can repent of our human spirit, live by faith, seek and follow the truth, and bear fruit of the Spirit. Today, ask the Lord to fight your personal battle for you.

*Read: Romans 5:5; John 16:4-15; Titus 3:3-8*

# WHEN FAITH FALTERS

*"I believe; help my unbelief!" (Mark 9:24).*

God's Word always tells the truth about humanity. The Bible shows people not only in their strengths, but also in their weaknesses. We who are often weak can grow stronger by understanding the weaknesses in biblical heroes whom God loved. Elijah, the Mountain Man, defeated the prophets of Baal in a spectacular trial by fire, yet afterward his faith faltered and he wanted to die. Peter, the Rock, claimed he never would forsake Jesus, but turned to shifting sand. John the Baptizer, confined in jail, began to falter in faith and question the validity of Jesus. "He sent word by his disciples and said to him, 'Are you he who is to come, or shall we look for another?' And Jesus answered them, 'Go and tell John what you hear and see: the blind receive their sight and the lame walk, lepers are cleansed and the deaf hear, and the dead are raised up, and the poor have good news preached to them'" (Matthew 11:2-5).

Our own faith falters from time to time. We feel uncertain that Jesus really can do all He says. We are bewildered by tragedies and injustices. We find it hard to see how God is leading and directing our lives. We wonder how we can be sure, and if it is worth all the time, talent, and treasure we invest. Thank God, He never gives up on us even when we give up on Him! Notice, it was after John sent messengers to question Jesus that Jesus said, "Truly, I say to you, among those born of women there has risen no one greater than John the Baptist" (v. 11). Jesus did not compliment John in his strength, but in his weakness, when his faith was temporarily detoured and he expressed doubts. Though John had faltering faith, Jesus's faith never faltered in John. Jesus still believed in John even when John had trouble believing in Jesus.

Jesus went on to say, "Yet he who is least in the kingdom of heaven is greater than he" (v. 11). That's us! Even when our faith falters, Jesus thinks we are great. If your faith is faltering today, try to be patient and trust the Lord to help your unbelief. Always remember to have faith in Jesus's faith in you.

*Read: Matthew 11:1-15; I Kings 19:1-8; Mark 14:66-72*

214

# HE MEANS IT!

*"He who is greatest among you shall be your servant; whoever exalts himself will be humbled, and whoever humbles himself will be exalted" (Matthew 23:11-12).*

Servanthood -- such a beautiful ideal, such a lofty goal! Jesus exemplified the life of servanthood and He calls us to live as He did. Generally, we agree with the principle of servanthood, but when it gets down to specifics, I am not sure we always take it seriously. Have you ever thought Jesus's words might apply to other people, but somehow you are an exception? "You mean, with my position, my salary, my skills, I must be a servant to that so-and-so? I am to wait upon others, when really, I should be waited on? I have to pick up after everybody?" Yes! Jesus means what He says, whether we like it or not. And Jesus is not telling us to do high-profile, glamorous, prestigious jobs. He is talking about jobs that are often menial, sometimes messy, and usually thankless.

Pride is a great barrier to servanthood. Our human nature makes us think we are just a bit better than other people, and we like to be treated that way. Instead of seeing what we can do for someone else, we expect others to do things for us. The Bible warns that pride is deceptive and dangerous, for those who exalt themselves will be humbled by God Himself. "The pride of your heart has deceived you, you who live in the clefts of the rock, whose dwelling is high, who say in your heart, 'Who will bring me down to the ground?' Though you soar aloft like the eagle, though your nest is set among the stars, thence I will bring you down, says the Lord" (Obadiah 3-4). If you think you are high above everyone else, invincible, set among the stars, too exalted for servanthood, watch out!

Greatness in the Kingdom comes in serving, so make the decision to live as a humble servant of Jesus Christ. "The Son of man came not to be served but to serve" (Matthew 20:28). That is what He expects of His followers today. Jesus does not grant exemptions from servanthood. He tells us plainly how He wants us to live, and be assured, He means it!

*Read: Matthew 23:1-12; Psalm 119:89-91; Proverbs 16:18*

# HELPS FOR HEALING

*Behold, God is my helper; the Lord is the upholder of my life (Psalm 54:4).*

Through Jesus's healing of a man during a worship service in a Capernaum synagogue, God gives us helps for healing in our lives. Consider how the sick man helped Jesus to heal him.

**He sought to be taught.** The Bible says the man had an "unclean spirit" (Mark 1:23), which could have referred to demon possession, mental illness, epilepsy, alcoholism, a nervous disorder -- we do not know for sure. Whatever it was, the afflicted man knew there was something wrong and was not afraid to admit it. He made the effort to search for somebody to teach him, to guide him, to heal him. He went to the right place, a house of worship, for there he met Jesus Christ.

**He fought with a new thought.** He was willing to struggle. Healing is never easy. We tend to fight against new ideas and suggestions even when we know they are right, because we do not want to change. I see the phenomenon frequently in the counseling room. I call it the IRS system. That is not the Internal Revenue Service. It means Intimidation, Rebellion, and Screams! Sometimes the closer we get to a life-changing breakthrough, the more violent is the reaction. The demoniac, though, had the courage to wrestle with Jesus's words, in spite of his anger, hostility, and turmoil.

**He caught what Christ wrought.** After he sought and after he fought, the sick man caught the healing only Jesus could give. He did not know how it happened, and he did not ask. Observers were shocked. "They were all amazed, so that they questioned among themselves, saying 'What is this?'" (v. 27). Not the healed man. He was just grateful to be well.

If you are hurting today, Jesus Christ came for you. "Those who are well have no need of a physician, but those who are sick; I have not come to call the righteous, but sinners to repentance" (Luke 5:31-32). God wants you to be healthy and whole in mind, body, and spirit. Trust Him to help you and uphold your life, in His own time and in His own way.

*Read: Mark 1:21-28; Matthew 8:16-17; Luke 9:11*

# WHERE TO FIND LOVE

*Beloved, let us love one another; for love is of God, and he who loves is born of God and knows God. He who does not love does not know God; for God is love. In this the love of God was made manifest among us, that God sent his only Son into the world, so that we might live through him. In this is love, not that we loved God but that he loved us and sent his Son to be the expiation for our sins. Beloved, if God so loved us, we also ought to love one another (I John 4:7-11).*

People have been looking for love in every generation of history, but many look in the wrong place. Some think, "If only I can get this car, this income, this house, this person, then I will have love." That is looking for love through possessions. Possessions only bring about the desire to have more possessions; they do not bring love. Others imagine, "If only I read more books, if only I get another degree, then I will know everything there is to know about love." No, we cannot find love in a book. The latest trend is datemaker ads. Telephone companies and newspapers make a few dollars while people look and hope for love, but love will not be found there either.

The Bible tells us we find love in this imperfect, sinful world through the perfect, sinless Christ. "For God so loved the world that he gave his only Son, that whoever believes in him should not perish but have eternal life" (John 3:16). God loved the world so much that He sent His Son, Jesus Christ, to tell each and every one of us, "I love you." We know what love is because God gave us love. "Love is patient and kind; love is not jealous or boastful; it is not arrogant or rude. Love does not insist on its own way; it is not irritable or resentful; it does not rejoice at wrong, but rejoices in the right. Love bears all things, believes all things, hopes all things, endures all things. Love never ends" (I Corinthians 13:4-8).

God is love and love is of God. To discover the meaning of love and of life, follow Jesus's command to love God with all your heart, soul, mind, and strength and love your neighbor as yourself. Love is not hard to find if you know where to look.

*Read: Mark 12:28-31; John 13:34-35; Romans 5:8*

# MIRACLES

*Jesus then took the loaves, and when he had given thanks, he distributed them to those who were seated; so also the fish, as much as they wanted. And when they had eaten their fill, he told his disciples, "Gather up the fragments left over, that nothing may be lost" (John 6:11-12).*

God can do anything, anytime, anywhere, in any way He wants. That is the sovereignty of God. God performs miracles that are startling, beyond explanation, seemingly impossible. He performed them in biblical times and still performs them today. Perhaps the most miraculous thing about God's miracles is that He allows people to help Him. God causes miracles, but He calls people to get involved in the making of miracles. All four Gospel writers talk about the feeding of the 5,000. That dramatic event shows what God uses to make miracles happen.

**Response.** Miracles begin when we respond to the incredible ideas God sends. Feeding 5,000 people with a few loaves and fish? We respond obediently to God's ideas only if we believe, "All things are possible with God" (Mark 10:27).

**Resources.** The size of our resources does not matter. God wants us to bring whatever we have and say, "Here, Lord, it may not be much, but it is all I have and I give it to you."

**Relaxation.** We cannot force God to create a miracle. Miracles happen by God's plan. We must wait upon Him to show us when the moment is right. Then comes the time to work, using our best common sense, dedication, and love.

**Remembrance.** Jesus did not send the disciples to gather up the fragments because He needed the crumbs and fish bones for another miracle. He knew their sore fingers and aching backs would remind them of what happened that day! When God involves us in a miracle, we should remember all we saw, did, and felt, so the experience strengthens our faith.

Thank God today for what He has done through you thus far and pray He will be able to do even greater things in the future. Never forget yesterday's miracles, for the miracles of yesterday prepare you for the miracles of tomorrow.

*Read: John 6:1-14; Acts 2:22-24; Daniel 4:3*

218

# DO NOT BE AFRAID OF FEAR

*"Will not his majesty terrify you?" (Job 13:11).*

"Fear not!" That phrase occurs throughout the Bible. It is great advice, except when we are scared to death, when our knees are shaking, when the earth is quaking, when our hearts are breaking, it does not work, does it? Trying to persuade a frightened person not to fear is like telling a drowning person to quit gasping for air, a person with an open cut to stop bleeding, or somebody who is choking to death to be quiet!

The women who went to the sepulchre on Easter morn knew fear. Suddenly the earth moved and an angel came down, rolled back the stone, and sat upon it, his radiance so blinding that the guards trembled and fainted. What did the angel say to the women? "Do not be afraid" (Matthew 28:5). I think I would want to punch anyone who gave advice like that in such an eerie situation! I would need reassurance, support, answers. I would not need someone saying, "Do not be afraid." I guess angels do not know fear the way we human beings do. Fear can be crippling and absolutely devastating if we allow it to control us, but fear is not always bad. In fact, if we cannot take a little fear, we will never have the experience of meeting Jesus. Confrontations with the Lord are dramatic, awesome, and frightening. "It is a fearful thing to fall into the hands of the living God" (Hebrews 10:31). We must be able to endure those fearful moments to see the glory of the risen Christ.

Perhaps you are frightened right now. Maybe you are in the darkest, loneliest moment of your life. You wonder if the suffering will ever stop. Maybe you are even considering ending your life. Do not give up! Never let troubles, whatever they are, destroy you. God loves you and He is coming with comfort and strength. Today you could sense His presence and power as never before. His majesty might terrify you, but praise God! You are on your way to new life in Jesus Christ.

Do not be afraid of fear. Rather, let fear lead you to put complete trust and confidence in Jesus Christ, who says, "Do not fear, only believe" (Mark 5:36). He alone brings peace.

*Read: Matthew 28:1-10; Psalm 111:10; John 14:27*

# SOUR SAINTS

*Here is a call for the endurance of the saints, those who keep the commandments of God and the faith of Jesus (Revelation 14:12).*

Luke 15 is one of the Bible's most powerful chapters. It not only offers advice for prodigals and their families. It also has counsel for hard-working, law-abiding, church-going people. The elder brother, a supposed saint, was the kind of individual churches need to be effective. Through him, we see how easy it is for decent people to become sullen, resentful, and harsh, sliding into subtle sins that turn them into sour saints.

Sainthood goes sour when we disassociate ourselves from people we do not like. Coming in from the field, the elder son heard music. A servant told him his father was throwing a party to celebrate his wayward brother's return. "He was angry and refused to go in" (Luke 15:28). Jesus never said we had to like one another, but He did command us to love one another as He loved us. When we do not, our Christianity spoils.

Also, sainthood goes sour when we think someone else has won what we rightfully deserve. "His father came out and entreated him, but he answered his father, 'Lo, these many years I have served you, and I never disobeyed your command; yet you never gave me a kid, that I might make merry with my friends'" (v. 28-29). God wants us to quit playing the game of winning and losing. He does not operate on the merit system, but on the grace system. We earn none of His blessings. He gives because He loves us. When we think God plays favorites and we are being slighted, our Christianity turns sour.

For almost 2,000 years, the dedicated, responsible brother has been known not as a hero, but as a sour saint. He ends up losing everything, missing the party, standing out in the field, angry, disgruntled, upset, defeated. Do not let that happen to you! God has given you creation, life, rebirth through Christ, and the power of His Holy Spirit to become a saint. He calls for your endurance in faith, so protect the sainthood bestowed upon you by God. You cannot lose it if you do not give it up.

*Read: Luke 15:11-32; I Corinthians 1:2-3; Psalm 31:23*

# GIVE, GIVE, GIVE

*God loves a cheerful giver (II Corinthians 9:7).*

According to Jesus, there are things we must be able to give away, give up, and give to, if we hope to find meaning in life.

**Give away: Money.** Money is not to be worshipped as a god nor wasted as garbage. It is to be given away in Christ's name to bring fulfillment to ourselves and others. **Talents.** Talents are natural abilities given at birth, and all our talents are important to the Kingdom. If we do not give them away to help people, we waste them. **Time.** We should give away our time to rescue those in need and teach the Good News.

**Give up: Rights.** As Christians, we do not live by rights. We live by grace. We do things that do not sound right to our culture because they are right in God's eyes: turn the other cheek, go the extra mile, give to those who beg. **Security.** Security has become a national obsession, yet it is only when we give up security and live in mystery that we are alert, awake, and open to new ventures. **Control.** We have to give up our desire to coerce, correct, and command people. We will never know peace if we try to be everybody's boss and direct the universe. The only person we can control is ourselves.

**Give to: Give to God** what He wants from us: praise and thanksgiving. "O give thanks to the Lord, for he is good; for his steadfast love endures for ever!" (Psalm 107:1). **Give to other people** love and forgiveness, no matter what they have done. We do not have to like people, but we do have to love them; when we do, we usually begin to like them as well. **Give to yourself** appreciation, for you are made in the image of God and there is no one like you in all the world. You have value!

Give, give, give . . . What do you get from all this giving? Life! Jesus said, "Whoever would save his life will lose it; and whoever loses his life for my sake and the gospel's will save it" (Mark 8:35). When you give everything you have and everything you are, you find the joy, purpose, and power God created you to have. Be a cheerful giver. The more you give, the more you will love Jesus Christ, who gave His life for you.

*Read: Matthew 5:38-42; Psalm 7:17; Proverbs 21:26*

## PACKING FOR JERUSALEM JOURNEYS

*Taking the twelve, he said to them, "Behold, we are going up to Jerusalem, and everything that is written of the Son of man by the prophets will be accomplished" (Luke 18:31).*

On Palm Sunday, Jesus made a journey to Jerusalem that He knew would end with His death on the Cross. In our lives, we, too, are forced to make Jerusalem journeys more often than we would like. They are awful times when we must confront what we do not want to confront, decide what we do not want to decide, meet what we do not want to meet. We fear those journeys, but we cannot always avoid them. If you face a Jerusalem journey today, be sure you know what to pack.

**Pack the presence of Jesus Christ.** God is omnipotent and omnipresent, but to have the assurance of His presence, you must acknowledge Him and believe He is present. Even in perilous emergencies and crises, Jesus Christ is with you. You are not alone, any time, any place, or in any experience.

**Pack the sense of preparedness.** God has prepared the experience even before you get to the destination. Wherever you are called to go, Jesus has been there before and He is there now to bring comfort and strength. He is your Shepherd.

**Pack the prophecy.** All the prophecy! Jesus told us we would suffer, so do not complain. Followers of Christ do not get an easy, free ride. Expect problems and remember, the prophecy ends in victory. Jesus's Jerusalem journey did not end with the crucifixion, but with the glory of the resurrection.

**Pack prayer.** In the midst of your Jerusalem journey, do not hesitate to ask God for guidance, strength, and wisdom. Persevere with your petition, no matter what people say or do, and believe He will direct you where He wants you to go.

**Pack praise!** Thank God for every blessing. Whenever any insight comes enabling you to see that Jesus Christ loves you and He is leading you to a great Jerusalem, praise God.

Wherever you are in the travels of life, be prepared for Jerusalem journeys. Pack your bags and get going! God will make sure you have all you need to accomplish your mission.

*Read: Psalm 139:7; I Corinthians 2:9; Matthew 5:17; Jude 20; Psalm 115:18*

# SIGNS OF REPENTANCE

*"Bear fruits that befit repentance" (Luke 3:8).*

Repentance is not merely a concept to think about or a sense of remorse for sin. Repentance involves drastic change. It means changing our direction, our minds, our priorities, the way we think, talk, and act. Signs of repentance are vastly different from our natural tendencies. If repentance is happening in our lives, we will see striking evidence of change.

**Sharing.** By nature we are selfish and self-indulgent. We try to keep all we have and get more. We resent the demands of destitute, needy people. A sign of repentance is sharing.

**Honesty.** Games and lies -- that is how we operate. We hide from the truth, deceiving ourselves and others, and cheat when we can get away with it. A sign of repentance is honesty.

**Kindness.** We like to bully and intimidate. We feel powerful when people fear us. We deal harshly and rudely with those whom we dislike. A sign of repentance is kindness.

**Contentment.** We become angry when other people are more successful than we are. We abuse ourselves and use others to get ahead. A sign of repentance is contentment.

No wonder signs of repentance are visible for all to see; they stand out so brightly against the dreary self-centeredness of natural humanity. Only God can bring about such incredible changes. What a powerful testimony of His transforming love! Peter said, "Repent therefore, and turn again, that your sins may be blotted out, that times of refreshing may come from the presence of the Lord" (Acts 3:19). The universal longing for times of refreshing that come from the presence of the Lord is satisfied only by the process of repentance.

Never think of repentance as a harsh deprivation of your self-indulgent pastimes. Repentance is the path to fellowship with God and to joy, and not only joy in your life, but joy in Heaven as well, for there is joy in Heaven over every person who repents. Turn yourself over to God and allow Him to work His amazing grace in you. The fruits of repentance you bear will bring joy in this world and throughout eternity.

*Read: Luke 3:1-14; Ezekiel 18:30-32; Luke 15:7*

# BLIND FAITH

*"I have come as light into the world, that whoever believes in me may not remain in darkness" (John 12:46).*

A poor, blind beggar who lived in Jericho nearly 2,000 years ago can teach us a great deal about our walk of faith today. His name was Bartimaeus, and his blind faith made him well and enabled him to see. It was the healing power of Jesus that brought blind Bartimaeus out of darkness and into the light, but Bartimaeus himself had a vital part in this miracle.

**Bartimaeus had a vision of what he could become.** He saw himself contributing, not begging; involved in life, not sitting by the roadside. He believed he would be healed. God gave him a vision and he caught it. That is how healing begins.

**Bartimaeus shouted for help.** People rebuked him and told him to keep quiet, but he repeatedly cried, "Jesus, Son of David, have mercy on me!" (Mark 10:47). He did not let embarrassment, timidity, or opposition keep him from the Lord, but made a noisy racket until Jesus stopped to listen.

**Bartimaeus obeyed Jesus's command to come to Him.** Throwing off his robe, feeling his way through the crowd, not knowing where he was going or what would happen, he sprang up and came to Jesus. He had no idea what Jesus would do. He simply trusted Jesus Christ to do what was best.

**Bartimaeus knew what his problem was and he asked for specific help from the Lord.** "Jesus said to him, 'What do you want me to do for you?' And the blind man said to him, 'Master, let me receive my sight'" (v. 51). Jesus did not have to ask Bartimaeus what he wanted. He knew Bartimaeus was blind. Jesus wanted Bartimaeus to understand his own problem. God is ready to supply our needs, but we must be willing and able to ask for specific help with our concerns.

"Walk by faith, not by sight" (II Corinthians 5:7). Blind faith! It is the kind of faith that brings miracles, heals hurts, solves problems, and takes people out of darkness and into the light. Put your faith in Jesus Christ, who came as light into the world, so you do not remain in darkness another moment.

*Read: Mark 10:46-52; Psalm 146; Isaiah 42:5-7*

# THE TWO FACES OF HYPOCRISY

*"Beware of practicing your piety before men in order to be seen by them; for then you will have no reward from your Father who is in heaven" (Matthew 6:1).*

Watch out for hypocrisy in your life.  Watch out for hypocrites!  Hypocrisy has two faces: some hypocrites try to look good, while others try to make everyone else look bad.

People who like to appear to be good present a pretty picture to the world.  They go to all the elite places.  They claim the prestigious pews at church.  They expect everyone to call them exemplary names.  "They love the place of honor at feasts and the best seat in the synagogues, and salutations in the market places" (Matthew 23:6-7).  They manufacture a sterling image for themselves, but there is just one problem: they are phonies who do not practice what they preach.  They are undependable, inconsistent, and insincere.  We can never be sure who the real person is: the one who speaks, or the one whose mean actions scream so loudly that we cannot hear any words.  They play games, wear masks, and care only about self.

People who try to make others look bad practice a more subtle, vicious hypocrisy.  These people, with their smug sense of religious superiority, look down on everyone.  They act as if they have supreme authority to judge others.  When they have power to help, they use their power to hurt.  "They bind heavy burdens, hard to bear, and lay them on men's shoulders; but they themselves will not move them with their finger" (Matthew 23:4).  They could lift people up, but instead load them down with harsh denunciation and criticism.  Tragically, they turn themselves and others into children of hell.

God does not like hypocrisy.  It is a waste of time and effort.  Hypocrisy is acting, not living.  When we are not honest and direct, we are of no value to the Lord.  Jesus warns that hypocrites will not enter the Kingdom, so guard against the two faces of hypocrisy.  It is a daily battle to keep hypocrisy out of our lives, but it is a battle we can win if we just remember that the answer to hypocrisy is good old-fashioned humility.

*Read:  Matthew 6:1-18;  Matthew 23:1-28;  Mark 7:1-8*

# A SPECIAL SENSITIVITY

*"Blessed are your eyes, for they see, and your ears, for they hear" (Matthew 13:16).*

So often Jesus is with us, in our midst, speaking, loving, trying to help, yet we do not recognize Him. We can be in the very presence of the Lord and not know it. Jesus Christ is alive today, but it takes a special sensitivity blessed by His Holy Spirit to feel and see and experience that He is here.

Of course, spiritual dullness is not unique to us. It has been a problem in all ages since Christ brought the Kingdom to earth. Jesus said to His own disciples, "Do you not yet perceive or understand? Are your hearts hardened? Having eyes do you not see, and having ears do you not hear?" (Mark 8:17-18). Even people who knew Jesus well during His ministry did not perceive His identity after His resurrection. The most difficult thing Jesus had to do on Easter morn was not to be resurrected; it was to convince people that He was resurrected! Mary Magdalene stood before Jesus in the cemetery and mistook Him for the gardener. Two men on the road to Emmaus walked with Jesus for some distance without realizing who He was. On Easter night in the Upper Room, Jesus came before the disciples and they thought He was a spirit. "Jesus himself stood among them. But they were startled and frightened" (Luke 24:36).

We need to cultivate a special sensitivity to believe Jesus is alive, He is here. When we feel at peace in the midst of chaos, that is Jesus. When we question tragedies and mysteries but still know God is in control, that is Jesus. When we grow stronger from our weaknesses, that is Jesus. When we are unsure what to do and suddenly an answer comes, that is Jesus. When our lives change miraculously and we want to tell people about it, that is Jesus. Do you see how He works? If you begin to look and listen for Him, you soon find Him everywhere.

The resurrection is not only a fact of history. It is an experience you can know today. The risen Lord is with you!

*Read: Matthew 13:10-17; Luke 24:1-43; Psalm 21:6*

# CONSIDER YOUR CONTROLLER

*Consider Jesus, the apostle and high priest of our confession (Hebrews 3:1).*

Everyone is controlled by somebody or something. We may not like to hear that, but it is true. You are controlled by somebody or something and so am I. It should be God who controls us, but people are controlled by money, power, popularity, physical satisfaction, friends, foes, family, cults, sickness, selfishness, and more. The disciples found three powerful controllers one night on the Sea of Galilee when Jesus walked on the water during a storm to reach their boat.

**Fear**. "When the disciples saw him walking on the sea, they were terrified, saying, 'It is a ghost!' And they cried out for fear" (Matthew 14:26). Fear and terror control many of us. When sudden storms howl, we see problems instead of potential, horror instead of hope, ghosts instead of God.

**Impulse**. Impulsive, impetuous Peter! Without consulting his friends or taking time to reason logically, he climbed out of the boat and started to walk on the raging water toward Jesus.

**Wind**. The wind of adversity! Peter walked on the sea until he took his eyes off Jesus and noticed the fury of the storm. Then he began to sink, just as we do when we take our eyes off Jesus. Often we concentrate too much on the wind of adversity and not enough on the words and promises of Christ.

"An upright man considers his ways" (Proverbs 21:29). Everybody has a controller, but each of us has the power to decide who or what controls us and to change controllers whenever we choose. Right now, try honestly to identify and evaluate the controlling force in your life. If your controller is not Jesus Christ, please consider your ways, for you are on your way to eventual disaster.

To make Jesus Christ the controller of your life, believe He is with you, call on Him to save you, and wait for Him to lead you. That is all it takes. Your new controller, Jesus Christ, the apostle and high priest of the Christian faith, promises that nothing will ever separate you from His love.

*Read: Matthew 14:22-33; Hebrews 12:3; Psalm 47:5-7*

# GOOD SOIL

*"And as for that in the good soil, they are those who, hearing the word, hold it fast in an honest and good heart, and bring forth fruit with patience" (Luke 8:15).*

Jesus tells the parable of the sower to explain that whenever the Word of God is cast, it falls upon people with different levels of receptivity. There are four kinds of soil.

**Hard soil.** Some seed falls on the path where the ground is hard. These are people who are indifferent to God's Word. They are not concerned about salvation; they think they already have all the answers and know everything there is to know. They are hard-headed, or, as the Bible says, hard-hearted.

**Shallow soil.** The seed immediately is caught. People become excited, faith begins to grow, but there is no depth, no thought. Soon the Word is snatched away. These people go to church enthusiastically for a while, then are not seen again.

**Thorny soil.** The seed is cast and begins to germinate, but other forces quickly choke the Word of God: anxieties, fears, troubles, false promises of wealth. These lives are cluttered, mixed-up, and confused. God's Holy Word is pushed out.

**Good soil.** Good soil is open, free, and cultivated. People receive the Word of God gladly, sincerely. They hold it fast, joyously and consistently bringing forth good, lasting fruit.

Good soil is the result of painstaking, laborious preparation. Tilling the ground takes the sharp blades of the plow, the continuous hacking of the hoe to break clumps of dirt, the deep piercing of the spade to separate the earth, keep the soil loose, and allow the seed to flourish. So it is with receptivity to the Word of the Lord. It can be a painful process to grow in faith. Often it takes tragedies and traumas to prepare us to hear and accept God's Word. If now your heart is aching and your foundations are shaking, it is difficult, but praise God! Hard soil is breaking up; shallow soil is deepening; thorny soil is clearing; good soil is being cultivated for you to receive the Word of God. Allow the Lord to work in your garden and thank Him today for the great harvest He will bring forth.

*Read: Luke 8:4-15; II Corinthians 9:10; James 1:22-25*

# TEST YOUR RELIGION

*Religion that is pure and undefiled before God and the Father is this: to visit orphans and widows in their affliction, and to keep oneself unstained from the world (James 1:27).*

There are many religions in the world. Christianity has three main branches: Roman Catholicism, Eastern Orthodoxy, and Protestantism, which has hundreds of denominations. Sadly, in addition there are hordes of deceivers claiming to be of the Almighty and countless dogmas that are far off target. No wonder people are bewildered! I offer four tests to help identify true religion.

1. True religion comes from wisdom from above rather than knowledge from below. It is founded on what God sends down, not on what some person dreams up. Religion is not based on how much we know; otherwise only Christian Phi Beta Kappas would enter the Kingdom! Religion is based on what we believe concerning the revelation and inspiration from God. True religion has authority. It does not offer suggestions, present alternatives, or give multiple choices. It commands!

2. True religion helps people use their emotions in the right way. It fosters growth in love, forgiveness, kindness, and patience. It enables us to conquer unhealthy fear and anger so we can live the productive, joyful lives God wants us to have.

3. True religion makes people honest. It inspires us to live with honor and integrity in a society filled with phonies and frauds. True religion motivates us to overcome our hardness of heart and recognize the need for correction and change.

4. True religion keeps people close to eternal values. It kindles integrity, compassion, and commitment to serve God in practical ways. Piety and good works are bound together, for "faith by itself, if it has no works, is dead" (James 2:17).

Cults, self-proclaimed messiahs, cultural fads that appear and disappear so often -- none can pass these four tests. Only God's Son, Jesus Christ, is the way, the truth, and the life. Do not let yourself be fooled by any other person or idea. Never allow anyone or anything to lure you away from Christianity, the only true religion and the only way to eternal life.

*Read: James 1:19-27; Lamentations 3:40; Isaiah 5:20*

# THE ARMOR OF GOD

*Be strong in the Lord and in the strength of his might. Put on the whole armor of God, that you may be able to stand against the wiles of the devil (Ephesians 6:10-11).*

It is distressing to see a Christian stumble, fall, and lose faith. It is frightening, too, because if we are honest, we realize any one of us can become a wreck upon the highway of life. Being a Christian in this fallen world is not easy. To be strong in the Lord, we must cooperate by accepting the grace of God and putting on the armor of God. The whole armor! We cannot venture out half-dressed if we hope to combat the diabolical, relentless forces of evil. Paul tells us what to wear.

**The Belt of Truth.** Truth is like a belt: not too expensive, but indispensable in holding everything together. Without the belt of truth, we have no freedom, firmness, or force.

**The Breastplate of Righteousness.** The breastplate shelters the heart. The power of evil will try to destroy us through our hearts: to break our hearts, cause us to lose heart, or make our hearts hard. We protect ourselves by doing right.

**Shoes equipped with Peace.** Shoes must be comfortable, flexible, durable. In your Christian walk, put on equipment that brings peace: love, forgiveness, patience, and tolerance.

**The Shield of Faith.** Faith is the most important part of the Christian's armor. Faith justifies us, heals us, empowers us, and enables us to believe. We cannot please God without faith.

**The Helmet of Salvation.** Helmets are designed to protect the head, which contains the mind, and also to identify clearly to whose army we belong.

**The Sword of the Spirit.** The sword is the only offensive weapon the Christian has; all the others are defensive. The sword of the Spirit is God's Word, which shall abide forever.

Do not risk spiritual suicide by going out unprotected. Put on the whole armor of God so you can be strong and live in the might of the Lord. And remember, the armor of God is not just a protective covering, but also a magnificent, impressive display. Wear it proudly! All the world ought to recognize you as a Christian marching under the banner of Jesus Christ.

*Read: Ephesians 6:10-20; Romans 13:11-14; I Thessalonians 5:8-10*

230

# A COSTLY INVESTMENT

*He loves righteousness and justice (Psalm 33:5).*

Anger is a serious and expensive emotion. Every time we get angry, physical changes occur that are costly to us: breathing deepens, the heart beats more rapidly, stored-up sugar in the liver is released, the spleen contracts, adrenaline is secreted, veins swell, and the complexion reddens. If we express anger rashly, we provoke people to become angry at us. If we suppress it, we induce headaches, hypertension, and other ailments. What a price the body pays for anger!

The only way to get a good return on our investment in anger is to use anger constructively. Jesus, the truest example of what humanity was created to be, became angry -- in the house of worship! He was so angry that He overturned tables and drove money changers out of the temple. Notice, though, Jesus directed His holy anger not against people, whom He loved, but against systems that were full of holes, broken down, deteriorating, ineffective: justice that was not just; religion that was not religious; processes that did not proceed; practices that violated what was preached. God blessed His anger because Jesus used it to restore wholeness, righteousness, and justice.

Like Jesus, we are to control anger and direct it against wrongs in society, communities, and churches. Investing in holy anger is not like putting money in the bank, where we collect interest without doing anything. Holy anger takes whole-hearted involvement. It is lazy and irresponsible just to pray about wrongs and expect God to fix everything. We need to take a moral stand, persevere in the face of opposition, and follow through until corrections are made. God created us to love people and get angry at wrongs that trap people in the holes and hells of life. He is depending on us to work for righteousness and justice, as Jesus Christ did.

Be careful how you spend your anger. If you are adding more hostility to the world, the cost will be misery for you and everyone around you, but if you use anger for the good of the Kingdom, your investment will bring a heavenly reward.

*Read: Matthew 21:12-17; Mark 3:1-5; Amos 5:24*

# THE LAST STEP

*"How hard it is to enter the kingdom of God!" (Mark 10:24).*

Jesus has a warning for people who claim to be disciples. "Not every one who says to me, 'Lord, Lord,' shall enter the kingdom of heaven" (Matthew 7:21). There are degrees of closeness to the Kingdom. In which category are you today?

**Acknowledgers.** Acknowledgers recognize the existence of God, Jesus, and the Church, but do not truly love God, Jesus, and the Church. They have Bibles, but seldom read them. They go to church on Christmas and Easter, for weddings and funerals. They pray when they need something or when they want to blame God for the vexing problems in their lives.

**Approachers.** Approachers come to church, listen, then drop out of sight, returning only when they have an emergency. They promise to get involved, but are all talk and no action.

**Askers.** Askers are willing to take questions to Jesus, but they argue with His answers. They think biblical demands are too difficult and prefer to find an easier philosophy to follow.

**Agreers.** Agreers assent intellectually to the answers Jesus gives, but not enough to make a commitment. They are close to the Kingdom, but still outside. There is one more step.

**Accepters.** Accepters have the courage to take the last step, the one that counts: they accept Jesus as Lord and Savior and Master of their lives, and never look back. Becoming an accepter is an act of will, a decision to honor and obey the commands of Jesus no matter how high the cost, saying, "I am going to love God with all my heart, soul, mind, and strength, and love that son-of-a-gun neighbor in spite of everything!"

If we travel 999.9 miles of a 1,000 mile trip and never go that last tenth, the trip is not complete. Many people will not know the beauty of life in Christ on earth or the beauty of life everlasting in Heaven, where "the righteous will shine like the sun in the kingdom of their Father" (Matthew 13:43).

How close are you to the Kingdom? God wants you there. "It is your Father's good pleasure to give you the Kingdom" (Luke 12:32). If you have not done it yet, take the last step.

*Read: Mark 12:28-34; Luke 12:32-34; Matthew 13:47-50*

# LITTLE PEOPLE AND LITTLE THINGS

*"'As you did it to one of the least of these my brethren, you did it to me'" (Matthew 25:40).*

To serve Jesus, one does not have to perform spectacular miracles and do great big things all the time. Jesus said, "Whoever gives to one of these little ones even a cup of cold water because he is a disciple, truly, I say to you, he shall not lose his reward" (Matthew 10:42). Throughout His earthly ministry, Jesus identified with "the least of these." He felt deep compassion for "little ones," not just little children, but little people of all ages who needed help to grow bigger and better.

As His disciples in the world today, it is our responsibility to identify little people with big hurts: little people who are hungry and need nourishment; who are tired and need refreshment; who are naked and need socks and shirts and dresses and coats; who are strangers and need recognition; who are sick and need comfort; who are in prison and need hope. We are to help in immediate, tangible, practical ways.

It is little things that count to Christ. Neglecting to do little things can make a big difference in our destiny. According to Jesus, a very little thing could separate us from the Kingdom of Heaven for eternity: a cup of cold water, a hamburger and French fries, some socks or shirts or dresses or coats, a greeting card or a phone call or a visit or a warm smile or a hug. Serving the needs of others in the name of Jesus ought to become a way of life for every Christian. When there is someone to help or something to do, we should not even have to think about it, but just instantly do whatever we can to help, with kindness, concern, enthusiasm, and perseverance. It is hard at first to reach out to others. It takes practice, but the more it is done, the easier it gets and the more Jesus loves it.

Never consider yourself unimportant in God's Kingdom. Do not put yourself down because you think you have not done anything big or spectacular or colossal for the Lord. Every day, you can help little people and do little things, and that is the way the Lord Jesus Christ wants you to serve Him.

*Read: Matthew 25:31-46; Galatians 5:13-15; Luke 16:10*

# HOW TO SAY YES

*Be rich in good deeds, liberal and generous (I Timothy 6:18).*

To be in the world but not of it, to deny ourselves and take up our crosses to follow Jesus, to present our bodies as living sacrifices, Christians must say No to many appeals. Yet sometimes we forget to say Yes to God. A Christian cannot grow by saying only No. The moment comes when we have to say Yes if we are to find the destiny for which we were created. God often speaks to us through the needs and requests of other people. When someone asks something of us and it is not opposed to our Christian ethics, we ought to do it!

Fear is perhaps the greatest hindrance to saying Yes to God. We are afraid we might look foolish, lose control, or not get our way. Overcome the fear! Throughout the Old and New Testaments, God tells people, "Fear not!" He gives us power to rise above fear through self-control and perfect love. That does not mean we should go around wearing a silly grin on our faces all the time, pretending nothing ever goes wrong. When we say Yes to God, we still will have struggles and tears, and people might even call us suckers and fools. Say Yes anyway!

Also, do not worry that a new responsibility will take too much of your time, talent, or treasure. Selfish people always look for what they can get, but usually end up losing what they have. Jesus said, "Whoever would save his life will lose it, and whoever loses his life for my sake will find it. For what will it profit a man, if he gains the whole world and forfeits his life? Or what shall a man give in return for his life? For the Son of man is to come with his angels in the glory of his Father, and then he will repay every man for what he has done" (Matthew 16:25-27). Say Yes to God and find life's true purpose.

Live as an energetic servant of Jesus Christ. When you are caring and honest in your Christian walk, many people will thank God for you, and you probably will not even know it. God knows, and you will be moving closer to the fulfillment of your unique destiny. Whenever God provides an opportunity to be rich in good deeds, liberal and generous, say Yes!

*Read: Luke 9:57-62; James 2:14-17; Galatians 5:13*

234

# LESSONS FROM LUKE 15

*"Just so, I tell you, there is joy before the angels of God over one sinner who repents" (Luke 15:10).*

Throughout my ministry, I have referred more people to Luke 15 than to any other chapter of the Bible. It teaches so many lessons of life and answers so many questions. Luke 15 tells us how people are lost and how they are found.

**The lost sheep -- the baa baa lost.** Sheep are soft, cute, and stupid. They do not deliberately decide to get lost. They just wander around with their heads down looking for grass. Suddenly they look up and see no shepherd, no flock. Lost sheep are found by **shepherds**, big, strong, conscientious, sometimes unorthodox people who worry about sheep. "What man of you, having a hundred sheep, if he has lost one of them, does not leave the ninety-nine in the wilderness, and go after the one which is lost, until he finds it?" (v. 4). Shepherds get involved, run risks, and persist despite daunting obstacles.

**The lost coin -- the clink clink lost.** Coins are not dumb or smart. They have no minds or wills. Coins do not lose themselves; they are lost by someone else. Many people are lost not because of anything they have done, but because of another person's cruel or careless treatment. Lost coins are found by **searchers**. "What woman, having ten silver coins, if she loses one coin, does not light a lamp and sweep the house and seek diligently until she finds it?" (v. 8). Searchers let the light in and look gently and untiringly until they find the lost.

**The lost pig -- the oink oink lost.** Some individuals, like the prodigal, leave home knowing exactly what they are doing. Their deliberate disobedience eventually leads to a pig sty. These individuals are found through **common sense**. The prodigal "came to himself" (v. 17). He experienced a moment of insight and learned in his suffering how to think right at last.

Jesus uses different ways to find the lost, and no person on earth is beyond hope of salvation. If you are lost today or if you are trying to help someone who is lost, never give up! Through Jesus Christ, anybody, anybody at all, can be found.

*Read: Luke 15; John 6:38-40; Proverbs 13:14*

# REMEMBER NATHANAEL

*If one loves God, one is known by him (I Corinthians 8:3).*

Nathanael is one of the less prominent disciples. He was not in the top three or four. He was a second-stringer. Still, he was first-rate in the opinion of Jesus, who complimented Nathanael when they met. "Jesus saw Nathanael coming to him, and said of him, 'Behold, an Israelite indeed, in whom is no guile!' Nathanael said to him, 'How do you know me?' Jesus answered him, 'Before Philip called you, when you were under the fig tree, I saw you'" (John 1:47-48). A person without guile is a seeking, truthful individual; a sinner, a little misdirected, but essentially a sincere person who, despite questions, seeks to know the one true God and is not easily persuaded by false doctrines. Jesus was telling Nathanael, "You are an authentic Israelite, a son of Jacob who is not merely talker, but one who proves by his actions he is honest. I like you. I appreciate you. I observed you under the fig tree, wrestling with problems, praying with supplication, struggling over what to do. I saw you, I know you, and I love you."

Nathanael had a little trouble understanding Jesus's love. Sometimes we do, too. Can you understand that Jesus knows your past, your thoughts, your temptations, your mistakes, everything about you, yet He still loves you? If you are unsure of God's love, I urge you now to open the Gospels and see yourself coming to Jesus. Allow the words of the Master to be spoken as though they are to you alone. Try to hear His compassionate voice saying, "Yes, you are a sinner. You are a little confused and mixed-up. You have some prejudices. You do not always believe things I say. Still, I love you. I trust you. You are without guile. You are conscious of your inconsistencies and trying to be honest. I love you because you seek to be a true follower of mine." Remember Nathanael today and accept the biblical assurance that if you love God, you are known by Him and He accepts you just as you are.

You do not have to explain yourself to Jesus Christ. He sees you. He knows you. And still, always, He loves you.

*Read: John 1:43-51; Job 34:21; Psalm 14:2*

# SPIRITUAL SOMNAMBULISM

*It is full time now for you to wake from sleep. For salvation is nearer to us now than when we first believed (Romans 13:11).*

Somnambulism is sleepwalking, a state of unconsciousness in which we have no awareness of what is going on; the foot walks, the mouth talks, the eyes gawk, but the mind chalks up nothing! Jesus exhorts us to stay awake and alert, for spiritual somnambulism can keep us out of the Kingdom. "Watch therefore -- for you do not know when the master of the house will come, in the evening, or at midnight, or at cockcrow, or in the morning -- lest he come suddenly and find you asleep. And what I say to you I say to all: Watch" (Mark 13:35-37). In spite of Jesus's warning, we are slow to learn spiritual lessons. We live as though we already know everything. The Word of God alone has eternal meaning, yet few people read it. God tries to direct us, but we are too mentally drowsy to notice Him.

Spiritual somnambulism has eternal consequences. Before it is too late, wake up! Be ready to meet Jesus. How?

**Wait expectantly.** God will guide if we wait expectantly for Him to show us the things He has in store. God moves in many ways, so do not be shocked by anything He does.

**Watch attentively.** Sometimes we miss God because we are too busy. God does not operate by our time schedules or calendars. Watch for His presence every moment.

**Pray intently.** We are to go to prayer not with answers, but with questions; not to get out of something, but to get into something. Ask, "What are you trying to say to me, Lord? What do you want me to do? Where do you want me to go?"

**Work faithfully.** While you await His answer, do not sit around idly, but work wherever He places you to the best of your ability. God will not call you to new challenges until you prove faithful and upright in your current responsibilities.

It is time to wake up, for salvation is nearer every day. Do not sleepwalk through life. Sure, you can spend your days just breathing and eating and moving around, but you really will never be alive till you wake up and see the leading of the Lord.

*Read: Mark 13:28-37; Matthew 25:1-13; Revelation 3:1-3*

# HERESIES OF THE HEART

*"Thou, thou only, knowest the hearts of all the children of men"*
*(I Kings 8:39).*

Medical research indicates that when a person has a heart attack, often that attack on the heart alters the thinking of the mind. Our spiritual hearts are affected in a similar way. As the spiritual heart is attacked by heresies, rational perceptions give way to irrational ideas, emotions, and attitudes. Heresies creep in innocently, but they are dangerous. They pollute our thoughts and keep us from having the mind of Christ.

**The heresy of hopelessness.** The hopeless heart moans, "What's the use? I give up. You can't fight city hall. It's too late." This sick heresy inevitably brings divisiveness and separation to homes, businesses, churches. Hopeless people build walls around themselves and live in self-imposed misery.

**The heresy of lovelessness.** The loveless heart whines, "Nobody cares about me." What damage this heresy does! Generally it leads to vindictiveness. "Nobody loves me, so I'm not going to love anybody else." Loveless people fail to recognize the Cross as proof of God's love; they break the heart of God, who, in love, gave His only begotten Son to save us all.

**The heresy of faithlessness.** The faithless heart cries, "Why should I follow the Word of God? I'm looking out for me!" Faithless people never try to do good in the world; they are indifferent to others. There is plenty of this heresy around.

If you have hopelessness or lovelessness or faithlessness in your heart, it is only a matter of time until it comes out in your words, thinking, and logic. Do not let that happen! As a Christian, you are to be controlled by the mind of Christ, not heresies of the heart. God knows what is in your heart. Do you? Inspect your spiritual heart daily. Even if you face discouraging problems, keep heresies out of your heart and use your heart instead to love God, others, and yourself. You can do it if you believe God still is in control and working for good in all things. Keep your heart strong and pure by trusting in the matchless love and kindness of the Lord, no matter what.

*Read: Luke 6:43-45; I Corinthians 2:16; Hebrews 8:10-12*

# ACCEPT THAT CALL

*Let me hear what God the Lord will speak (Psalm 85:8).*

God calls people. God calls specific people at specific times to do specific tasks. We need to remember, though, that the voice of evil also gives us messages. Some people have claimed to hear a voice urging, "Kill, kill!" God would not give that message. It is wise to ask ourselves whether or not a voice we hear is truly a call from God before we act upon it.

Fortunately, it is not difficult to test a message to determine if it is of God. Ask three questions. 1. "Am I equipped to accomplish what God is asking me to do?" God never calls us to do anything without giving us the tools, skills, and gifts to fulfill it. If I get a message to swim across the Atlantic Ocean, I will know it is not from God. He knows I could not make it across Bakerstown creek! 2. "If I do not do it, is it something that someone else will do?" If you realize the job will not get done unless you do it, you can be pretty sure your message is of God. 3. "Is this something Jesus would do?" This is the supreme test. If it violates the teaching of Jesus in any way, it is not of God, for God cannot lie or contradict Himself. Run your message by those tests and you will know who is calling.

God calls in different ways: through His Word, the still small voice within, preachers and teachers, pastors and friends. He is an equal-opportunity caller. He calls men and women, young and old. He never calls on a conference call or station-to-station. It is always person-to-person, first class. How you answer His call is up to you. You can hang up. You can put Him on call-waiting and take other calls, hoping He will get tired and go away. You can put Him on call-forwarding so He will find somebody else. Or you can just let Him talk and do nothing. Those are not wise ways to answer the call of God. Little Samuel knew how to answer when God spoke. "Here I am! ... Speak, for thy servant hears" (I Samuel 3:4,10). Let that be your response the next time the Lord calls you.

Perhaps you will receive a call this very day. Whatever task He calls you to do, accept that call without delay!

*Read: I Samuel 3:1-18; Hebrews 1:1-2; John 10:27*

# HOW TO BE A HERO

*When I look at thy heavens, the work of thy fingers, the moon and the stars which thou hast established; what is man that thou art mindful of him, and the son of man that thou dost care for him? Yet thou hast made him little less than God, and dost crown him with glory and honor (Psalm 8:3-5).*

If you dream about becoming a hero, that's wonderful! God created every one of us to be heroic. We must understand, though, what it means to be a hero in the Kingdom. Even Jesus's first disciples were confused about spiritual greatness. Jesus Christ, the hero of all heroes, explained many times how to be great in the eyes of God. From the story of the rich young ruler, we learn that good works and obedience to the law are not enough. We also must have the right attitude about our possessions. How do you become a hero in God's sight?

**Be a part-time adventurer.** God placed within us the good instinct to reach for adventure. We are to use this instinct for spiritual gain by accepting challenges and taking risks to multiply our gifts, then share our resources with the needy.

**Be a full-time merchant.** The free enterprise system is biblical. It is good to make a profit so we can do more for God. "Honor the Lord with your substance" (Proverbs 3:9). Whatever God allows us to earn, we are to use to His glory.

**Be a some-time fool.** Sometimes we have to take our possessions and give them away, expecting nothing in return. "Give to him who begs from you" (Matthew 5:42). Giving to a beggar might seem foolish, but God commands us to do it.

**Be an all-time follower.** We usually think heroes are leaders, but that is not Kingdom theology. Kingdom heroes are followers of Christ who forsake everything to be His disciples.

We use possessions wisely if we remember they do not belong to us. "Whatever is under the whole heaven is mine" (Job 41:11). God created the heavens, moon, stars, everything; yet He cares for us and crowns us with glory and honor. In gratitude for His myriad blessings, let us strive to be Kingdom heroes by giving all that we have and all that we are to Him.

*Read: Luke 9:46-48; Mark 10:17-22; Mark 8:34-35*

# HOW TO PLEASE JESUS

*Try to learn what is pleasing to the Lord (Ephesians 5:10).*

Here are some suggestions on how to please Jesus today.

**Look Him up.** Nicodemus, a respected ruler of the Jews, took time at night to seek out Jesus to ask Him questions. Jesus is pleased when we humbly look for Him. Jesus Christ is everywhere, but He will never force His way into our lives. He comes in only by invitation. "The Lord is near to all who call upon him, to all who call upon him in truth" (Psalm 145:18). Look for Jesus in the Bible, the Church, and other people, even your enemies. You will find Him when you look Him up.

**Lift Him up.** "As Moses lifted up the serpent in the wilderness, so must the Son of man be lifted up, that whoever believes in him may have eternal life" (John 3:14-15). We lift Him up with our belief. Believe in Jesus as the Son of Man, who understands every experience a person can have, who knew rejection and temptation yet never yielded to sin, and as the Son of God, the perfect portrait of the Father. When we believe, though we cannot understand or explain, we are saved.

**Let up.** Let up on yourself and others; stop beating on everyone. "God sent the Son into the world, not to condemn the world, but that the world might be saved through him" (v. 17). Do not condemn what God saves! As followers of Jesus Christ, we are to build up, not tear down; compliment, not criticize; help people to learn, not teach them a lesson. God is pleased when we let up and lean upon Him.

**Live up to the truth.** Knowing the truth sets us free; living the truth makes us Christ-like. Do not make a show of religion. Simply live the truth. "He who does what is true comes to the light" (v. 21). No matter how difficult it is, keep loving and forgiving, never returning evil for evil. Jesus is pleased by people who not only know the truth, but do the truth.

As you try to learn what is pleasing to the Lord, remember, "without faith it is impossible to please him" (Hebrews 11:6). What counts most in pleasing the Lord is faith in Him.

*Read: John 3:1-21; Numbers 21:4-9; II Corinthians 5:9*

## "FOR"-"GIVE"-NESS

*O the depth of the riches and wisdom and knowledge of God!
(Romans 11:33).*

Words are fascinating, yet often we skip over familiar
words thoughtlessly, missing their subtle insight. Consider the
make-up of that important theological term, "forgiveness".

The word "for" has twenty-seven definitions in my edition
of Webster's Dictionary. Here are three: substitute or in place
of; in favor of; being able to do something for someone else.
Think about it. The Bible says, "All have sinned and fall short
of the glory of God" (Romans 3:23). To be forgiven of sin, we
need a substitute; we need somebody who is on our side; we
need somebody to do something we cannot do for ourselves.
In the Old Testament sacrificial system, priests burned guilt
offerings on the altar daily; each new sin required a new
sacrifice. Jesus, though, paid the price for sin once and for all
with His death on the Cross. "For God so loved the world"
(John 3:16). Jesus was "for" us in every sense of the word.

Now look at "give". To give means to yield or present
something to someone, expecting nothing in return. In the act
of giving, we relinquish ownership. What we give is no longer
ours. That is how forgiveness works. We give our guilt to
Jesus Christ. He takes it and it is no longer ours, because He
paid the price for our sin with His own blood. He sits now at
the right hand of God, waiting to make intercession for you and
for me. No matter what we have done in the past, what we do
today, or what we do in the future, we can give our guilt to
Jesus Christ and be renewed, refreshed, and redeemed.

When we understand the meaning of the words "for" and
"give", we understand a great deal about forgiveness!

Keep a dictionary beside your Bible and try to study more
diligently the eternal truth and startling beauty of the Holy
Scriptures. You will find unforgettable, priceless treasures on
every page if you look for them. Enrich your life beyond
measure today and every day by immersing yourself in the
depth of the riches and wisdom and knowledge of God.

*Read: Exodus 24:5-8; Hebrews 10:11-18; Proverbs 2:1-10*

# THOSE GRAVE SITUATIONS

*Behold, Jesus met them and said, "Hail!" And they came up and took hold of his feet and worshiped him (Matthew 28:9).*

This may not be an uplifting thought, but it is the truth: people usually do not have a vital, life-changing confrontation with Jesus Christ until first they face some very grave and serious experiences and hear some very sobering words. Even the resurrection began with the open grave. In Matthew 28:9, we see people meeting Jesus for the first time in His resurrected body, enjoying a vibrant, worshipful, wonderful experience with Him. Hallelujah! But though they met Jesus in verse nine, they spent the first eight verses in the graveyard.

The grave experiences we face are many: fear, sorrow, depression, loneliness, illness, loss, death. I know the pain of grave situations. I counsel parents who pray desperately for rebellious, wayward children. I sit in hospitals with people who try to hope in spite of a devastating diagnosis. I stand at the graveside with heartbroken people who want to believe they will see their loved ones again. Like people in all eras of history, many cry out to God, "Why is my pain unceasing?" (Jeremiah 15:18), sometimes wondering if God is even there.

If you are in a grave, serious, sobering situation today, do not give in to despair. It could be that you are ready to meet God in a life-changing way. The Psalmist wrote, "The snares of death encompassed me; the pangs of Sheol laid hold on me; I suffered distress and anguish. Then I called on the name of the Lord: 'O Lord, I beseech thee, save my life!' ... when I was brought low, he saved me" (Psalm 116:3-4,6). Like him, most of us wait until "then," times when we feel encompassed by the snares of death, trapped in the depths of hell, to call upon the name of the Lord for salvation, but when we do, He is there.

God has not forsaken you. He is with you wherever you are, whether you know it or not. Take hold of His Holy Word and meditate upon the words of Jesus, for there you will find strength to endure those grave situations. The darkest moment comes before dawn. Trust in the Lord. The light will come.

*Read: Matthew 28:1-9; Psalm 118:5; James 1:2-4*

# A SAD IRONY

*People came to see what it was that had happened. And they came to Jesus, and saw the demoniac sitting there, clothed and in his right mind, the man who had had the legion; and they were afraid. And those who had seen it told what had happened to the demoniac and to the swine. And they began to beg Jesus to depart from their neighborhood (Mark 5:14-17).*

Often when the Lord is working powerfully, effectively, and miraculously, people do not like it. That is a sad irony of history. It was true in Jesus's day and it is still true today.

In the Bible, we see it in the healing of Mr. Legion from Ten Cities. At the instant Mr. Legion was made well, two thousand pigs ran down a hillside, plunged into a lake, and drowned. That's a lot of soggy pork chops! The pig farmers were furious at losing their business. Instead of praising God for a miracle, they tried to chase Jesus out of town. Jesus never stays when He is not wanted, so He boarded a boat and left.

A woman came to me once because of her alcoholic, abusive husband. She said she would do anything to get him straightened out. Well, the Lord met that man. He was converted and he quit his destructive habits. What happened? His wife could not stand him anymore. She divorced him!

It is sad. When God brings help and healing, why don't people rejoice? Why are they so often frightened and angry? It may be partly our fault. We Christians do not always show excitement, happiness, and joy ourselves when God works miracles in our lives. We often fail to tell people of the amazing, marvelous changes Jesus has brought. Sometimes we are quite boring in our faith. We make God's work seem commonplace and routine. People get turned off and look for fulfillment elsewhere. The Bible tells us, "Rejoice in the Lord" (Philippians 3:1). When God changes your life, communicate your gratitude and excitement to others. Each of us can be a vivid advertisement for the joy, happiness, peace, and power Jesus Christ brings into a life. When God works in you, rejoice and be glad, and let all the world see your joy and gladness!

*Read: Mark 5:1-20; Psalm 75:1; Psalm 150*

# STRONG FAITH IN WEAK TIMES

*Yet I will rejoice in the Lord, I will joy in the God of my salvation. God, the Lord, is my strength (Habakkuk 3:18-19).*

What should we do when we are in weak times and we lack strong faith, when we feel trapped, strapped, imprisoned, abused, misused, and misunderstood? We ought to do what Paul and Silas did when they were attacked, beaten, and thrown into a dark prison for invoking the name of Jesus Christ.

**Say prayers.** Paul and Silas did not pray to escape jail. They prayed for courage, comfort, and wisdom to obey whatever God would ask of them. We should remember that prayer is not to be used to try to change the will of God, but to bring the will of God into our lives. Prayer is meant to help us endure suffering and pain, not avoid it. We cannot expect to escape hardships in life, but we can pray for strength and trust God to use even a horrible situation to bring about good.

**Sway with the music.** Paul and Silas sang hymns in prison at midnight and their spirits soared. Since the beginning of time, God has used the beauty of music to revitalize people. Music can reach us at moments when the written or spoken word does not seem to make sense. If we sway with the music, we will be lifted up even when we think we cannot go on.

**Stay, do not go away.** A great earthquake shook open the prison doors. Paul and Silas easily could have fled. They stayed, and as a result, the jailer and his entire household were saved. Wherever we find ourselves, we can lead people to the Lord. Never miss any opportunity to share the Good News.

Weak times are difficult to endure, but Paul wrote, "It has been granted to you that for the sake of Christ you should not only believe in him, but also suffer for his sake" (Philippians 1:29). Regardless of what is happening, God still reigns. He is in charge. Do not try to control other people or situations. Let God run His universe. Trust Him. Even in the darkest prison, our faith can grow, for we can do all things through Christ who strengthens us. Rejoice in the Lord today! Strong faith comes out of weak times when God, the Lord, is our strength.

*Read: Acts 16:16-34; Philippians 4:13; Psalm 29:1*

# WHEN SURROUNDED BY A CLOUD

*Therefore, since we are surrounded by so great a cloud of witnesses, let us also lay aside every weight, and sin which clings so closely, and let us run with perseverance the race that is set before us, looking to Jesus the pioneer and perfecter of our faith (Hebrews 12:1-2).*

Though the writer of Hebrews says we are surrounded by a great cloud of witnesses, sometimes we feel surrounded instead by a cloud of confusion, a mist of mystery. We feel alone, lost, bewildered. We want to move, but do not know how or where.

The Bible tells us faith works in a cloud of mystery! Faith grows if we know what to do when surrounded by a cloud.

**Lay aside every weight.** Christians are pioneers who should travel light. Instead, we love to collect things. We do not dare move because we are so tied to our possessions. Get rid of excess weight, the weight of materialism and also the weight of anxiety, fear, retribution, indecision, and negativity. Only then will you be alert to the leading of God's Holy Spirit.

**Get rid of the sin that clings.** The sin of selfishness clings like skin. Though we can be forgiven of sin if we repent, the desire to serve self will be with us to the grave. It is only as we forget ourselves and begin to think about God, His Kingdom, and other people that we temporarily get rid of the sin that clings so closely and start to see light through the clouds.

**Start running!** Though you are in a cloud, rouse yourself and charge into that darkness and uncertainty. If you fall, pick yourself up and start again. If you feel like quitting, don't! You cannot know your destiny until you get into the race. Look to Jesus Christ and listen to Him through the Bible and through the still small voice of His Spirit working in your subconscious. When He gives you some insight and light, shift into second gear and run to Him. Do not crawl or stroll or trot. Run! He will dispel the cloud of confusion and the mist of mystery and lead you into the clear light of His eternal truth.

There is a silver lining in the cloud. Look for it. Run for it. He will find you.

*Read: Psalm 99; Matthew 17:1-8; Revelation 1:7*

# THE PRESIDENT IN YOUR LIFE

*"The Kingdom of God is within you" (Luke 17:21, KJV).*

The complexity and depth of the human psyche are not discoveries of modern psychology. Classical theology gave Greek names to four spirits within us: Cosmos, the worldly spirit; Sarcos, the animal appetites; Diablos, the source of evil; and Logos, the Word of God. Those four forces, today and every day, vie for the position of President in our lives. It is false theology to say Logos causes the others to disappear. Cosmos, Sarcos, and Diablos will fight to gain the presidency over Logos until we die. Who presides over you today?

Only you can decide who will preside in your life. You can choose Cosmos: strive for fame, fortune, glamour, and prestige; lead the parade and get your name in the paper. But you will lose your soul in trying to win the world. There is Sarcos: take whatever you want whenever you can get it; go for thrills! The thrills, though, soon wane. You could pick Diablos: put yourself first; do your own thing! The trouble is, you will not like yourself later. Cosmos, Sarcos, and Diablos will fail you, leaving you empty and miserable. The only spirit that overcomes the emptiness and brings enduring joy is Logos.

Most likely you feel the tug and pull of Logos calling you now. Make the decision to abide with Jesus. Ask Him to be your President and to preside over the other forces residing in you. Simply pray, "Lord God, preside over my life. Help me to abide with you. You lead the way, and give me the courage to follow, for without you, I can do nothing. Lord, you are the President of my world and I will follow you." If you slip, and we all do, ask for forgiveness and re-appoint Jesus as President, then pick up where you left off in His grace and love.

Jesus is "the blessed and only Sovereign, the King of kings and Lord of lords, who alone has immortality and dwells in unapproachable light" (I Timothy 6:15-16), yet the Almighty King of kings and Lord of lords will never use His great power to force His way into your heart. You and you alone decide whether or not Jesus Christ will be the President in your life.

*Read: Matthew 6:25; Psalm 25:4-5; Romans 8:9-11*

# WILDERNESS WANDERINGS

*"For the Lord your God is bringing you into a good land, a land of brooks of water, of fountains and springs, flowing forth in valleys and hills, a land of wheat and barley, of vines and fig trees and pomegranates, a land of olive trees and honey, a land in which you will eat bread without scarcity, in which you will lack nothing" (Deuteronomy 8:7-9).*

Many people cannot understand the Gospel message until they go through wilderness wanderings, deserts of darkness, plains of pain. If you are in some horrible, hellish experience right now, do not lose hope. Ultimately, your wilderness wanderings can change your life and strengthen your faith.

It is in the wilderness that we best hear the messengers of the eternal Word. While life is comfortable, we often do not even think about God. It is when we feel forgotten, unloved, alone, and helpless that we begin to listen to the Lord. The anguish of wilderness wanderings brings changes in our priorities and values more quickly than anything else. We learn to depend upon God's Holy Spirit. It is easy to sit in church and talk about the Holy Spirit, but in the wilderness we entrust our lives to Him, for there is no one else. Paul knew that sense of desolation. "We were so utterly, unbearably crushed that we despaired of life itself. Why, we felt that we had received the sentence of death; but that was to make us rely not on ourselves but on God" (II Corinthians 1:8-9). Through our wilderness wanderings, we come to see that we do not have to understand or explain God, just believe and trust Him.

The Israelites, John the Baptizer, and Jesus Himself spent time in the wilderness. If today you feel heartbroken, hurt, and hopeless, remember "the Son of Man came to seek and to save the lost" (Luke 19:10). God knows where you are this moment. He knows your pain, even if no one else in the whole world understands. "Cast all your anxieties on him, for he cares about you" (I Peter 5:7). Believe it! Trust Him and He will lead you out of the wilderness and bring you into a good land where His many blessings will flow bountifully.

*Read: Deuteronomy 8:1-10; Luke 1:80; Matthew 4:1*

# THE MIGHTINESS OF GOD

*Mightier than the thunders of many waters, mightier than the waves of the sea, the Lord on high is mighty! (Psalm 93:4).*

Our God is not only a God of love, but a God of majesty and dominion as well. He is a mighty God! When Jesus came to earth to reveal the character of God, He easily could have demonstrated His mightiness with spectacular displays of force: crashing thunder, earthquakes, exploding stars, anything! Why not? He is God! Yet God chose to reveal His mighty abilities through three abilities He gives to all human beings.

**Astonishment** is the sense of shock and surprise we experience when the unexpected happens and we exclaim, "That's awesome!" It is God's way of gently showing us we are not as powerful as we think, there are many things we cannot comprehend or control, and someone else is in charge.

**Belief** comes when we recognize that the someone else who is in charge is God, that it is God who, in His might, created all things, it is God who created our very lives. God gives everyone the ability to believe, but what we believe is up to us. There is unbelief and disbelief, but there really is no such thing as no belief, for we either believe in Jesus Christ as the Savior of mankind or we believe in something or someone else.

**Common sense** is our ability to interpret impressions we get from our five senses. We do not need a theological degree to understand the mightiness of God. All we have to do is to look around, to see and touch and smell and taste and hear all that is in this beautiful world, to be astonished, and to believe.

How magnificently David expresses the mightiness of God! "Thine, O Lord, is the greatness, and the power, and the glory, and the victory, and the majesty; for all that is in the heavens and in the earth is thine; thine is the kingdom, O Lord, and thou art exalted as head above all. Both riches and honor come from thee, and thou rulest over all. In thy hand are power and might; and in thy hand it is to make great and to give strength to all. And now we thank thee, our God, and praise thy glorious name" (I Chronicles 29:11-13). Praise His name today!

*Read: Job 9:4-10; Isaiah 40:10-26; Revelation 1:8*

## DOES GOD OWE US?

*"He who believes in me will also do the works that I do" (John 14:12).*

It is so easy to think we can earn our way into Heaven, buy our forgiveness, and work for our salvation. Our society is achievement-oriented. We expect our paychecks. We want to be rewarded for our efforts. We go to church and think, "Hey, God, do you see me sitting here? Did you see that big check I put in the offering plate? By the way, did you notice all the people who aren't here today? Don't you think I'm good, God? Didn't I do a good piece of work?" Works theology. We actually believe God owes us all the good things. (Surely no problems.) We think we earn our acceptance into the Kingdom through good works and right living. We vainly imagine the Lord is obligated to us, and we deserve it! Do not be fooled by that popular line of thought. God owes us nothing, no matter how brilliant and generous our works may be. Works are important, very important, but we are saved by faith.

There has been a controversy in the Church for almost 2,000 years over faith and works. Many people think there is a conflict between the theology of Paul and the Book of James. I happen to disagree with that disagreement. The heart of Pauline theology is that we are saved by grace through faith. Salvation is a gift. We are forgiven and justified not because of what we do, but because of what God has done for us. We are not saved because we are good, but because God is good. We are not made righteous because of our goodness, but because of the goodness of God. James agrees! But James says faith is not merely something to talk about or pray about. It is something to do. Faith must be evidenced with works or it is not true faith. Faith is practical. Faith brings results: dreams become reality, lives are transformed, and great things happen.

We owe God everything, even our lives. Our good works express to Him our belief, gratitude, love, and willingness to serve. Work your faith! Do the works that Jesus did, and your faith and works together will help to change the world.

*Read: Ephesians 2:1-10; James 2:14-26; John 15:14*

# A GOOD SAMARITAN

*"A man was going down from Jerusalem to Jericho, and he fell among robbers, who stripped him and beat him, and departed, leaving him half dead. ...a Samaritan, as he journeyed, came to where he was; and when he saw him, he had compassion, and went to him and bound up his wounds" (Luke 10:30,33-34).*

The parable of the good Samaritan teaches that whenever we come across someone in trouble, we are to help that individual in a personal and practical way. Admittedly, the man who was beaten and abandoned on the road from Jerusalem to Jericho was a little foolhardy. Everyone knew the "bloody way" was dangerous. At least he was not ashamed to cry for help when he was hurt! People react so differently to pain. Some enjoy it and feel proud of their agony. Others deny it, huff and puff and look half-dead, but claim they feel great. Sometimes we are afraid to divulge our pain for fear of a second hurt, that of being passed by. We are stunned when people we count on for support just ignore us and relief comes instead from someone we might not even know or like.

Jesus told the parable of the good Samaritan in response to a lawyer who asked how to inherit eternal life. Surely, then, being a good Samaritan is important in God's eyes. A merciful spirit toward the needy reveals the presence of God's love in us. "If any one has the world's goods and sees his brother in need, yet closes his heart against him, how does God's love abide in him?" (I John 3:17). When we find a person in need, we ought to remember times when we were a little foolhardy, times when we were hurt and passed by, yet someone came along and bound up our wounds, paid our bills, and took care of us. No one likes those terrible, humiliating experiences, but usually we only learn compassion when we suffer ourselves. We must know need before we can supply another's need.

The good Samaritan showed mercy, and Jesus says to us, "Go and do likewise" (Luke 10:37). When people are knocked down, lift them back up. Be patient, kind, and practical. Share yourself with others, as Jesus Christ gave His life for you.

*Read: Luke 10:25-37; Hebrews 13:1-2; Proverbs 19:17*

# KNOWING WHEN YOU ARE IN LOVE

*So faith, hope, love abide, these three; but the greatest of these is love (I Corinthians 13:13).*

Love is the greatest thing in the whole world. Love is greater than eloquence, power, knowledge, wealth, everything! Jesus Christ proved from the Cross that the greatest thing that ever has been, is, or will be, is love. Love never ends. Love can do anything. And each one of us can know love in our lives. We do not create love; God does. "We love, because he first loved us" (I John 4:19). Jesus commands us to love, and He never commands us to do something without equipping us to do it. Take a little inventory right now to see if you are living this day in love. Love has three requirements.

**Obedience.** Jesus said, "If you keep my commandments, you will abide in my love, just as I have kept my Father's commandments and abide in His love" (John 15:10). The words of Jesus are the perfect guideline to love. When we obey His commands to love, forgive, serve, and treat others as we would wish to be treated, we know we are in love.

**Communication.** Love is not possible without honest communication. The great enemy of communication is fear. Many people are afraid to say something they believe needs to be said. John wrote, "Perfect love casts out fear" (I John 4:18). When we have the freedom and courage to speak from the heart, kindly but honestly, we know we are in love.

**Commitment.** After dedicating ourselves to obedience and communication, we then can commit ourselves to a relationship with the certainty that no matter what happens, we will never, ever quit on our loved one. If we are willing to invest such commitment in a relationship, we know we are in love.

Love is the greatest thing in the world, but love takes time and effort. If you want to help your love life today, do not grab the bestseller list and rush to the bookstore. Go to the true authority on love, God's Holy Word. Read I Corinthians 13 every week. Memorize it. Make it part of your life. Then you will know you are in love, and so will everyone around you.

*Read: I Corinthians 13; I John 4:7-21; Psalm 89:1-2*

# MEANINGFUL MEMBERSHIP

*Make a joyful noise to the Lord, all the lands! Serve the Lord with gladness! Come into his presence with singing! Know that the Lord is God! It is he that made us, and we are his; we are his people, and the sheep of his pasture. Enter his gates with thanksgiving, and his courts with praise! Give thanks to him, bless his name! For the Lord is good; his steadfast love endures for ever, and his faithfulness to all generations (Psalm 100).*

Nowadays it seems people base decisions on their feelings more than on any other factor. Some people join churches when they find one that makes them "feel good." That upsets me! As a pastor, I try not to be offensive or rude. If people feel good after a worship service, I am glad. But "feeling good" should not be a reason to join a church. People should not join because it is good for business, because they hope to meet new friends, or because they want to be uplifted once a week. Those reasons put them far from the Kingdom.

Other people avoid church membership because they do not "feel" like coming. They do not "feel" they will miss anything.

Feelings: if that is all we count on, we will be a group of flimsy, flopsy people with no substance, strength, or stamina!

We need greater commitment in the Church. Feelings have nothing to do with commitment; a person's commitment is to control his or her feelings. We should make the decision about church membership and everything else we do based on commitment to Christ as our personal Lord and Savior. Jesus spoke of the shallow worship of the Pharisees. "This people honors me with their lips, but their heart is far from me; in vain do they worship me" (Matthew 15:8-9). Do not worship in vain! For meaningful membership in the Body of Christ, go to church to serve the Lord with gladness, to come into His presence with singing, to offer thanksgiving and praise.

Make a commitment to Jesus Christ and keep it. Your steadfast love and faithfulness for God should endure forever, just as His steadfast love and faithfulness endures for you.

*Read: Isaiah 29:13-14; Psalm 84:10; Psalm 135:1-3*

# THE FACE OF KINDNESS

*Put on then, as God's chosen ones, holy and beloved,...*
*kindness (Colossians 3:12).*

Sometimes we think more about what we want to put off than what we ought to put on. I have a suggestion today: put on kindness. This world needs more kindness. Kindness is fruit of the Spirit. If we profess Jesus as Lord and Savior, kindness is within us; our responsibility is to show it. One of the best things we can do for our Father in Heaven is to be kind to His children on earth. Kindness is revealed in the face.

**The eyes.** The eye is the window of the soul, and a window has two directions, in and out. Our eyes not only enable us to see others; they permit others to observe us. Kindness is shown through the eyes, but so are lying, cruelty, rudeness, contempt. Probably the most unkind act is to look at people and pretend not to see them. Allow people to look into the depths of your soul to see God's kindness expressed in you.

**The ears.** Do not let noise and confusion drown out the forlorn cries of needy people. Keep your ears open and listen with kindness to what people have to say. Too often our ears are clogged. We do not listen because we are busy rehearsing what we are going to say, or we only hear what we want to hear, or listen part of the time. Be kind and pay attention.

**The nose.** Noses let us know what's cooking! Have a nose that knows what's going on. It is unkind to ignore the moods and seasons of life. There is a time to weep and a time to laugh, a time to mourn and a time to dance. Be sensitive.

**The mouth.** Words not only heal; they can hurt and destroy. Do not let your words come out in 3-D: discouraging, disheartening, disparaging. Jesus says we will have to give an account for every careless word, so be careful. Though we cannot always control what our eyes see, our ears hear, and our noses sense, we can control what our mouths say, if we try.

Do not put off being kind. Today, as one of God's chosen, holy, beloved disciples, put on the face of kindness and wear it with a smile, and God will make His face to shine upon you.

*Read: Job 6:14; Ecclesiastes 3:1-8; Psalm 67:1*

# UNDERSTANDING BY STANDING UNDER

*Do not be foolish, but understand what the will of the Lord is (Ephesians 5:17).*

Some people think they have an inside line to God's will and can speak correctly for God without hesitation. Others do not care about God's will; they only want to serve themselves. Many simply refuse to take time to understand the will of the Lord. I hope you are not in one of those categories, because you will never be wise, fulfilled, or happy unless you devote time and effort to discovering God's will for you. Fortunately, you do not need a Ph.D. to do it. I offer three guidelines:

**1. Stand under the authority of Scripture.** We cannot rely on stories we learned back in fourth grade Sunday School classes. We must get into His Word now, brood over it, struggle with it, and ask Holy Spirit, "What does this Word say to me today?" Accept God's Word as your authority on how to live. Look to Scripture for guidance and wisdom. "The unfolding of thy words gives light; it imparts understanding" (Psalm 119:130). Read the Bible and try to learn about God.

**2. Stand under the practice of prayer.** We must come regularly, daily, to the throne of grace to talk with the Lord, to listen, and to meditate upon His matchless love, goodness, and mercy. "Pray at all times in the Spirit" (Ephesians 6:18). In prayer, we should not try to impose our will on God, but rather seek to discover and follow God's will for us.

**3. Stand under the wisdom of people of faith.** We can learn so much from the prophets, apostles, and people we know personally who have wrestled with the Word of God for years. Take every opportunity to speak with people who are a little bit older and a little bit wiser, people who may have been walking with the Lord since before you were born. Be willing to be taught! "He who ignores instruction despises himself, but he who heeds admonition gains understanding" (Proverbs 15:32).

If you take time to stand under the authority of Scripture, the practice of prayer, and the wisdom of faithful Christians, you soon will understand God's wise, wonderful plan for you.

*Read: Proverbs 3:13-14; Colossians 1:9-10; II Timothy 2:1-7*

## YOUR EMOTIONAL HOUSE

*Peter went up on the housetop to pray (Acts 10:9).*

The Gentiles came into the universality of the Gospel through Cornelius, a Roman centurion who was converted under Peter's ministry. Peter approached Cornelius following a housetop experience. While waiting for a meal at the home of Simon the tanner, Peter went to the housetop to pray. There he fell into a trance and saw a vision of a sheet holding animals, reptiles, and birds. After the Lord explained three times that these creatures were not to be called common or unclean, Peter understood he had to give up some of his personal prejudices and traditions. When Cornelius sent for him to ask about Jesus, Peter was prepared to go, believing it was God's will to preach to the Gentiles. The lives of Peter and countless other people were changed because Peter went up to a housetop to pray.

Housetop experiences always have lasting consequences. God uses housetop experiences to reveal to people what He wants them to do. Each one of us, though, must decide for ourselves if we want to climb up to the housetop. We choose on what level of our emotional house we wish to dwell and in what frame of mind we live. We can choose to live in the dark, damp, dismal, cobweb-draped **basement**, feuding, bickering, criticizing, retaliating all the time. We can live in the **game room**, playing charades, lying, deceiving ourselves and others. We can live **upstairs** and just be spectators, observers, never getting involved. If we want to live in one of those areas, no one can stop us, but thank God, we can make the decision to live on the **housetop** where God wants us to live. As the crown of God's creation, we are born to live on the rooftops, where we can bask in the warmth of the sun, appreciate the splendor of God's beautiful world, and daily, triumphantly, face strong blasts of wind from any direction and live victoriously, with confidence in the heart and a smile on the face.

Where is your emotional house? If you would like to dwell in the house of the Lord all the days of your life to behold the beauty of the Lord, choose to climb up to the housetop today.

*Read: Acts 10:1-23; Psalm 27:4; Hebrews 3:1-6*

# HOW GOD TAPS YOUR SHOULDER

*In the year that King Uzziah died I saw the Lord sitting upon a throne, high and lifted up (Isaiah 6:1).*

Has God tapped your shoulder lately? I am not, of course, asking if He has reached out of the heavens with a great big hand and pointed finger and literally touched you. But have you thought perhaps the Lord was calling you to do some particular thing? Isaiah's experience demonstrates that God's method of tapping us on the shoulder is four-fold.

**A Show.** Isaiah saw a spectacular, terrifying show: seraphim, those burning, talking birds with six wings; shaking thresholds; a smoke-filled temple. When God taps your shoulder, He begins by sending a show, an unforgettable vision of His awesome power, might, and majesty. Before He speaks a word, He gives a wonder so you recognize, "God is here!"

**A Woe.** "Woe is me! For I am lost; for I am a man of unclean lips" (Isaiah 6:5). When God taps your shoulder, you sense your inadequacy. "Lord, I can't do it!" Suddenly you realize you are small, imperfect, unworthy. Near the holiness of God, you feel full of holes. It is painful, but being humbled teaches you to rely on God's strength, not your own.

**A Glow.** Isaiah glowed when one of the seraphim took a burning coal from the altar and touched it to his lips. When you understand you are cleansed and forgiven by God's love, your face glows with joy that only comes through grateful acceptance of His grace and obedient submission to His will.

**Go!** "Here am I! Send me" (v. 8). Finally, you are ready. "I will go, Lord. Use me as you wish. I can't wait to serve you!" Once you realize God has a special plan for you to fulfill, you will be edgy and restless until you begin to do it.

Isaiah's shoulder was tapped when he saw the Lord sitting upon a throne. For Moses, the tap came through a burning bush. For Saul, through a blinding light. Have you felt His tap yet? If you haven't, you will. It can happen anywhere, anytime. It is scary, but go! Accept the challenge of your calling. It will change your life, and you will never regret it.

*Read: Isaiah 6:1-8; Exodus 3:1-6; Acts 9:3-19*

257

# KEEPING SCORE

*You will forget your misery; you will remember it as waters that have passed away. And your life will be brighter than the noonday (Job 11:16-17).*

The Christian life is a call to excellence, but there is one task Christians should try to do poorly: score keeping. All of us ought to be lousy at keeping score of wrongs, injustices, and abuses done against us. It is a huge mistake to engrave past heartaches and traumas in the mind, replay them incessantly, and pity ourselves. Painful memories debilitate us and prevent us from becoming the triumphant people we are meant to be.

Few of us get through a day without some kind of frustration caused by people who are rude, crude, and ought to be sued. Usually it is minor: a friend is late; an automobile driver cuts in front of us; a co-worker habitually goofs. Sometimes it is serious: someone receives credit for our ideas; a competitor lands a promotion we deserve. Occasionally it is heart-breaking: a friend betrays us; a spouse leaves; people gossip viciously; someone is brutal. The ways we can be hurt by people are countless, and it is difficult to forget unpleasant experiences. What we can try to forget and overcome is the painful impact of those experiences: bitterness, anger, sadness, rejection. We have the power to erase those griefs from the mind. How? Forgiveness. With God's help, we can forgive anybody of anything. In fact, forgiveness is not an option but a necessity. Jesus said, "If you forgive men their trespasses, your heavenly Father also will forgive you; but if you do not forgive men their trespasses, neither will your Father forgive your trespasses" (Matthew 6:14-15). Once we forgive, we are right with God and free to enjoy life fully again.

If you are upset about the way you have been treated in the past, ask God to give you a big eraser filled with forgiveness to blot out the unhappiness once and for all. It is over and done. Do not dwell on it or you will ruin your future. Erase it. Let it pass away. Forget your misery. Forgive people who hurt you. Be a lousy score keeper; it is a great way to brighten your life.

*Read: Matthew 18:21-35; Exodus 21:24; Matthew 5:38-48*

# THE ONLY SAFE WAY TO GO

*Do not throw away your confidence, which has a great reward.*
*For you have need of endurance, so that you may do the will of*
*God and receive what is promised. "For yet a little while, and*
*the coming one shall come..., but my righteous one shall live by*
*faith, and if he shrinks back, my soul has no pleasure in him."*
*But we are not of those who shrink back and are destroyed, but*
*of those who have faith (Hebrews 10:35-39).*

We tend to remember Thomas for his doubts after the
resurrection. That is too bad, because Thomas exhibited bold
faith in an incident about ten days before Jesus's death on the
Cross. Word came that Jesus's friend Lazarus was ill. After
two days, Jesus made plans to go to Bethany, but the disciples
nervously objected. "Rabbi, the Jews were but now seeking to
stone you, and are you going there again?" (John 11:8). They
were frightened, with good reason. There was danger in
returning. Only Thomas trusted Jesus enough to say, "Let us
also go, that we may die with him" (v. 16). Thomas was
saying, "Let's follow Jesus, no matter what." That is courage.

Most of us, when frightened, say, "No, thanks, I'll pass."
We stall, go back to bed, hope the danger evaporates. Thomas
did not throw away his confidence, but made the decision to
follow Jesus. Notice, he did not form a committee, take a poll,
or conduct a survey, as we often do to avoid personal
responsibility for a tough decision. Can you picture Jesus
calling a committee meeting to discuss His plans? People
today are afraid to take a stand, so they ask for a show of
hands. That is no way to be a disciple! "Let us also go."
Going with Jesus means we might be despised and persecuted,
but thank God for Thomas and other disciples of Christ who do
not shrink back, but say "Let us also go, that we may die with
him." People with such faith are used mightily by God.

Do not throw away your confidence or shrink back from
the destiny Jesus wants for you. Go with Him, wherever He
leads. Follow Him this day, every day. It can be a frightening
route to take, but in truth, it is the only safe way to go.

*Read: John 11:1-16; John 12:25-26; Psalm 34:15-22*

# OUR CERTAIN WAY ACROSS THE DARK

*Jesus was born in Bethlehem of Judea (Matthew 2:1).*

How certain is your way today? This week? This year?

In 1934, my father, Dr. Joseph S. Morledge, former pastor of the Sixth Presbyterian Church of Pittsburgh, designed a unique format for a Christmas candlelight service. In 1960, the tradition began at the First Presbyterian Church of Bakerstown and has continued for thirty-five years. To many, the poem recited prior to the lighting of candles has been an inspiration.

> Lord, it is dark, and the road is rough to go;
> I lift an unlit candle in the night,
> Behold it, Lord, within my upraised hand;
> Touch it to flame with Thine own heavenly light.
>
> This slender waxen thing that is my faith,
> Fire it, Lord, with some divine white spark,
> Until its circle, widening at my feet,
> Will mark my certain path across the dark.
>
> "Thou will light my candle" ...thus assured
> I shall go forward throughout this unknown land;
> The way shall never grow too dark, too long,
> For I shall bear Thy light within my hand.
> Grace Noll Crowell

The most important meetings of all time took place when Jesus was born: Heaven met earth, as God revealed Himself in His Son; salvation met the sinner, for Jesus came to defeat the power of sin; harmony met disharmony, for all people can meet at the manger. Today, we can know with certainty that whatever happens, we will be all right. Even our loved ones on the other side are all right, for God takes care of them in Heaven as He takes care of us on earth. Praise God that in this unknown land, His Heavenly light will mark our certain way across the dark and guide us to our eternal home. Believe it! Believe it with your heart, soul, mind, and strength. Trusting in God's presence, care, guidance, and love even when the road is rough will make every day a great day in the Kingdom for you.

*Read: Luke 2:1-20; I John 4:14-16; Romans 10:13*